JOURNAL

'Kate Paul's *Journal* is a treasure trove for
ways in which British culture and society (
1960s. Few archives so accurately and poignantly capture this country's miraculous transition from austere greyness to the multicoloured world of 'swinging' pop.'
Dr.Alex Seago; author of Burning the Box of Beautiful Things: The Development of a Postmodern Sensibility (Oxford University Press, 1995)

'I read the *Journal* straight through and was transported through the years. It has an urgency, a determination, a willingness to tell the truth and avoid cant; it is critical of self, family, society, God. Of course it contains inconsistencies and contradictions but at the age at which it was written, which of us did otherwise? - supposing, that is, we were given to any reflective thought at all.'
Laurie Fricker - Associate: University of Portsmouth

'Sitting in the candlelit gloom of *The Troubadour*, watching the passing show of personalities, many to make their mark in later years - Kate Paul, with her hilarious sense of humour, at the same time broodingly recording her progress to self-awareness and making a document that so recalled that peculiarly vivid time - the early Sixties. Read it!'
Josh Kirby - Cover artist for 'Discworld'

'Reading the *Journal* was an emotional experience; I found a great resonance with my own experience as a young woman in the 60s, struggling to find an identity in the art world; the difficulty of reconciling one's sense of what it was to be a woman with a full identity as a thinking, critical, creative person. The Journal gives a fascinating insight into some of those tensions. The writing of such an extensive, intense, thoughtful and honest document at such a young age is impressive and significant in its own right.'
Sue Watling - Lecturer, Somerset College of Art

'I liked the *Journal* a lot and found myself sniggering sympathetically.'
Julie Christie

Other Books by Kate Paul
(as Kate Clarke)

*

Murder At The Priory: The Mysterious Poisoning of Charles Bravo
Co-author, Bernard Taylor

The Pimlico Murder: The Strange Case of Adelaide Bartlett

Who Killed Simon Dale?

The Book of Hay

*

Kate Paul

JOURNAL

Volume One
1958 - 1963

*

*

Carrington Press

Carrington Press
PO Box 18
Hay-on-Wye
Hereford HR3 5YN

First Published by Carrington Press 1997
Reprinted by Carrington Press 2000

*

ISBN 0-9530761-0-5

Produced by
The Short Run Book Company
St Stephen's House
Arthur Road
Windsor
Berkshire SL4 1RY

Printed and bound in Great Britain

For Chilli Lauren Mahendra

*

Acknowledgements

I should like to thank Caroline Edwards for permission to use the photographs of Derek Boshier, Brian Rice and myself taken by her late husband, Tony Evans.
Also Roy Lichtenstein for permission to reproduce his painting *'Hopeless'* as part of the cover design.
Terry Green for permission to use his ARK 25 Spring 1960 Cover image of Brigitte Bardot.
Geoffrey Reeve for permission to reproduce his photographs of David Hockney, Derek Boshier, Peter Phillips and Peter Crutch in the Royal College of Art Painting School, 1961.
Tom Watt for permission to use his photographs of the Troubadour, Coleherne Road, Earls Court and Enid Faers.
I regret I have been unable to ascertain the photographers of the images of James Dean, Elvis Presley, J F Kennedy and David Hockney which form part of the cover photomontage.

I should like to thank the following for their help and encouragement in the months preceding the publication of the Journal:
Tom Watt, Brian Rice, Julie Christie, Duncan McAra, Bernard Taylor, David Bambridge, Duncan Campbell, Derek Boshier, Alex Seago, Christopher Frayling, Eugene Rae, Laurie Fricker, Jasmine Grassie, Josh Kirby, John Porter Davison, Sue Watling, Sarah Jackman, Anne and Dan Dewell, Nick Jensen, Roger Tarr, George Burroughs, Richard Madelin, Roger Capps, Bob Organ, Kate Pemberton, Liz Calder, Peter Webb, Shelley Lee, Giles Morgan, Jennifer Preston, Kate Beaver, Terry Murphy, Sasha and Anil Mahendra, Lara Bingham, Hugo Schofield and Margaret Brett.

*

Introduction

My father was a British Army officer serving in North Africa during the last war and my mother and brother joined him there. So it was that I was born in Jerusalem in 1940. My father died soon after and we spent the next five years, with other Service families, constantly on the move, finally reaching Durban, South Africa, before returning to England in 1945. My childhood was, thereafter, fairly typical of the post-war years: austere, in many ways - rationing, strict church attendance, no music, except on the wireless, and a few books.

In 1956, aged fifteen, I left Yeovil High School for Girls and enrolled at the local School of Art. I had hoped to study journalism, but with no such course available I turned intsead to Fine Art.

Already having the sense of being an 'outsider', on entering the Art School I felt an immediate kinship with the other students and my life changed irrevocably. It was here that I met the painter, Derek Boshier, who at eighteen had just been accepted by the Royal College of Art; but he, like others of his age, had first to complete his two years' National Service. For many this constituted a frustrating and untimely break at the onset of their careers, one that today's young artists and designers would find inconceivable.

Amongst the rubbish littering the cupboards of the Art School I found an old, discarded ledger and felt compelled to write in it. Thus began the Journal, the original handwritten version eventually filling seven notebooks. It provides merely a glimpse of one particular young person's life, who, like many thousands more, felt uncertain and alienated, living with not only the threat but, as it seemed at the time, the imminent possibility of a nuclear war.

The first section of the Journal covers a period of two years spent at Somerset College of Art, in Taunton, where the painting tutor was Terry Murphy. He had been a contemporary of Peter Blake and Leon Kossoff at the Royal College of Art, at a time when Frank Auerbach, Bridget Riley and John Bratby were also studying there and John Minton was working as a part-time painting tutor. Through Terry Murphy I learned much about life at the RCA in the mid-Fifties, little knowing that I would subsequently become involved with many of its students.

The second section of the Journal covers the time when, having graduated from Somerset College of Art, I moved to London, working for a while as a chambermaid in an hotel in Cromwell Road, West London and frequenting the celebrated Troubadour coffee-bar and the gay pub, the Coleherne, at night. Then to Birmingham on the Art Teachers' course for a postgraduate degree, where I lived in the notorious Varna Road, Balsall Heath, then a red-light district where cock-fights were regularly held in the streets after dark.

Finally, the third section, the longed-for return to London. The year was 1961, the beginning of an extraordinary era, one of escalating protest - anti-nuclear weapons, anti-apartheid, anti-capital punishment - a time when old-established attitudes were at last beginning to change, marking the emergence of a society that at least acknowledges the long overdue need to embrace the gay community, stamp out racism and further augment equality of the sexes.

At the same time there was a great surge of innovative creative energy emanating from the art schools in the wake of artists like Peter Blake, Jo Tilson and Bridget Riley; people like David Hockney, Derek Boshier, Peter Phillips, Pauline Boty, Zandra Rhodes, Sally Tuffin, Marion Foale, Ossie Clark, Celia Birtwell and Janice Wainwright - linking Pop Artists, fashion designers and pop musicians and all contributing to the emergence of a definable youth culture, epitomised by the vibrant, defiant optimism and excitement of the Sixties.

The Journal ends in 1963, the year when the winter was so harsh that London froze for weeks on end and President John F Kennedy was assassinated.

Naturally, reading the Journal again after so many years, I longed to make changes, extend the vocabulary and improve the style but I have resisted the temptation. It remains, therefore, as it was written, with all the arrogance, inconsistency, false assumption and rotten syntax of an eighteen year old at odds with the world.

Whether it has any validity is a matter for the reader. Besides the desire to record aspects of social history, diarists' compulsion to 'talk to themselves' is essential to their sanity, performing perhaps a function whereby they can decipher and assimilate the constant barrage of ideas and feelings with which they are bombarded, especially in late adolescence. And if one is feeling alienated or isolated there is, undoubtedly, a profound comfort in reading the thoughts of others who have felt the same way. At such times, through reading their journals and letters, I have felt a great affinity with the Russian painter, Marie Bashkirtseff, the naturalist and essayist, Barbellion, the painter, Carrington, and many others and I should, in turn, like to think that another struggling soul might find some solace in mine.

*

Kate Paul 1997

SOMERSET

Friday 22 December 1958, Yeovil
Now that I've found this book to hide in, where should I begin? I could start, I suppose, by gathering up these little notes from last year, scribbled on scraps of paper and the backs of envelopes, thoughts so fleeting that I sometimes wonder at their usefulness.

...it's a sad and inevitable day when one realises that one is *not* going to be the most beautiful woman in the world, the greatest surgeon, the greatest musician, the greatest artist or even really good at something one considers important. One struggles to prevent oneself from realising that one is just ordinary - but I am *me!* But where? A surgeon may cut me up but find nothing for I'm an invisible spirit in a body. Love, I suppose, is a sympathetic mobility of spirit.

... and it's a lonely day, too, when one realises that one is an individual. An individual spirit set loose to wander, always alone, not an extension or part of another. In a crowd, if the others run off, you are left standing unless you run too. You remain *I* and the rest remain *Them.* You desperately want to rush across, mix in the crowd and become one of Them but you can't - you remain I. There is no escape.

...it seems that as we grow older, unlike flowers that unfurl, we fold inwards, and begin to discover ourselves, become aware of our actual self inside our body - we fold inwards and get to know who we are.

Saturday 23 December 1958, Yeovil
I find myself in the most despairing of moods; moods of utter inability to see the point in anything whatsoever. My work is at a standstill. I am ahead of my ability in my craft, a most frustrating state to be in. My work is hopeless yet it seems to me it should somehow reflect the sheer will to produce what is in my mind. I was talking to Tim [*fellow student, painter*] about this and he feels the same. The hands and feet he loves to paint, he feels that through the sheer impact of his conception and the mental and physical will to recreate it in terms of paint, he should be able to achieve his aim. I envy his capacity for concentration. I know I could work better alone. I could concentrate so much better. I always write alone but I cannot tuck a canvas under my arm and paint. I hate my thoughts and feelings to be seen.

Before the Arts Ball I was beside myself with excitement. The murals were wonderful. I enjoy these parties for one and a half hours and then feel disappointed, miserable and very tired and I want to curl up and sleep. Frustration, that's what it is. I'm so self-centred that when I come across a man who doesn't succumb to my charms I'm hurt and feel annoyed when people don't like me. Does everyone suffer from this? I'm sure they do. Surely one cannot help liking oneself and yet, at the same time, see a thousand faults.

After each weekend I return to Taunton [*Somerset College of Art*] with my paints untouched and a horrid feeling. A couple of weeks ago I borrowed Beaver's *[Kate Beaver, fellow student]* edition of Voltaire's *Candide* which I will read again soon. New digs next term, thank God.

Monday 25 December 1958, Yeovil
This business of believing in a spirit. How can one admire, love and understand works of art and acknowledge the genius that created them? Where did that genius come from? God? The whole business of life puzzles me. I want to force my brain to its furthest, furthest point, to delve into its chasms and creep up and pounce upon a revelation that I know is lurking there.

A few days ago I bought the most lovely petticoat of black nylon with lace frills, its very own blue artificial rose and layers of pink nylon net underneath. My Bach record has come and it's beautiful. It makes me want to smile and trip about and move my hands.

Saturday 27 December 1958, Yeovil

This morning I found the key to my box and rummaged happily for hours like a pig in its swill. Life fragments. I was thinking as I was listening to one of my records that one can buy a masterpiece of music for a matter of shillings. Is this the advantage music has over the visual arts? Even so there's no excuse for not going to concerts. I have never been to a concert in my life and am thoroughly ashamed of it.

Imagine buying an original painting for a couple of shillings. To be able to take it to one's room and savour it to one's heart's content! But music is plagued by its interpretation. This must be the eternal heartbreak of dead composers. How they must reach the depths of despair to hear their divine compositions so often misinterpreted and sometimes even mutilated. Surely, no matter how magnificently a work is conducted and rendered in all good faith, the composer must hang over heaven's walls and long to put it right? Surely only *he* knows how it should sound and only *his* rendering with *his* brain and hands is the original and anything else, however good, is merely a reproduction?

As for the artist, when his work is done it is done, but then he has interpreters in his beholders. Maybe there is no difference between the artist and the composer. The artist has to bear his work violated by misguided eyes and lack of conception. When the composer dies he leaves his music sheets, the artist his paintings, but the reasoning, the brain and the true explanation is gone.

A doubting postcard viewer can go to the original painting and see for himself, be his own interpreter. But with music the original is gone. We hear only a secondary conception and our conception is the *third* conception to take place. With the visual arts there are two.

This afternoon on the wireless there was a recital of works by Bach, Mozart and Brahms. I have the idea of making the end of my desk [*made from an old chair and a piece of plywood*] into a bookshelf but

the planks and bricks I need are in the shed and I'm afraid of spiders. In front of me is my jug of brushes - each one as dry as a bone.
The wind is whining like it does in desert and Arctic films. There's hardly any other sound and the cabbages are turning yellow. It's very damp. I can hear the ten past three bus. I can see it over the hedge; written along one side *Woodbine - The Great Little Cigarette*. I can hear the driver and the conductor talking. I wonder what happens to the spirit when our bodies are asleep? I like the Tibetan explanation, if there is any truth in it.

Monday 29 December 1958, Yeovil
How long is an existence? How long am I to go on? What is eternity? We cannot comprehend a thing which does not end. Ever. I am stuck with myself for ever. Never to be extinguished. These thoughts always come when the wheel of life slows down a little. Once thrown into the wheel once more there's no escape. No stopping. Forced to live on and dreading to stop. A running play. A packed theatre of actors. No audience, that's the thing. One cannot sit and watch. One can't even switch parts - the same part for ever.

There was something about the Pope [*John XX111*] on the television. He was visiting a prison and one prisoner was so overcome by being near the Pope that he said: 'This has made my day.' And the Pope said: 'And mine.'
I wonder what I shall be thinking in twenty years time? Whatever I write down now will only be of interest to me. I will read it on wet afternoons and let the fire go out and feel odd when I came round. I ask myself why I write these things. I don't know. Maybe it's to have something in black and white, not just fleeting thoughts, unhaltered.

Tuesday 30 December 1958, Yeovil
I had in my red book some notes I managed to get down on a broadcast about Dr Schweitzer. About his absolute reverence for life and the debt he felt he owed to all coloured people for the way they've been wronged for so long. He has taken this debt on his own shoulders and has dedicated his life to repaying it. He has a deeply embedded hatred of machinery and he is often criticised for having only the bare essentials

in his hospital. He has contrived to make it as much like his patients' own homes as possible. He's always open to new inventions and discoveries in medicine, however, and the efficiency and standard of his care is outstanding
In 1952 he was awarded the Nobel Peace Prize. He firmly believes in manual work and is respected to the point of worship by his patients. He's a very imperious man and once said to his workers: 'You have come to Olympia and I am Zeus.' He is cautious of other people's abilities and is always right. He maintains that the more superhuman we become the more inhumane. This sentiment was held by Delacroix in his *Journal.* Dr Schweitzer is a very learned scholar and was also a fine organist and organ builder before he became a doctor. He's written books on Jesus, Bach and St Paul. He is not, however, willing to admit his faults and when he was given a new organ and his mistakes were magnified, he returned it, declaring it wrong. A great man. How few greats we have left. We have Picasso and, but only just, Matisse and Braque, great men in an age of their own.

The book that has made the most impression on me is, without hesitation, Delacroix's *Journal.* I think it's because I had so many hours of interest and pleasure out of reading this marvellous book that it made me want to gather my own meagre thoughts and memories. I remember coming across the book as I rummaged through the library at Taunton. I thought about taking it out, not through any great interest in Delacroix - in fact, I knew little about him - but it appealed to me because it was written *by* him. I didn't take the book out at first. Instead I took a very good book of Cézanne's letters which I hope to buy some day. Eventually I went back for Delacroix's *Journal* and now cannot express my admiration enough. A great man who I only came to know about by chance.

A book I loved very much was Balzac's *Old Goriot.* A masterpiece of sadness and love of living. I feel a deep affection for books and it gives me pleasure just to hold them in my hand knowing the wealth of things they contain. As I look at my small row of richness I see the three Shakespeare volumes, little green books with other people's markings in them, which I bought for one and six in Schooling's junk shop. I see

Voltaire's *Candide* which belongs to Beaver; she can afford books so I don't intend to give it back if I can help it. Along the row to *The Grapes of Wrath*, which belongs to Anne [*Anne Cornelius, fellow student, painter*]. I am constantly reminded to give it back but have forestalled this catastrophe for nearly two years.

Now I must stop writing and get on with other things. I would like to write down the things that Beaver and our friends find unbearably funny but it's impossible. We laugh all the time. Sometimes we find everything funny, especially social embarrassments. We laugh at ourselves too for we know all our physical defects and funny points.

Wednesday 31 December 1958, Yeovil

Met Beaver in town and she bought five bottles of champagne for the party. Decorated the house [*Kate Beaver's home, Glebe Farm, an old rectory at Rampisham, near Dorchester*] till four then started cooking the sausages. It was marvellous seeing everyone again. I looked hideous. Dreadful, a real ugh! Beaver felt foul too. I sat and talked to Derek[1] most of the time as we'd hidden a bottle of sherry in the drawing room.

Next morning, everyone sitting around the fire, draped with miserable strips of weed and the occasional ivy stem, very hung-over and glum.

Back in Yeovil now, full of happy memories and looking forward to visiting David Chant [*fellow-student, amateur actor*] tonight. As

---

[1]Derek Boshier: artist. One of the most prominent exponents of the British Pop Art Movement in the early 60's, with other contemporaries at the Royal College of Art: Patrick Caulfield, David Hockney and R B Kitaj. His work has always contained a strong political/social stance. Apart from painting he has worked in areas of film, drawing, sculpture, photography and documentation. He has lived in the USA since 1980 (returning to live in Britain for a 4-year period, 1993-7). Is currently living in Los Angeles, California. He has exhibited world-wide and is represented in many collections, including the Tate Gallery, London: Museum of Modern Art, New York: Kunsthalle, Hamburg: National Gallery of Art, Canberra, Australia: Menil Collection, Houston, Texas: Museum of Contemporary Art, San Diego, California: National Gallery of Poland, Warsaw: Contemporary Art Museum, Honolulu, Hawaii.

always, when I come back from a party at Beaver's, Mother is tight-lipped and silent.

Friday 2 January 1959, Yeovil

And my mood has changed. Miserable, sick and very tired. I bet Derek won't come this afternoon. The clouds are blue-black with a reddish tint in them. I can see clump after clump of cabbages and a line of washing, two dirty prefabs and the most delightful shit-coloured, flat-fronted council house - with a turquoise door for good measure. One bare Shumac tree. One corrugated shed. A delightful assortment of dead plants. The whole thing is unbelievably dreary. [*The estate was built as post-war emergency housing in 1946 by German internees.*]

Saturday 3 January 1959, Yeovil

Last night, when Derek had gone back to Montecute,[2] I had a terrible pain in my lungs. I love my records. I'm hoping to scrape up enough money for Beethoven's *Fantasia in C Minor,* the *Juna Symphony* and the *String Quartet No 10.* Out of the ten Classic Club records to choose from, some I don't want and some are too expensive. For example, records by Haydn and Mozart are expensive, those by Beethoven less so.

My skin is a mess, my hair too. My eyes are aching and like dull slits. I am quietly desperate. I love Beethoven's *Piano Concerto No 3* so much. It never fails to make me feel better. It's very hard to voice any appreciation of music. I don't know why. I think maybe because one has to recite the name, title, rank and creed of the work before making any comment; it sounds so pompous and knocks all the sincerity out of

---

[2] Home of Brian Rice: painter. Known for his geometric forms in the early Sixties: has combined a career in art with teaching - Brighton, Hornsey and Croydon Colleges of Art and as Visiting Tutor in Print Making at Central School of Art, Royal College of Art, St Martin's and the Slade School of Art; has exhibited widely in a number of galleries and collaborated with the late photographer, Tony Evans, on a treble award-winning book entitled *The English Sunrise* (1972), also *A Pictorial History of Santa Claus* (1995).

what you have to say. I think one must just love it alone or be lucky enough to have an intimate friendship that needs no words. Sometimes the human voice is a bad interpreter.
This reminds me of an interview with John Osborne[3] on the television. He's a playwright of some controversy, unluckily labelled 'an angry young man'. He had great difficulty expressing himself before four fat lumpy journalists. I was very surprised and pleased to hear this John Osborne, an honest and very sincere young man, saying words that I have written in this book. Exact thoughts. It makes one happy to find a fellow thinker. It restores one's faith in oneself.
He was stressing the vital importance of the unique existence, a theme always winding through my brain. He said that people on the whole were not happy and that the biggest problem of the human mind is the problem of existence. He was trying to say that the answer is in oneself, to be fought out alone.
He denounced Royalty, as I do, and presented it in its true light, debunking the Queen's Christmas Speech in all its insincerity and uselessness, giving millions a momentary feeling of communal safety and international love that does not exist - it only leads to a dangerous sense of false security. Just when a rather insipid young woman sits in rich surroundings, a suitably royal and docile smile on her face, perfect elocution, all is well if she bows her head and peace reigns in all corners of the earth. What rot it is! Millions abroad in poverty and misery couldn't care a damn about her. It's completely false, this united love of England and its royalty. She's just a rather redundant symbol of something that has passed.

Young people who express any opinion about the running of the world are denounced and made fun of. Fine, the ones who are making a mess of the world won't be here long - *we* will. I have pages and pages of thoughts I want to get down about war, peace, the minds of people and yet I cannot express them.
I get so angry I can't even write them down. The right to hang a person is one subject I feel so strongly about I can only think about it.

---

[3] John Osborne: 1929-94: playwright. His play *Look Back in Anger* had been produced at The Royal Court Theatre in 1956 to great acclaim.

Sometimes I cry with sheer anger. I'm going to write about capital punishment another day when I'm thinking more clearly.

I can be incredibly ugly. I just looked out of the window and there was a beautiful rainbow - the rain trickling and seeping. This past year I have completely changed. I'm beginning to think more seriously. I am finding myself. Derek is wrong when he says one doesn't change between sixteen and twenty. This is the time of folding into oneself.
It's getting dark now; still raining. I've played my records many times and I wonder where Derek is. I'm so unsettled. Reading Longfellow.

Oh, why do people get mixed up with the filth of politics? I hate them. An excuse for hatred, grabbing power and showing off. Sometimes I'm so engulfed with feelings about all the wars and cruelty that I want to be a coward and run and hide myself in a forgotten place far away and pray myself sick for peace. When I think of the great learning centres in the Soviet Union, every facility for learning for the young, far in advance of ours. All that and for what? To make things to destroy everything.

I feel like hiding away somewhere so I need not watch the destruction coming, to forget and let the blow come suddenly, not watch it crawl. Terrible things like the Hungarian massacre have only just touched the fringes of our brains when along comes something else. More hatred. More brutal killings. Young people like myself, just killed off. I *mind* being destroyed so young. Bloody men, always fighting. Showing off. Power. Strength. Soldiers. Guns. Die a hero. Bloody men. The stupidity. There would be no war with women. They have more understanding. All is hatred in the world.

Sunday 4 January 1959, Yeovil
I must rid myself of this silly, seeping desperation. I read today that Russia has set off a rocket that has passed the Moon and will now become a planet around the Sun. What an achievement. It doesn't really interest me so very much, though. I want to see Derek. I wish he were in the same place so that I could see him nearly all the time. Still, I've sent him a letter.

I've just seen a certain young Texan on the television, Van Cliburn, a brilliant pianist. His interpretation is very sensitive and unique. He has spots, horrible hair and the most beautiful hands. On the same programme Maria Callas said that she only lost her temper for the sake of art. Stravinsky was also saying what I was trying to say a few pages back about the composer being the only one able to give the original concept of a piece of music. He is so aware of this fact that he says he will conduct until he no longer has the strength.

Monday 5 January 1959, Yeovil
I am much brighter this morning. Beaver, Anne and I are going to a secondhand bookshop in Beaminster. I hope to buy a few cheap books, one of Longfellow especially so that I won't have to spend precious hours copying down. I can't send for my Classic Club records because I have no money. My total is £1 Christmas money plus 4/6 from last week's pocket money. The records, if I send for them, will come to £1 13s 6d. I can't borrow from next week's pocket money as it's back to college next week and I'll need every penny. Oh, for some money for some books and records. I'll get a job in the last term - can't go to Florence on ten shillings.

So many fields to run in, so many paths to take; too many countries, too many people and I am only one spirit here for only one innings! I want to live everyone's life, to partake of everything that is going, go to every single place on this earth - I want so much. I want to do something I shall be remembered by, not remembered for a few months by a few but for ever, by everyone. I want to be necessary.

The Russians are behind the West in their painting. They just haven't gleaned anything from the discoveries and progress of other countries. There's no sophistication, no tackling of problems; there's something *Victorian* about their work. Like very competent Intermediate compositions, naïve and coarse but the icons are very beautiful. I hope to buy a small book of poems by Boris Pasternak.

It has rained all day. I wish Derek was here. I feel a little lonely. I look really nasty today; my hair needs washing. Maybe he's got my letter.

Tuesday 6 January 1959, Yeovil
I had a letter from Derek this morning and I hope to go up to Basingstoke where his parents live [*Bill Boshier, his father, was landlord of the Railway Arms at the time*] on Sunday if I can borrow the money from somewhere. I want to go with him to London the following weekend to see the Russian Exhibition.

Back to college on Monday. I can't say if I'm pleased or not. In a way, but my room, this lovely, odd, familiar room will take on its awful damp weekday feeling. All quiet, unused and the chair sticking to the damp floor. This room always has a quiet, watching feeling but in term time it's much worse. Now it's thawing and quite friendly towards me.

Records, books, painting - all this, who'd ever know there's this strange, colourful world inside four grey, peeling aluminium walls, that people in the bus look at while they're waiting to go, little guessing the glorious cave within.
If Derek and I go to London we can see Tintoretto's *Christ Washing the Disciples' Feet* in the Bond Street Gallery. It's soon to be sold to someone in Canada for £30,000.

It's the age of space travel, bases on the Moon. No doubt who owns the Moon will be the next excuse for another war and people will rocket into the universe, into nothingness and they will meet God in the end. I am sure each man thinks he will be here to see the end of the world. After all, we are nearly in the Brave New World of Huxley. Smelly films are here - space travel very nearly here. Test Tube Babies, Deep Freeze People, radioactive horrors. Sometimes it frightens me but sometimes I accept it all - but all that beauty, the treasures produced by great men - *destroyed!*
Oh, the bliss, the glory of nail-varnish! Gold and silver. Liquid lushness smelling of pear drops.

A child's work is so often brilliant, a work of genius in design, colour and conception and even in drawing sometimes but it's never accepted as a work of art. Why?

If a grown-up, mature person had done it, it would be considered wonderful. Why? I think because the sheer point of conflict for a work is that one has to overcome the problems that impede the mature mind, knock down the obstacles and return to the pure and simple. That is the test, the crux of the matter. A saturated mind, sorted out, cancelled.

I don't want to play another record or write anymore and yet I'm not wanting to go into the bare, colourless, impersonal living room where Mother is doing school work. [*She worked as a secretary in a secondary modern school.*] I think I shall sit in this warm, glowing room and look in the mirror or comb my hair or re-read Derek's letter - or just listen to the rain.

Thursday 7 January 1959, Yeovil
Yesterday was a very happy one. Beaver fetched me [*she was the only one to have transport - if unable to borrow her father's car she drove a battered old Lambretta; it was rare for students to have cars*] and we went to fetch Anne. Trundled to Beaminster to a shop that sold books but was closed. On the way we had cider and then to West Bay where we climbed over slot machines to spend, or rather, to save, a penny, and then to Ray's old flat. Then to Weymouth, coffee, noughts and crosses on the tablecoth, more laughing. Then to Dorchester, the Nappers' Mite, then Rampisham and scrambled eggs. Then back to the Nappers' Mite, rude conversations, much laughter, great fun, fish and chips. A wonderful laughing day. Home to Yeovil. Stopped by police looking for two Dartmoor prisoners on the run.

People who are too busy living don't have time to think about life. Activity destroys thought. Too much thought makes activity pointless.
Mr Bates[4] called at lunchtime to invite Beaver and myself to tea. I have no drawings to show him and will have to confess my lack of enthusiasm.

---

[4] David Bates: painter. Studied under George Sweet at West of England College of Art, Bristol, 1945-9: at the Royal College of Art, 1950-3: contemporary of John Bratby, Frank Auerbach, Jack Smith and Bill Goldsmith. Taught at Lancaster College of Art, Boot's College, Nottingham and Yeovil School of Art, 1954-61. Senior lecturer in Drawing at Preston

I've written to Derek and I'm desperate to know where to get the money for the fare. The truth is I have only 7/6 left and the fare is £1 5s 8d.
For nearly two hours I've been dreaming in front of the fire and it's a queer feeling when you come to and there's the rest of the afternoon to be lived through. The fire is right down now and I'm longing to see Derek. I hate the cold and the light. I like warmth and half-light. I hate having to keep appointments. Beaver will be all nervous. I can't think why we're so scared of Bates for I consider him a pattern of honesty, enthusiasm and all that is good.

Friday 8 January 1959, Yeovil
We had a wonderful evening with the Bateses. Their home is beautiful; wonderful proportions and the way they've decorated it is very good. The stairs are straight and wide and the rooms spacious. [*It was an ordinary late-Victorian semi-detached house but compared to the prefab in which I was living at the time, it was the epitome of elegance.*] We talked about art in general and Russian art in particular. Bates is going to the CND [*Campaign For Nuclear Disarmament*] demonstration at Swaffam but Mrs Bates can't go because she's pregnant. Bates said there's enough radioactivity in the air already to kill or malform babies still in the womb. It's a frightening thought and yet those bloody brutes carry on blindly, stupidly creating more bombs.

The answer is, of course, for the workers at the base to refuse but then they're so damned stupid they only care about their pay packets. They live in the pointless world of the present and we are led into a hopeless, horrible future. Last night I tried to get Mother to see the crisis we are all in and that it is her responsibility as much as anybody else not to just sit and watch, not even realising the terrifying reality of the atom bomb. She didn't really take it in and can't see that in the next war

---

Polytechnic: Manager, Arts Centre, 1961-78. Exhibitions: West of England Academy; Royal Academy; Abbot Hall, Kendal. One-man shows; Keele University, 1967; Tib Lane, Manchester, 1974. Paintings in a number of collections in the north of England.

there won't be time for *coping* or anything human like there was in the last one. It'll be too quick and terrible and yet she just shrugs and doesn't bother to even think about it. I'm almost as bad. I think about it and talk about it but what else? There's Bates, a man with so much to just sit and be pleased about yet *he's* going to Swaffam. Even if the demonstrators are laughed at, at least there are a few people who care about being blown sky high and producing deformed children. What is the hope for our children? At every moment we dread that some madman is preparing world extinction. It could happen now, this minute, or tomorrow, any time. England would be the first to go, I expect; we're pretty well disliked and very small. Yet, the young are up and shouting all over the world, protesting at the insanity of so much that goes on - in Cuba, Hungary, France, England, Germany and a faint, far away whisper from Russia.

Back to college on Monday and what have I done? Nothing. Only a book begun here, a note-book that is proof of nothing of importance to anyone except me. I haven't touched my paints or done any drawing. I always used to be drawing and painting. Talking with Bates helped a bit but I feel I am to be an admiring onlooker in art as well as in music and literature. I think next term will be an important and decisive one. I will have to make some headway or quit and do something else. I must work. The Taunton people will be all frosty and humped in a corner and they won't talk to me unless forced. I'll be in Basingstoke on Sunday. I'm sure Derek doesn't really want me to go; I look particularly hideous lately. I have no bust whatsoever today and no back to my head - many spots.

Saturday 9 January 1959, Yeovil
Started to snow a little. I had a letter from Derek; he may be there to meet me and maybe not. I saw a programme on reincarnation yesterday and there was so much for and against. Who cares anyway? I don't feel very well today.

Monday 11 January 1959, Yeovil
And I'm still here in Yeovil - snow, snow, snow. My hands can hardly hold my pen and I have two fires on. I missed the 9.58 am train and so

must catch the 2.32 pm instead. I'm glad, now I have time to write. The whole country seems frozen into silence.
Yesterday I went to Basingstoke and had a very happy day. In the morning, however, I had to leave at 6.15 am and it was deathly white and absolutely deserted and I was scared. I had to walk through the town - oh, the comfort of a light in a window! I seemed to be the only one in the streets but I heard the jangle of a milk lorry in the distance.
The world in the early morning, especially in the snow, is like a fairyland belonging to cats and goblins. Completely alone, walking through deserted, echoing streets, empty shops with their lights on, an illusion of life where there is none, not a soul. And zebra crossings, redundant, with the orange balls still blinking.

As I passed Boots, the chemist, the long hand of the clock clanked up a minute with so loud a noise, performing its duty unseen through every minute of the night. The train was very weird and the other people, the porter, the driver, the train itself, seemed remote, run by silent clockwork. Early morning is a different world. As the train went on the light was seeping through, somewhere, and the whole countryside had the look of an old and faded photograph. As it got lighter more detail was revealed like magic.

Arrived at Basingstoke and started to walk down the hill and I saw Derek and Rynty [*his Alsatian dog*] at the bottom, coming up to meet me. Their pub is wonderful, very low, thick-beamed and very rambling - little narrow staircases. Mr and Mrs Boshier are very sweet. Derek and I took Rynty for a walk, about six miles - really bitterly cold, biting coldness. Basingstoke is an odd, jumbled, untidy little town, with many grey railway bridges and funny churches. I want to go up next weekend but have no money. Had a filthy journey back; had to wait at Yeovil Junction for nearly half an hour in the bitter cold and then, no buses in Yeovil so I walked all the way home in the ice and snow.

I had that dreadful stitch pain in my lungs again when I got home. Had an awful argument with my brother and mother about the terrible situation the world is in. I was desperately depressed and saw the future as one of horror and hopelessness. They are right, I know, when they say there is no place for people like me who think everything is hopeless but I say there is no place for sitters who just dismiss the horror and shut their eyes to what is happening. Still, what good is it for me to praise the fighters at Swaffam? I'm not for them; how can I be when I am full of despair? They are full of hope, that's why they fight. If they thought it was all hopeless they wouldn't bother. So I am the fool, on neither side.

In America, Mr Mikoan, Russian big-bod, is being demonstrated against as 'a bloody henchman'. Rebel freedom fighter, Fidel Castro, has taken over Cuba. The Communist epidemic is creeping throughout the world - Russia, China. I can't see how the Communists can fail to overpower the whole world in the end. Britain is undermined with it.

I heard Artur Rubenstein talking on the wireless last night and playing a superb Mendelssohn sonata. When I hear great men voicing perfectly the thoughts I too share, it's a great comfort. But this hopelessness of mine is a grave fault. These men are very distressed but they have hope. There are musicians in Warsaw watched by Russian hawks, great men, with a great deal to say and yet they have hope. And they could be shot tomorrow! And here I am, sheltered, with very little hardship in my life and only my mind to worry me.

At Derek's I was reading about the new UNESCO Headquarters in Paris; a fabulous building, crescent-shaped, and inside, murals by Picasso and other great painters of today. I believe art is coming back a little, i.e. in Coventry Cathedral. Brazil is a paradise for mural painters. Derek will make a good mural painter. He's had work in the Royal Academy, for what that's worth, and a Brighton gallery.
I feel and look awful - my face all flushed and blotchy and my eyes are dull, my hair hanging limp. I've just been reading Longfellow and some other American poets.

Monday evening and I'm in bed in Taunton in dreary digs. I hate this place so much and I want to get away. I feel sick at the thought of this term. I'll never write in this book properly again. I just don't think here.

Tuesday 12 January 1959, Taunton
Evening. Utterly depressed. I have no interest in art at all. No letter from Derek.

Monday 18 January 1959, Taunton
And so much had happened. Went to Basingstoke for the weekend and had a wonderful time - creeping upstairs. Last week I was in the deepest despair but this week I am a little brighter but broke already. A man, a teacher in Exeter, offered me fifteen shillings an hour to pose nude. I never have time to write in this book. My thoughts are a shallow stream and I think of Derek a lot of the time.

Saturday 19 January 1959, Yeovil
I have regained a certain amount of interest in my work again. Thank God I have shed a little of that horrible despair. At last I am home in my room with my records and time to think clearly and above all to write. Mother and I have been discussing the possibility of my moving to Bristol but the problem is money - *money!* Socially, Taunton is a stagnant pool compared to the rushing rivers of Bristol or London - people, lectures, films, parties, discussions, influences. There is absolutely nothing in Taunton and what a waste to be cooped up here when I could be learning - there's so little time.

What is the end for women in this business? Teaching in primary schools! Anyway, with this new system only the Royal College people will get the few jobs going. I must get my ATD [*Art Teachers' Diploma, postgraduate degree*] but I feel incapable. The thought of teacher training horrifies me. The shadow of parentage and sacrifice, not even allowed to make one's own mistakes. I must keep on painting. I've just begun two life studies, a still life and a mother and child composition. Holterman [*the Principal, Somerset College of Art*] liked the first nude but I'm getting bogged on the second. I hate the feeling of getting bogged down, forgetting the whole, fiddling. I want to keep the work broad, honest and open. My work is constipated and I'm striving all the time for looseness.

Derek wrote me a long letter when he was on guard on Wednesday night.[5]

Next weekend I'm meeting him in London. We'll do some exhibitions and go back to Basingstoke for Sunday. No money. I'm going to take some old clothes to a shop in Taunton and sell them. I met some girls I knew at school and they were like strangers. I could see they thought me an oddity and didn't like me at all. I left them with a feeling of hopelessness and feeling very shabby and wondering which existence is the most use and which brings peace of mind. But peace of mind only comes to minds that have known other than peace - if a mind has no turmoils and trouble, then happiness or peace of mind can only be slight.

At Laurie Fricker's[6] house we were talking about the age at which a person has something to express - we put forward thirty as a good age. I will be in London with Derek looking shabby and he will be ashamed of me. I do want to look nicer. I wish I had some money. It's wonderful to be here in my room with my records on and time to think. Anne and Beaver will be in Weston now and maybe going tonight to a jazz thing at Bristol but I couldn't go. Even hitching costs money - fags, cups of tea, etc. Longing for next weekend.

I was upset when I heard of the death of Mike Hawthorn [*racing driver*]. To think he was a living personality, moving, talking, laughing and now he's just an empty case, dead, nothing and no earthly power whatever can bring him back. It's a sad and sombre thought.

---

[5] He was doing his compulsory two-year National Service, stationed at Haslemere, Surrey, prior to starting at the Royal College of Art. Some painters, David Hockney, Bob Organ and others, were conscientious objectors and served their time working as auxiliaries in Mental Asylums or as Mortuary Assistants.

[6] Laurie Fricker: Lecturer in Landscape Architecture at University of Edinburgh, 1962 -93.

It's freezing cold and my hands are shaking. The oil stove has had it and the stupid electric one-bar is pathetic. I look frightful this morning. My hair is like straw and my legs are blue and blotchy - *ugh!* What is more I can't have the fire and the gramophone on at the same time - only one plug. I was going to make some pretty garters out of mauve and pink ribbon but can't face touching the ice-cold sewing machine.

I'm longing for the summer. I have a hidey-hole - a dream of a place where I can go and paint all day near French Weir in Taunton. From every angle there's a painting. A year's work lined up. As to Florence in the summer, Beaver keeps asking so many people to accompany us that to date there are about two hundred and five coming. I refuse to include any more women. Of course, I would like more than anything to go with Derek but he wouldn't think to ask me.

Tuesday 3 February 1959, Taunton

There is certainly plenty to write about but it's no longer fresh in my mind. Drinking oxtail soup with Derek in the Hayloft in South Kensington, near the Royal College. When you are with a person who is intent on getting away from and pushing aside the orthodox 'good design', with its good proportion and balance, you see that it begins to irritate the eye and that a conscious disorder, a deliberate re-arangement, is refreshing to the eye. Being with Derek, with his abstraction, you can see how realism (i.e. Augustus John, Spear, Sickert, etc.) has been on the compost heap too long and become stale. It's essential to learn and move on to prevent the mind stagnating.
I don't think I shall be seeing much more of Derek, though this will make me sad.

Thursday 5 February 1959, Taunton

Derek wrote only the shortest line on Monday and hasn't written since. I hope he really wants me to come to London or it'll be embarrassing. I'm very wary of telling him about the Valentine's Party at college because he'll go off with hundreds of girls and I'll die of jealousy.

Thursday 12 February 1959, Taunton

Alone in hideous digs. Thursday again and no night-school. Beaver has gone home and I have a few moments to myself. I made a mess of two life paintings this week and one still life. Bitty, badly drawn and completely unrealised as a whole. It's amazing how long it takes to make a mess. I've thrown away my small brushes to help cure my static, hideous constipation and I'm freer and slightly better for it. I was looking at some Daumier, wonderful use of paint. Tim is on the list for prizes. Poor thing - he was getting on quite well with the still life until Murphy[7] came and scrubbed it out and demonstrated on it!

It's amazing how precious one gets over the most horrible efforts in paint.

I suddenly feel lonely. Why is there something so sad about being alone and hearing a wireless in another room?

I shall be sad when Beaver's gone, especially in the evenings. No more parties, laughs - I shall be lost for a while.

Mrs S, the gruesome landlady and that revolting child are in bed and it's only 6.25 pm and cold down here in this bare room. Patches [*art student in Weston-super-Mare*] says the Post Office is going to to take action against us because of the rude drawings we do on the envelopes we send him.

Once I've drunk my allotted flask of weak tea there'll be nothing else to do but go to bed. No wireless, no gramophone, silence. 6.40 pm now. I'll go and get my tea at seven and not before. It's like a Samuel Beckett play. Here I am wishing my training was over; how I'll kick myself later for wasting time. I realise that this time should be wonderful but it isn't. I get moments, an hour at most, of enthusiasm and then watch the clock for hour after hour, day after day - waiting for what?

---

[7] Terry Murphy: painter. Studied at the Royal College of Art, 1953-6, at the time when Peter Blake, Leon Kossoff, John Bratby, Frank Auerbach and Bridget Riley were also students and John Minton was a part-time painting tutor. Tutor at Somerset College of Art, 1958-64 and thereafter at Cheltenham College of Art.

A gnawing boredom. I wish I had a wireless. I never listen to music any more. I hardly ever read. I'm in a state of decay, but fully conscious, which is dreadful.
Five minutes past seven and I've had my allotted cup of tea and two rock cakes, both tasteless and now my pleasures have gone for the evening. It's like when the lights in the street go out.

Saturday 7 February 1959, Yeovil
And now I am home and in my room once more. No letter from Derek. Anne and I hitched back last evening and got picked up in a Rolls-Royce, a direct run. We did 100 mph without realising it. I still want to move to Bristol; the prospectus reflects the spirit of the place and the emphasis is on a serious study course, drawing being the basis. I don't know if they'll take me for the second-year NDD. [*National Diploma in Design*]. I must creep at Taunton to get a scholarship and then push off. The whole place is upside down, everyone's leaving, hating the place. There's no Students' Union, no communication whatsoever, except to moan about the place. It's a very third-rate school though Murphy works wonders.

Most of the exhibits at the Russian Exhibition were appalling though the icons were wonderful, beauties of design, yet their followers completely ignore design and seem oblivious of their heritage.

I've just spent a few hours on something hopeless. Is an accidental masterpiece art? Why do modern painters pick *one* aspect of all the great art and pursue it to an extreme? Take colour, for example. There are countless works produced today consisting purely of colour contrasts. Some are quite pleasing but what a limitation. In a painting by Giotto there's a wealth of colour, in Piero, in Gauguin, but how much more - there lies the genius. Do painters who follow one aspect, one theme, do so because they lack the ability to go further? A good painting, containing all aspects, is rarely done today. There lies the genius, the work well done, the combination of all these factors to create a work of beauty.
Is the modern mind incapable of a wider concept or have we lost the capacity for concentration and gruelling effort? Generally, the bad

modern painter produces a small canvas on a small theme. Picasso is a genius of output, if nothing else - a wide scope, fantastic versatility. Is it just that the modern mind doesn't want to include all aspects at once - or is it incapable?

Monday 9 February 1959, Taunton
The work I did yesterday looks even worse today. Beaver has been to collect her things. She's going to Corsham Court of all things, a place of pretentious idiots. A good life pose today.

Wednesday 11 February 1959, Taunton
A row about a letter sent to the college by David Chant. Idiot, a very amusing letter. I've started a new still-life - two apples on a drawing board. I do hope I hear from Derek tomorrow.

Friday 13 February 1959, Yeovil
Oh, the luxury of a stolen morning in my room, a stolen afternoon yet to come, a huge pile of notes, odd bits, things to sort through, an oil stove, a head full of things to write, a stolen pen I can write with, my beloved records and the luxury of time I don't normally have. Escape is sweet. It's only when one's alone that one becomes familiar once more with one's own spirit, detached from the body that one is always conscious of in company. People who are never alone have no time, no inclination, no necessity, to search for their own souls.

I wish I could express my thoughts more easily and more clearly. Are they natural human thoughts or are they minute oddities of my own mind? Only rarely does another person voice my mind exactly. Second-hand thoughts are easily agreed upon; it's the original turn of reasoning that is unique and therefore, to a certain extent, incomprehensible to others.

I have the feeling that if I'd been lucky enough to have had music lessons and learned an instrument I would have played the cello. I wonder at such beautiful, unearthly sounds coming from an instrument made from something as solid and earthbound as a tree.

I heard a journalist say on the televison last night that the Russians have agreed to let Boris Pasternak out of Russia for a lecture tour.

We were talking about Dadaists yesterday. Fur-lined cups and saucers and spoons, irons with nails in them. I think this is an essential element in all of us brought sharply into focus, making us shudder. It's all to do with dreams, spirits, surrealism. I hope Tachism follows Dadaism in its brief triumph, looked back on as an oddity, a joke, fun, strange, anything - but not painting.

Is there any new good music being written, any new good writing, any new good painting? Or does every decade say it's all been done, what now? We have Picasso, a great pioneer, now seventy-six. He can die knowing he's achieved so much, used his mind and many talents to the full and never became stale. A pioneer in every sense, treading new ground with confidence and doing it so well. A great capacity for work and an extremely inquisitive, sensitive mind. I would love to meet him.

I said to Murphy yesterday that Holterman is very clever in the way he's often *not* at college yet when he *does* come in he makes such a noise that you think he's always there. Whenever he sees me he grins like an idiot; his eyes are slightly mad and he vibrates with nervous tension.

The party tomorrow. I've reached such a pitch of excitement over it that now it's nearly here I've no energy to anticipate it. As I was waiting to phone Beaver there was a man in a call box making arrangements for a wedding and the conversation was a complete study in human nature - he was angry, mellow, peeved, creeping, jovial, businesslike - all in one conversation.

As I went down the road I passed three giggling girls and one said: 'Well, Lil, I'll be honest with you, one Babycham and I'm happy!'

I had a letter from Derek and roared when I remembered the couple on the train, plus child and dog. The woman spent the whole journey ordering her husband about: 'Put the light on, rock the baby, mind the dog, get the magazines, gimme a fag, mind the kid, get the tickets...' Derek did a wonderful drawing of them.

I want a super old Valentine card or flowers or something but I won't get them. We're going to have old records and long beads at the party. Old friends, much laughter, drink; I'll be so happy I'll feel physically sick knowing it won't last long and the clock ticks on.

I often wonder, when I see a couple, the man all jolly and twinkling and the woman all tight-lipped. I suppose if they've been married long enough she's probably heard the same jokes so many times before but I feel sorry for a man who can't have an almighty roar with his wife. The Taunton men-students haven't the capacity for being vulgar, that's why they're so dull. Bob Organ[8] was very rude and Bates had his moments. Beaver's deliciously rude.

Saturday 14 February 1959, *Yeovil*
Mother and I have just had an argument about what she calls 'anticipating marriage'. Anticipating marriage! Good Lord, is that all there is to anticipate in marriage? I hate to upset her but she will stick to ideas without considering them, their use or the case in particular.

Sunday 15 February 1959, Yeovil
A good party but they're wearing thin and I felt moments of boredom. One of the twins from Weston was sick on vodka and slept all through under the coats on Beaver's bed. I missed Derek. I have no real interest in anyone else and just danced all night. I was exhausted by five o'clock and slept till eleven. I'm in my room, lonely and homesick for Rampisham. Mother is so bad-tempered it's impossible to live with her. Nothing is right and every time she speaks, she snaps.
On the bus to Rampisham there was a strangely beautiful little girl holding her ballet shoes. She had perfect carriage and prominent bones.

---

[8] Bob Organ: painter, architect. Slade Scholar; painting tutor, Falmouth School of Art, 1958-70. Tutor, Architectural Association, London, 1975-77. Visiting tutor at Bristol and Cambridge Universities, Architecture Depts. Lecturer, RIBA and Art Workers' Guild, SPAB. Has had six one-man shows and exhibits widely in London and the South West.

I found a bright yellow paper heart whilst clearing up the rubbish.

Monday 16 February 1959, Yeovil
There's a knock on the door but I won't answer. I hate people coming to the door. I look indescribably hideous today, really ugly and vaguely unhappy. It's as if the present doesn't exist because I'm doing things I don't normally do on a Monday. I'm in my room, playing old records which belong to another section of time. I bless this book - for me, it partly justifies things. Here is something, perhaps wrong, probably stupid, but something, proof of someone existing. I've always written things down. I make useless lists, never referred to, purely for the sake of writing things down and seeing thoughts, ideas, hopes and promises in material form.

What of the future? Beaver has gone. Anne is going. Derek is far away and doesn't care a damn. I feel happier now the sun has gone in. I wish I had a bigger bust. Derek is the only one who has anything originally funny to say about it now. It's a pretty exhausted subject, anyway. There's Beaver, encumbered by Nature's goods and there's me, forgotten and unbestowed.

There's an unwelcome fug in this room. Monty Sunshine playing *Wildcat Blues*. The Frank Sinatra record reminds me of Derek and Yeovil Art School and being happy. The Bach brings me up to date. It has a nice alive feeling, in the present. The feelings I had a few moments ago are as remote as the feelings I had last week, a month ago.

Bishop Makarios has a beautiful face - a strong, intense, *biblical* face.

Cubism has a huge influence on advertising; small doses of it are constantly thrown at the public with beer and soapflakes and they don't notice. Posters are cubistic, linear, startling colour contrasts, oddities, tricks - all accepted without so much as a whimper.

Tuesday 17 February 1959, Taunton

Back in Taunton. This evening we had a prize giving. Holterman told many speechy lies about the place and the painter, Carel Weight[9], talked with simplicity and good sense. Afterwards we had a booze-up in the Common Room with a crate of beer.

There was no letter waiting for me. Derek hasn't written since last Thursday. I'm starved of company and feel like talking to complete strangers. Mother and I were arguing about John Bratby[10] last night and she said that if she met him she'd ask what he meant by his 'messes' on walls. I told her Bratby hadn't asked her to like them - if she does, well and good. He is fundamentally one step ahead of her in that he has made the 'messes', she has not. To do something is far better than being a mere spectator.

Thursday 19 February 1959, Taunton

Another miserable day. I abandoned the landscape as there's a thick fog and went into the reading room instead and wrote a poem. I don't want to go to the party but I don't know how to get out of it. For one thing, there are no interesting men at all and I've no money for drink, ticket or cigarettes and I'm not interested in the people who'll be there. My hair needs washing but I can't afford a shampoo. I want to meet people in other fields - our outlook down here is appalling narrow. We don't even know much about art. Beaver has flu and won't be going.

---

[9] Carel Weight: painter. Lecturer at the Royal College of Art: Professor of Painting, 1957-73. Work mixes realism and fantasy. Major exhibitions, Bernard Jacobson Gallery, 1988, and *Strange Happenings in the Common Place,* at Christie's, 1993.

[10] John Bratby: [1928-92]: painter. Studied at the Royal College of Art 1951-4. Generally termed a 'kitchen sink' painter: introduced popular brand-name images in advance of the Pop artists of the early Sixties. Prolific and widely exhibited, his work is flamboyant and heavily impastoed. At 26 he had his first one-man show at the Beaux Arts Gallery: Guggenheim Awards in 1956/7/8. Member of the Royal Academy. Major retrospective, National Portrait Gallery, 1991.

Anne will go with that man and I'll be left ugly and unattached, smiling as if I don't mind.

I've just read some astonishing facts - that 700,000 people each night sleep out on the streets of Bombay. This was disclosed by Arthur Koestler,[11] one-time Communist writer. He was once only concerned with politics but now, at fifty-three, he's a humanitarian and a philosopher.
I'm reading one of Aldous Huxley's essays and he's horribly longwinded, repeating himself appallingly; the writing is jerky which adds to the general dullness.

Friday 20 February 1959, Yeovil
I'm at home and I want it to be gone two o'clock so I know I'm not missing anything at the party. I just felt so vile and dull and dirty, I just couldn't go. I'm playing one of my records and I'm happy. I've re-read Derek's last letter. I must go up next weekend. My books, my records, my chair - oh, I'm so happy.

Last night I was very frightened, buzziness and nightmares and when I woke I felt a strong presence in the room. I imagined something supernatural moving about on my pillow. The room, my brain, everything, was alive, electric with some power.

I hear there is a peace settlement over Cyprus - wonderful news. Anne's so lucky having Laurie for company, always amusing and interesting company and a super place to lodge. I hate my digs. In half an hour there's some Handel and Beethoven on the wireless. Derek says the Bratby exhibition at the Beaux Arts is very good. I've just done a quick self-portrait. Of course, in this lantern light this absurd mess is just brilliant. Now to Handel and Beethoven and some real brilliance.

---

[11] Arthur Koestler:[1905-1983] Hungarian-born British writer, humanist, escaped imprisonment by the Nazis in France, 1940, and soon after published '*Darkness At Noon*'. He wrote extensively on creativity, politics and culture and was a fierce opponent of Captial Punishment. A member of the Voluntary Euthanasia Society he died in a suicide pact with his wife.

Saturday 21 February 1959, *Yeovil*
Mother has just said that my head is full of myself, which is true. We are always at loggerheads. She's very nervy and irritable. I'm forgetful, untidy and also nervy and irritable. Sometimes, when she goes on and on about something it irritates me so much I almost scream and have to bite my mouth to stop myself. We are always irritating each other from the moment I come in. It would seem that my very presence and the sight of me irritates her.

I loathe this miserable town. I want to shut myself away for ever and never have to go out again. This endless frustration, not seeing the end of anything, knowing that Derek doesn't really care much one way or the other, having no real friends, always frustrated in everything I do. Looking awful, feeling awkward and wretched. No laughs. No holiday hitching to Italy now Beaver's left. No nothing.

Sunday 22 February 1959, Yeovil
Yesterday I read Tolstoy's *The First Distiller* and am in the middle of *The Power of Darkness*. I've yet to read my other books, Aristotle, etc. I'm in the middle of *Antic Hay* and still reading Tolstoy's *The Fruits of Enlightenment* and will write to Derek later. He obviously doesn't want me to go up until Sunday but it's a lot of money for one day. Taunton tomorrow. The loneliness I feel there at nights I find hard to imagine now but how strong it'll be in a few hours time.

Tuesday 24 February 1959, Taunton
Last night was awful. In the evening after night-school C and I went to the Snug for cider. He's a staunch believer in Black Magic and we discussed the power of evil, the reason for existence etc. I dreaded going back to my digs. Waking nightmares of familiar faces becoming hideous with evil grins and hands turning into claws.
This morning I felt gloriously happy to be alive and in my right mind and the sun was shining. In the day I forget the horrors but at night the whole world changes and becomes a lonely nightmare, a battle against oneself and the supernatural.

Completed a nasty portrait of June, the model. I can only see the future as it is now, without real friends. I walk about as I did last evening - people working, Murphy printing, Guy doing something, everyone not lonely at all, no need of me whatever. Beaver has a job in Oxford and wants Anne, Laurie and me to go over to Rampisham for the weekend. But I must go to Basingstoke to see Derek.

Thursday 26 February 1959, Taunton
Much happier now. On Tuesday night I overcame that dreadful thing that hung over me and slept without mishap and had a wonderful time last evening. Pubbing with Anne, Laurie and C. Skittles, singing in the car, C playing the piano and Laurie singing - so funny, marvellous. Driving through Taunton at three o'clock in the morning, pissed as newts. And now it's Thursday morning and my head feels like lead.

Derek wrote to say he has the flu but to still go up on Sunday. He's got two paintings in *The Young Contemporaries*. I think he has terrific ambition and besides, he hasn't even begun at the Royal College yet and is very up and coming.

It was wonderful last night. I was happy for a while. People, company, laughs. Completely broke now. Nothing at all, not even three pence to stamp a letter to Beaver to say I won't be over to Rampisham this weekend.

I went to the place by the Weir and did a small oil sketch then a very nasty painting. Today I started another monstrosity of Liz [*the other nude model*]. Holterman says I'm improving but I say *'phhtt phutt burp'*. Tonight I'm going out and I'm so happy!

Friday 27 February 1959, Yeovil
Now at home. My records. I feel physically sick with the beauty of the music. Hitched home with Anne, singing. Wonderfully happy, straightforward lorry drivers. They're so kind and very witty without knowing it.

Saturday 28 February 1959, Yeovil
Today I have been industrious. I've cut four lino blocks ready to print on Monday evening and roughed a design for a fabric print. Basingstoke tomorrow. I must get some money somehow. My head aches.
C, who believes that evil is prominent in Man and therefore right, believes that he has no spirit and the only reason he can think, feel any emotion, etc. is merely the pumping of his heart, the co-operation of his various muscles and organs and that's all. When his heart stops he is nothing. We argued for hours on the point of existence. He says that Man is basically evil, what he calls 'basic man'.
But I think it's just as natural to be good as bad but evil is very easy to accomplish. He says, as a basic man, he is drawn towards evil and as it's hard to be good it's much simpler to worship evil. As a basic man he denounces civilisation yet when the barman leaned over and asked him to pass a few empty glasses he jumped up and, smiling, did as he was bid. I said: 'If you are naturally evil, and seeing as you are basically uncivilised, why didn't you screw one of the glasses into his face?' Instead, it was natural for him to be courteous. Each man for himself, he says, and then helps collect a stranger's glasses for him.

At the moment I'm inclined to think that maybe when the mortal human body ceases to function, the spirit, the force of life, the soul, is expelled, merging with the other life forces in the atmosphere and so continues as part of the great life force pool that revolves from one thing to another, never dying. A life force, whether in a planet, an atom, a vibration, heat, plants, animals, anything that lives.

Sunday 1 March 1959, Yeovil
That horrible empty feeling coming home in the train away from Derek. People reading, talking, bustling about. All alone again, leaving him behind, not knowing when I'll see him again. knowing he's already dismissed me from his mind. He takes me for granted now. Taunton again in a few hours - on and on, leaving people, more loneliness, more boredom, more terrors and yet he knows nothing of this. He's not interested. I'm just a thing that comes up now and again to make his Sunday a little less boring.

I do like Derek's painting, *Creation of Eve*. Conventional 'good' design is so irritating - it hurts the mind to see it reproduced in a thousand paintings that say nothing.

Monday 2 March 1959, Taunton
I felt so ashamed at the bus-stop this evening and boiling angry inside. Next to me, sheltering from the rain, was a coloured woman in a navy macintosh and a rather ugly beret. She was very ordinary and silent. Then a bunch of hideous girls walked by and laughed and jeered at her. I felt like kicking their teeth in. I was watching her and for a moment a sort of horror, or fear, or plain misery crossed her face and her eyes looked wet but the next minute her face was blank and it was as if she hadn't heard.

Today, on the train, when I saw a hundred subjects for paintings all around me, on either side, flashing past - willows, flat plains, people working in fields - I felt determined to stay in Taunton after all and just paint and paint, but now, after one dismal attempt I'm once more disillusioned and the enthusiasm has passed as quickly as it came.

Tuesday 3 March 1959, Taunton
A new life pose, a good one. No decent-sized canvasses, only square boards. I'll prepare some callico tomorrow. Printing my lino cuts this evening. Worked hard and feel better but the prints aren't very good. Every other minute I think about Derek and mountains are built without foundations.

Wednesday 4 March 1959, *Taunton*
Rain, bleak rain and no money. I've got to save up 12/6 for my Beethoven Harp record and next week we have a trip to London. Where can I get some money? My coat is threadbare, my shoes worn out. I've no lipstick, no scent to speak of, and very few, nasty clothes. I dream of finding some money or being left some. I must buy Zola's *Germinal* as soon as possible. My painting of willows is too hopeless for words.

Later - washed and in bed and my ears are burning. The romantic in me imagines that Derek is in his sentry-box (this is the night he does his

guard duty) thinking of me. However, the pessimistic and sane side of me wonders if I have caught his flu.
There's a howling wind and the rain is lashing down, wonderful. The sound of the dustbin lids rattling down the streets. I wish the college was open all night. I dread the bell at 8.30 pm; everyone hurrying off. I'd like to stay and work and not feel lonely.

It's strange, there's Mother living in much the same way, at work all day and alone at nights. I feel sorry for her, having no one to talk to and feeling no one cares about her but when we see each other we squabble and get on each other's nerves to screaming pitch. What a life she's had, all those years with no one to turn to.

Thursday 5 March 1959, Taunton
Today I had to paint next to Holterman. It's good to have the Head painting near you, a much better atmosphere. A painters' day - just Tim, Holterman, Murphy and me, no other students, no part-timers and plenty to do. This was one of the very few days when time has gone quickly and I barely looked at the clock. Holterman uses browns, whites and ochres. When you see a person painting you see them as they are, with all the veils drawn aside.

Saturday 7 March 1959, Yeovil
Yesterday evening was wonderful. Anne and I hitched to Weston - kind lorry drivers again. One bought us a cup of coffee between us, huddled in his lorry, all squashed up and wet. Bouncing into Weston, walking the last two miles, singing, wet and dirty. Patches had to stay and work in the coffee bar and all the arrangements were mucked up so we got out of Weston and hitched another lorry. Lorry drivers work day and night and take pleasure in the simplest things. They seem to have no ambition, perhaps a few half-hearted daydreams but they are content. They stay with people like themselves because they like them best and therefore they have no social problems. They have enough money and are masters of their lorries. Lined, wrinkled faces, eyes screwed up, glued to the road, their strong arms turning the great wheels, laughter; they don't criticise, they just accept.

No letter from Derek. I've just been looking through an old sketch-book and I'm ashamed to say that my drawing hasn't improved. We were always drawing, anything and everything - now, I don't even know where my sketch-book is. Anne has a sketch-book full of damn good drawings. My life painting has improved beyond recognition but as for my other work I am ashamed and uneasy.
I wonder what Derek is doing in London? At some party or other, I suppose. It's sad that I must think of a future without him. If I became a streak of green paint on his canvas he might at least bother to get up and scrape me off.

Much of the journal for the period March 1959 to March 1960 has been omitted. The following brief extracts may suffice to effect some continuity.

How sad that I have to buy my own artificial rose because nobody would think of giving me one, not even a single violet. When I was in London with Derek an old flower-seller tried to sell him a small bunch of violets to give to me but he didn't seem to notice her and just kept on walking. If only he knew how much I would have loved to have been given just *one* violet.

And when we went to find out the time of the train back to Basingstoke he rushed me on and we caught it. I wanted to stay in London till the last train but just because all the galleries were shut and he couldn't take his dog for a walk he thought there was nothing to do. On our own in London, Saturday night, unlimited time! He hasn't got blood in his veins - he's got turps and slightly diluted at that. Being him I suppose I must accept it but how wonderful it would be if he wrote more often or said *one* nice thing to me.

Wednesday 11 March 1959, Taunton
Saw *The Inn of the Sixth Happiness* with Anne. Once more I wanted to scream at the futility of war and shudder at the unspeakable horrors it will bring. The next one won't be running around with tanks and guns, etc; it will be deadly quick. It'll be a scientists' war. Every day there's

fighting somewhere - why? Dictators, power-mad lunatics, insane men hiding behind politics.

Bad art is distributed everywhere; why is art overlooked and second-rate work accepted? Why can't people *see*? Surely if they're going to look at something on their posters, papers, soap packets, etc. why not something good? Good design costs no more to produce.

But things are improving - some posters, at least, are better, photography used brilliantly in some instances. Today, the camera man's conception has come closer to that of the painter. But painting will always win because it's to do with re-creation, not just brilliant shovelling around of objects to make a good design.

Thursday 12 March 1959, Taunton
This morning a summons from Sheikh Boshier himself requiring the first woman of the harem to Basingstoke when the sun is high to await his command. It was on the back of a relief map.

Tuesday 17 March 1959, Taunton
A pleasant weekend at Basingstoke. On the train a young man with green eyes who came from London asked me to write to him because something about me amazed him because he couldn't take his eyes off me, all the time staring and biting his lip - very odd. He stared intensely out of the window and made improper suggestions and stroked his knees as though he were trying to fathom something. I never make that journey without something like that happening.

On the train coming back there was a beautiful young soldier with Malayan blood in him I guessed - anyway, whatever exotic, sordid, ordinary or rash fusion was the cause, the result was very beautiful indeed.

Derek took me to Burghclere to see some of Stanley Spencer's[12] paintings. Very good, in a funny chapel where you ask for the key and sign the visitors' book. It was freezing on the back of the scooter. I like him so much but he takes me for granted, leaves me for ages at a time, never speaks to me but talks to his dog all the time.

Thursday March 1959, Taunton

Today I bought some wonderful record bargains - a Bach and a Beethoven Quartet for 2/-, a Ravel for 1/-, a Handel for 1/- and two Yehudi Menuhin's for 1/- each. I want all the terrific records in the whole world. Happy, happy, happy.

Anne and I are going to join the Anti-Nuclear march from the atomic station at Aldermaston to London.

To Bristol yesterday: exhibiton of *Twentieth-Century Watercolours* on loan from the Tate and the V & A. John Minton, Graham Sutherland, John Piper, Henry Moore, Ruskin Spear, Keith Vaughan, Paul Nash, John Nash, Leonard Rosoman, Epstein, Sickert and Stanley Spencer. Well worth seeing. In another gallery - three Matthew Smiths, wonderful, and a terrific still-life by Lawrence Gowing - a Pissarro, a Utrillo, a Sickert, two Ruskin Spears, a John Bratby self-portrait, a Ben Nicholson and a Reg Butler.

Thursday [no date]

Term at an end. In London bought a Gigli 78 for 2/- and saw the Bratby Exhibition in the Beaux Arts, off Bond Street. Interesting, very definite statement on people, humanity - size, about 6ft by 4ft, about the size of Derek's *Creation of Eve*.

Stranded the night in the bog at Paddington Station; no food and no money. Five and a half hours! Fumes, dirt, grime, hunger - charged 17/- for trying to get through with a day return ticket, so expecting a summons. I refuse to pay it as it was a tube cancellation at Earls Court that did it, missed the train by a minute.

---

[12] Stanley Spencer: painter[1891-1959]. Born and died in Cookham, Berkshire; eccentric personality and prolific painter of large allegorical works using figures and scenes from the contemporary village life around him.

Foul old woman with snuff and sores and rolled-down crepe stockings and a bucket scrubbing all night. Only four pence between us; not a cigarette or enough for a cup of tea. An old prostitute snoring away, emitting unhealthy splurts and snores.

Caught the 5.30 am train, got to Taunton at 10.00 am via everywhere one doesn't want to via. An Italian sat on my Gigli but it didn't break. Later we met Laurie and had a happy time and a few drinks. He's wonderful company. On Monday we hitch to Studland to get a job. No letter from Derek.

When I'm in London I feel so insignificant that I want to crawl away but now I want to be there again. Taunton College has bought a painting by Carel Weight.

I'm very ashamed that I didn't go on the Aldermaston March; we fully intended to go but honestly had no money with which to get up to London to start with let alone the four days of the march. You can't even protest without money. I hope it does some good. They've reached Reading so far. How this supposedly Christian country can be so apathetic - surely such weapons of mass destruction must be anti-Christian. And yet most people don't even know what's being made in the next field and the rest sit back and say there's nothing we can do. There is - protest!

What is needed is a 'guinea-pig' nation, strong and brave enough to disarm and be completely without atomic weapons; one can't have good uses of atomic energy and not the aggressive - that's impossible - we must rid ourselves completely. This might be the move that is needed to start to solve this terrible crisis and it can't make things worse.

Macmillan has signed a Cultural Treaty between the Soviet Union and Britain; this is wonderful. If men concentrated on the mind there would be peace. Unless we protest the government will never know what we demand, how we feel, it's through the people that this so-called democracy should work. So the only answer is to demonstrate, wake people up, show them the issue in hand; if public opinion is strong enough, if the whole country *demands* disarmanment, then disarm we will.

Yves St Laurent is so perfect it's unbearable. I wish he were very ordinary and I could meet him. But if you write to him he doesn't get letters. He's completely unapproachable. He's my ideal man.

The situation in Tibet is heart-breaking and terrible.[13] It makes me want to weep. All this war and hatred. These bloody Communist madmen. They've killed 20,000 Tibetans and thrown thousands more into labour camps, mostly monks - terrible, hideous and all those treasures destroyed. Tibet, of all places, country of my dreams. [*At sometime during that year I was working on a triptych depicting the Dalai Lama's flight into India.*] The Dalai Lama is so fascinating, disturbingly fascinating. I'm hoping all the time for his safety and happiness - a beautiful man.

On Sunday afternoon we went to Portsmouth. [*Derek's father had been a sailor and Derek was born in Portsmouth.*] A fascinating place, full of memories of sea-faring, taverns and old creaking ships. And all the lights and piers and fairs, bumpers and noise and bright lights and the dark silent sea and lots of cafes selling hamburgers and hot-dogs.
Yesterday we went to London in the van. Derek had to deliver his two 6ft x 4ft paintings for the RBA gallery and collect the two he'd had in *The Young Contemporaries*. We met his friend Peter who chars in the mornings to keep himself at St Martin's and hopes to get into the Royal College. It was raining in London. Derek's completely opposite to me; his whole being is epitomised in his paintings - very simple, straight-forward, clear, forthright abstractions. He has no sentiment, doesn't

---

[13] In 1950, Communist China invaded Tibet, killing thousands of Tibetan people and destroying monasteries and irreplaceable religious artifacts. In 1959, His Holiness, the Dalai Lama, urging his fellow Tibetans to adhere to their code of non-aggression, escaped to the Himalayan village of Dharamsala, in northern India, where he has lived in exile ever since.

cling to memories, things; he destroys all letters, is completely independent and lives wholely in the present, disregarding the past. He hates the old and creates the new. His whole existence is based in the present, newness. There's not an atom of the old, the fusty in him; he's brand new, like aluminium. I cling to memories, a shadow creature; he's neon lighting, I'm candles and lanterns. I keep old letters, old friendships, memories. He doesn't need them.

Sunday 12 April 1959
So now the government is making plans for evacuation to the Welsh mountains in case of nuclear war - idiots. We're a sitting target, it's absolutely futile - radiation is inescapable. I suppose it won't be long now.

Derek has got one of his paintings accepted; I'm very pleased. They're all getting together in Yeovil at Whitsun. What a terrific lawyer Laurie would make. Derek thinks this intense, widespread appreciation of the French Impressionists is a phase and that the German Expressionists should be next. Life is all phases, cycles, time itself. Fashion, taste, humour, people are all subject to phases. I'm sure this cold war of ours, always there, the tension, the predestined disaster, will bring them, the German Expressionists, in again. Abstraction is too cold for this cold war. The fire of Expressionism will be needed to quench the tension. John Bratby's an example and just look at his success.

Wednesday 25 April 1959, Taunton
At lunch time we met Laurie and went to see an old and very beautiful gazebo - old cast-iron spiral staircase and a little fireplace and lovely trees, blossoms and lime, and a garden gate, all overgrown, very beautiful, crumbling - and very sad because it's to be pulled down in a matter of weeks.

Friday 27 April 1959, Taunton
My report will be lousy. Everywhere I go Murphy pops up, 'What are you doing?' I walk down the stairs and Holterman pops out of his office, 'Where are you going?' I walk two steps and Simmons says 'What d'you think you're doing?' Then Thomas, 'What? No work to

do?' Hell, I can't move in any direction; nobody else suffers from this staff plague. Other people can give the impression of working like blazes when they're really skiving yet when I'm working I'm accused of slacking. I must save up for the Big Bill Broonzy record.

On Thursday a happy evening at Laurie's - Mrs Fricker's super food - and then we went to the Victory. Laurie's delicious and witty as always. 'A lovely young man', that's what he is.

I read today that Aneurin Bevan of the Labour Party has promised on the point of election to ban *all* H-bomb tests and abolish, as an example to other nations, all atomic power. I was very excited. This is what we need, a move at last from the top. They couldn't go back on a promise like that. Macmillan, bloody fool, says that fall-out has doubled in the last year and that within a year the amount of Strontium-90 in food, water, air, etc. will probably be at danger point but never mind, we'll wait till that happens, won't we? We bloody well won't, mate, fat bloated plutocrats.
At least Bevan will have the 3000-odd Aldermaston marchers behind him. God, I wish I were old enough to vote.

Friday night and I'm sitting up late on my own, a trifle love-sick. I didn't get a letter this morning. I was listening to a short thing on Buddhism and my interest was aroused once more. Very, very interesting and perhaps I could find some answers to the endless questions of this life.

Tuesday 1 May 1959, Taunton
Today it's sunny and I'm quite enthusiastic about a new life-pose. Yesterday Hazel, the great fatty in the café, asked me to leave because my knees were showing and I was showing too much leg. 'We're not 'aving none of that in 'ere,' she said, pressing her lips together. Good gracious me.

I still maintain there's a basic life-force, a basic energy in the explosion, the vibration that is life. Life is one long vibration, a chemical explosion, a split second long; we're aware of only the present

second, the previous second is gone and the only way we can record it is by memory. And this hemisphere is only a grain of dust. The whole universe is at the pitch of chemical explosion and the whole molecular structure we call Earth, civilisation, houses, social systems, ships, cars, roads, can go just like that as if a foot had squashed it. The whole structure is shifting and temporary, the falling together in an explosion; a temporary thing like a kaleidoscope, so easily shifted into another form.
If then we are grains of dust, refined to such detail, what of the rest of the galaxy? Inconceivable - and for what reason? Science surely rules out the Golden Gates and the keys of St Peter. Religion is surely a primitive safety hold. I can see the time when the religions of today will be like worshipping stones.

I saw a big American car, wide and open, with a man wearing a white shirt, sunglasses, elbow over the edge of the window; and in the back a blonde woman, also in white and sunglasses and a lovely looking baby in a carrying cot. They were all summery and young and happy. How lucky to have a beautiful husband, a car with the radio on, and a lovely child and life, the sun and time. Glorious. They were gone in a minute but they were the epitome of happiness and when they had gone I felt sad and shabby and tired.

The tall house at the end of this road speaks to me of affairs and warm evenings. It has wide, deep rooms. I have a feeling about the big room which I can see from the bus stop; it's as if it has many undeciphered memories for me - as if I have lived there in another time or that perhaps one day I shall live there. The familiar way the curtains hang, I can *smell* the room, I know its feeling, its atmosphere. Like people you somehow *know* yet watch them pass by, unable to do anything about it. Life goes too fast sometimes.
Mrs Murphy wore a beautiful dress today. Carl gave me a camel dung fag today. There's a vogue in college amongst the male specimens for fag trying-out.

Saturday - a beautiful hot day yesterday. We sat by the canal all day and my back is brown. Laurie has donned his boater and gone to

Reading. A very happy day until we got back to college to find Tim had gone back to Yeovil without us at 4 o'clock. We had to hitch in the sweltering heat. Very tired and hot.
A letter from Derek - he's coming today but only passing through with three others. Passing through - hell.
I have an idea for a painting of Anne in Laurie's 'painter's hat', a wonderful floppy straw. She has lovely weather for her dirty weekend in Oxford and is very excited.

Sunday - a surprise; Derek arrived on the doorstep at 1.30 pm looking wonderful. His scooter had broken down. We went to meet the others. It was a beautiful day but I was sad. I didn't get a chance to see him alone and he went at 4 o'clock.. He appeared to be very bored to be back in Yeovil which is understandable. I shall always remember him sitting at a table in the Cadena café, hundreds of people shopping in summer dresses, and he was bored and not saying anything and Anne and Beaver were talking and I couldn't help watching him. But I felt no nearer to him than they did. Very sad. He talked to Anne more than to me and I watched him go off on his scooter, a stranger.

Finished with digs till September, thank God. The bliss of hot water and no more positively sickening smells. No more of the landlady's twisted, purple, claw-like joints. Nor her backward daughter, backward yet slowly developing, sexually at any rate, braving this harsh world for the first time without her ankle socks, not Persil white, but humbly grey and kicked at the ankles, shapeless, limp, like the girl herself, pitiful. Thin, with the hopeful beginnings of a bust, rather plain, in a cherry pink hand-knitted cardigan, dull stupid eyes, blushing face, fumbling fingers feeling her mouth, the cherry button, tugging at the shapeless brown skirt. The clank of her bicycle, too small, seeing her through her last weeks at school. Like her shrunken macintosh, shiny-seated and hideously hooded. Poor thing. Plain, kindhearted, unhappy, aware of spotty crackly-voiced boys on bikes yet not equipped to attract them.
Her mother, bone idle, a moaner, poor as a church mouse, strongly resembling a church rat, musty, nosy, supposedly kind, incredibly stupid, wasting every hour of her life, bored, clinging, almost

friendless. The bare rooms, the old bus seat, the orange living room suite - the bareness, the meanness, the dull drabness, the poverty, the bored idleness. The geyser. The tin jug without handles. The crumb covered stale fruit cake covered each night by a pink chipped grubby saucer. The green tea, luke-warm, in a grubby flask. The one spoonful of sugar, the couple of teaspoons of milk, stale, just enough if you're careful. The faded strips of orange material for curtains that didn't meet across the window. Thank God I'm out of that house.

People joke about landladies being old, wizened, scratchy, mean widows and spinsters with smelly dogs and cats yet it's only these people, poor things, who are forced by circumstance - because someone from the family is missing and there's no money coming in - to take in lodgers.

However, Mrs Fricker is a widow and a landlady but she's one of the exceptions and a very nice one. Anne's so lucky. A paradise of a lodging place with a delicious unattached landlord like Laurie thrown in. What could be finer?
All last week I've been trying to design a 20ft by 12ft mural for the Summer Exhibition.
I've just watched a programme on Mars which was very interesting. There's a theory that life as we know it is in the process of beginning - that is, primitive organic structures, such as a species of moss, are growing there, in the process of photosynthesis. But they can't find any positive proof of oxygen on Mars. But plants will produce oxygen through photosynthesis so perhaps in years hence positive reactions will prove that oxygen is being produced and very slowly higher species of organisms will grow. Moss can survive in intense heat and extreme cold. The Russians have been studying Juno, next to Mars, and as it is wobbling noticeably on its axis, some of them believe it's a synthetic satellite such as their own and ejected by Martians millions of years ago.

Saturday 6 June 1959, Yeovil
If I paint I don't write and if I write I don't paint. The day after tomorrow I shall be camping [*West Monkton, landscape painting*

project]. Peter [*my brother*] is home; it's nice to see him. I started a portrait of him, very much to his annoyance. I've covered nearly all my work to paint on next month. Soon I shall be a chamber-maid [*summer job*].

Friday 12 June 1959

Why can't I settle down to some writing? Because I've been camping for the last week. At times it was hell, no water, no lights, dirt, muck, hard ground, cold, damp and hideous. Anne came daily to paint with us. Beaver came and camped too; we had some fun and saw Tony Newley[14] at the flicks. It seems funny seeing him on the screen, hearing his voice again.

I'm browning in the sun. Oh, the joy of being back in my room with one of my beautiful records on. Only three more weeks of outdoor shambles. I loathe it but we're painting all day. There are some really fabulous landscapes - monumental, lush and green.

Holterman and Murphy have paid strolling visits. Having lived amongst sheep for a week I know them to be the stupidest of creatures. Some dog's pinched a 24 in. x 30 in. canvas I took great pains in stretching. A cow shat on my other canvas and another monster calmly crushed my already frail easel to pieces with one flick of its shitty hoof. I stood on a tube of cadmium yellow tint and now I have one pinky brown leg with a cadmium yellow foot. Tim has flaunted himself without his vest and is lobster red. We play skittles all night.

Derek and I are losing contact and perhaps this is just as well. But I mind, that's the sadness. To be of no concern in his life; I want to know, to share what happens to him, know how he gets on, how he develops, but it's no longer my business.

---

[14] Anthony Newley: actor. He had recently appeared in the film *Pirates on Parade* and got to know students at Yeovil School of Art whilst visiting friends who ran a coffee bar called the Matador in the town. He went on to take the lead in a number of stage musicals, including *Stop The World, I Want To Get Off.*

Sunday - painting all day; more on *The Green Lantern* and some more on *Susanna and The Elders*. I've found some perfect small frames but no boards to fit them. I detect a disadvantage here. Now I'm packed and ready to return to the wilderness. I hate living in a tent - to think that some idiots love it and actually *plan* such tortures!
Great enthusiasm for work. And prickly heat rash which has resulted in a large broccolli-type ear, very flattering.

Friday - back in my room. Today I began a painting of an old disused cart under some trees. A fantastic subject, beautiful colours, and the composition in nature is brilliant. Can't wait to get back to it on Monday. I left it under the cart; I hope it'll be all right.
Last evening skittled the night away and then Laurie came very late and I slept with the sound of ecstatic grunts and passionate air intake not two feet from my head. I wasn't the least bit embarrassed or even sad and if there was any loneliness it quickly passed for I was convulsed with my own wit and fell asleep while they battered on with grunts and groans and sounds of joy well into the morning, which was as hot and tiring as the last. There was no sign of Laurie.

Saturday - I've done a small oil sketch of children in long grass up to their waists in the shade. It sounds much better than it looks. I wish someone wanted me; I hate to feel ugly. The 'dump' painting, if I may call it that, is on a small 2ft x 1ft piece of callico stretched on a drawing board - not ideal, but serviceable. However, it's unpleasant to work on as the paint soaks in even after several coats of size. The colour is muddy. This annoys me so much. I haven't the talent to use pure colours with any atom of success. I hate muddy colours as much as bad design and am brilliant at both these vices. I would love to do *good* paintings.

I'm amazingly drab and ugly today and am sporting a large and very painful blister that's causing me to walk embarrassingly. I quite thought Anne would be up to see me but obviously over-estimated my popularity for the second time today. I have a feeling I shall remain unmarried.

Late June - painted solidly this week. I feel I have new outlets, new ideas, new aims and enthusiasm. I'm working on eight paintings and am full of ideas for more. A bad week with many disturbances, quarrels and bad atmosphere. We've been turned out of the van and have made a splendid home for ourselves in an old pig pen. It's quite cosy. Holterman hasn't been out but Laurie has. Beaver's been with us since Tuesday, much fun. The freedom and the laughing, it's idyllic.
I've a still life set up waiting for me across the room, like a meal ready to devour but this beautiful Vivaldi record holds me a while. I'm so content today, the irritation of yesterday melted away, chased by beauty and the exquisite bliss of this music and of life itself. Why are we given individual feelings, precious only to ourselves? It's a cruel set-up, a frustrating game, a tragicomedy.
I've almost completed a small still life of a blue china pot and a pear on a green spotted saucer. I can't stop painting. I can't stop adding when it's screaming to be left alone.

Sunday - churned up and inside out. It was a roaring party; danced, exploited sex until it bored me. Let's drink, let's dance - jazzy records and stone passages, noise, people grinning, girls being sexy, men prowling, couples dancing, electric, all switched on, much harmless sex and loud music. Great fun but it rang hollow because Derek wasn't there.

Tuesday - painting has begun on the Exhibition mural; my design and a bloody grim one too. Jumping about on ladders all day.

Sunday - last night we had a glorious party at Rampisham - absolutely wonderful, nearly one hundred persons, assorted, varied, alien, friendly. Much noise, fun, drink, music and dancing. Beautiful John Porter Davison[15]. He's interesting, extremely funny and altogether gorgeous. He looks like a handsome ape. He's a drama student in London. Many

---

[15] John Porter Davison: actor. An eccentric, humorous and irreverent personality. He had recently appeared in the film *The Loneliness of The Long Distance Runner*, starring Tom Courtney. He remained a stage actor for a further ten years after which he and his wife started a successful antique business.

strangers and funny people. Beetle was lying with his legs above his head, singing in a low mournful voice. Laurie was there, the Murphies, the Andersons, some Frenchmen, some New Zealanders. Anne in a black dress. Colonel Beaver muttering. About thirty people stayed the night; it was chaos, blanketed lumps all over the place, bodies littering up everywhere. Anne's off to Weston to work as a chambermaid.
JPD knows Adam Faith and Danny Williams and poses nude.
College on my own next week. I'm dreading the next year.

Bombs, bombs, bombs - ban them, keep them, test them, make them, crop them, hide them - it's the ever-looming menace of every man, woman and child. It's the final horror. The Labour Party has split over whether we should disarm or keep them as a deterrent, which is nonsense as our measly couple of bombs are ludicrous against Russia's anyway - like a little fat man throwing stones at a brick wall. Khrushchev knows this and has said as much - that he will just tread on us in passing on the power trail. The situation is hopeless. Russia will never give up their bombs, nor those pig-headed idiots in America.

I want to be with my friends, the few I have. At parties we become puppets, mincing, smiling, dancing, grappling sexy puppets. Samuel Beckett wasn't in it before the party - we dressed and minced about, moaned, declared our ugliness hoping for compliments, confidences, encouragements, eyeing each other jealously; who is the prettiest? Who is the most attractive? Whose night is it? Putting on too much make-up [*Leichner stage make-up, black-pencilled eyes, very pale, sugar-pink lipstick*], many petticoats [*hooped*], tapping heels, sitting on beds, smoking, whipping drinks, a nervous babble, fumbling in drawers, nervous, anticipating silences - zip me up - can I borrow your eye pencil? hell, I look a mess - God, I'm really ugly tonight - hell, where's the fags? hell, I'm past my prime - no, honestly, I was much better looking a year ago - is this too low? is that a car? Beaver's mother always standing around, looking vague in gum boots: 'Catherine, *do* something about that skirt, darling.' 'I wish someone would come - hell, what if *no*body comes? Give them half an hour and we'll start ringing...'

Puppets, partying puppets, flushed up, powdered, pencilled eyes, hair up, hair down, fronts low, backs low, shirts high, scent too. Scent and powder and the click of heels in stone passages, the creak of heavy oak doors, the records already on, the candles lit, the front door open, Becky [*the dog*] over-excited and running around.

In the morning we scrambled seventy-five eggs and made at least a dozen huge pots of tea. People, eyes bleary, eyes triumphant, eyes shifting, bodies slumping, feet dragging, wit flagging, familiar lumps sleeping, unfamiliar lumps waking, walking about in blankets, a room full of bodies blearily, wearily forking scrambled eggs - conversations, mutterings, calling to people up the stairs. A chance to see who was there - a daylight tot-up, eyes shifting or shut; thick smoke and cups of too strong tea and Becky being stroked by odd males without any tea and too tired or shy to ask for any. Looking properly at persons in the light of the kitchen, cautiously, without appearing to - blotchy skins, ringed, smudgy eyes, shuffling feet, the smell of tea, cigarettes and stale scent.
What puppets we are and what energy we muster!

Another party on Saturday and then to Studland to work.
The sound of Chico Hamilton, slight rain, drawn curtains, the feel of last winter.

Sometimes life is like a hollow dream I shall wake from and all will be clear - that I'm not a human being after all but just in the guise of a puppet in this dream and when I wake all will be explicit, brilliant, ice-cold, ice-clear, adjusted.

Finished work on the mural. P asked me to design one for a jazz cellar in Bristol but nothing will come of it. We went to Weston to see Anne turning down beds in a tatty hotel. Tomorrow I'm off to Studland; how I could do with these eight weeks to myself but I must earn some money. I want to stay here in this room; in here I'm fully conscious, elsewhere I'm a misfitting puppet itching to be back in its box where it can be itself.

August 1959
Sometime next week I'll be nineteen. It's a nasty, neuter, an ageing age, somehow older than twenty.

September 1959
[*copied from scraps*] I lost my book last night which is just as well as I was so pent-up I would have written pages of love-sick dribble. In the light of this cheerless morning I've re-addressed Derek's letter in a better hand. I'm calmer now and realise the hopelessness of it and that I must get over it quickly and start again. It seems so unfair that people *do* have the joy of falling in love with someone who not only loves them - this in itself is a wonder that has escaped me - but also wants to marry them. It happens all the time. Other people pass on to a happy conclusion - I've slithered to a bitter stop and don't know what to do.

At the exhibition [*work by ex-Yeovil Art School students*], which was mediocre and the exhibits were badly framed, I was talking to Freddy Friar [*a Franciscan monk who worked with maladjusted boys in the monastery at Cerne Abbas, in Dorset; he attended evening classes at the art school and spent a lot of time swinging from the rafters*] who looked interestingly religious with his new beard. Miss Kohler looked straight through me and I talked to Mr Boshier for sometime and he called me Valerie. Everybody was there, Jo, John, Brian and Derek, looking wonderful - as sophisticated as Murphy in a beautiful Italian suit and a stark white shirt. They all had the money gleam in their eyes and they greedily licked red stars, their fingers itching to slap them on Derek's paintings which were justly priced far too high for Yeovil. They were the only decent exhibits, the others were mediocre. Derek was the highlight of the whole affair with his vast abstractions; sun-tanned, new suit and he knew it. He had the air of 'local boy made good' and in his element but he didn't overdo it. He's not so handsome as he was but to me he's beautiful.

Camberley, Surrey, 1959 [*Staying with an aunt*]
Last night we went to a tatty little circus. There were about six artistes, vast muscular orange painted females in mucky vests with faded tassles and penguins on them. Two or three middle-aged but wiry men and a

spectacularly small collection of thin, mangy, mostly untalented and wholely pathetic animals with vacant eyes. The whole place, the small cluster of caravans, the grim jolliness, the show business loud voices, the worn-out Sid Phillips records that crackled along accompanied by a fat man in evening dress bashing his guts out on some drums all night, glumly chewing what may have been his supper; the haunted tired animals running round obediently, eyes vacant, necks forward, tatty pastel satin bows flopping on their rumps. It was all very sad and the phony gesturing and blaring fanfares rang hollow.

We passed the Railway Arms, right past the window and along the tree-lined road out of Basingstoke where we so often walked with Rynty when it was cold and everything was new; and we walked for miles to the pub opposite the Pied Piper on the road to London in the bitter cold, laughing, the warm gin and back in the bus and we would go to separate rooms and then after an hour I'd creep up the narrow stairs to his room in the pitch-dark, climb over Rynty, all warm and soft, and jump into his bed - the curtains across the window, all snug, the narrow room and the smell of paint.
And I passed in that damned impersonal bus.

I went to the Tate and saw many Turners, Constable sketches, a Samuel Palmer which I'd never seen before, it was really exquisite. Hundreds of Blakes, some Sickert, Cézanne's *Passage d'Aix* and *Self-Portrait*. I couldn't believe I was actually seeing them - Manet, Degas, Van Gogh, Seurat and many others. Sutherland, Bratby, Nash, Stanley Spencer.
In many ways I hate London. The endless surge of glum, hard-eyed faces, there's nothing to cling to. I want to live each life in turn, pick just one at random and find out everything about them. It makes me weep with frustration being one mere mortal. I want to live up that road, down that street, be this person, that person. I wonder what they're going back to, what they're thinking, what they feel about things.
I'm at a loss and so inside myself I'm out of focus. I've become totally self-centred and, I think, not very nice to know but I'm so biased and self-concentrated that even this is a matter of some doubt in my mind.

Sometimes I think it was better a few years ago when things were so simple they were crystal clear, when I didn't even know myself. Now I've got to know myself so well I can't break off the friendship.
Another morning - no letters at all, just one long wait from one post to the next.
I've reached the last page in *Germinal* - a masterpiece.

Thursday September 1959
I'm in the stupid position of having begun a book, got four people eating carrots in a room at eight o'clock and no earthly idea of anything else. I just don't know how to write a book, tell a story, make up a story. I can only write bits. Two more poems today.
Now it's 12 o'clock but I have the beginnings of a story and I'm working on a family tree now; the book may be in three parts, three generations of love affairs, each unique yet similar. It may not work out but it's a beginning
No letter from Derek.

Sunday September 1959
So little time to write now; for five days I've worked at my book all day, every hour and now I'm interested in the people I have created and this morning I cried as I wrote the death of Katrin in part one. Now I feel I'm writing something that people may read. This is very exhilarating and I am hopeful. And it all started by forcing four people into a room and giving them names; now there are three generations and many names. Two poems came back but I'm not interested in them.

September 1959, Park Street, Taunton
Back at college [*having worked as a waitress and washer-up at Forte's, in Swanage*] thoroughly miserable and not the slightest enthusiasm; at screaming pitch just to pick up a pencil. A whole year! My only interest is my book and the books I have yet to write. This is an ideal room, ideal if I wasn't so lonely. Finished at 4.31 pm., came back here and worked for four hours and finished part two, now on part three. What a waste of a lovely place without friends to ask up. Derek hasn't written. I can imagine the misery of this winter, the darkness,

other people in cosy rooms with families, people out in cars, going places and me stuck in this room on my own watching the clock.

September 1959, Park Street, Taunton
I've sent my book to Rider & Co. and have collected material for another one. All my poems sent back. I feel a bit discouraged again. I've had many letters from Anne and from JPD. Reading the book I fear it's dull and only of personal interest; however, I'm full of hope for it - until it comes back.

Saturday - very lonely tonight. Beaver came and went. Now that my book's finished I'm lost, back to emptiness, there's a great hole in my life. God, I wish someone would come to see me. I can't get on with the other book. All my poems are back on my desk. I imagine Derek at some foul party in London; he starts at the Royal College on Monday.

Just finished Flaubert's *Madame Bovary*. I wish I could write like that!

Last night I had some twelve students in here but I was so lonely in the midst of them. No reply from my book. Letters from Anne. Reading some of Chekhov's plays. What a frustrated blank, what a blank existence. I long to write some more but I can't.
This evening we went drinking again, Tim, Roger[16] and me. Boring. I'm so uprooted and nowhere and each day at college is a dragging eternity. I'm not eating properly, drinking too much beer and smoking too much. I hate it here.
Monday 5 October 1959, Park Street, Taunton
This weekend I did an etching of a life-pose and countless designs for the Arts Ball poster and started two paintings. Tonight eternal talk in a pub and then went our separate ways, wondering. No word from my book; how I long for it to be published though I realise more and more I

---

[16] Roger Tarr: painter. He was filling in a year before taking up his place at Oxford. After reading English he studied at the Courtauld Institute in London. Now Senior Lecturer in History of Art at Edinburgh University.

have nothing to say. I've forgotten to bring my books - what a catastrophe! I've borrowed one on Oscar Wilde.

October 1959, Park Street, Taunton

Tonight an argument, a futile one, on whether art is for oneself or for other people's reaction. It seems to me obvious that a person writes partly to be read. No person writes or paints purely for himself; subconsciously at least, he hopes for approval, whether in two thousand years or a hundred. It's too ridiculous to imagine otherwise let alone argue about it.

Today my book came back. Dogs. Bastards. Philistines.

I've applied for colleges: London, Bristol, Leicester.

Friday - This morning my chest is heavy again and my cough is dreadful. It's cold and foggy outside. I like it like that. No money and in debt to Roger. Fed-up with the world - no food, a bit of rice, no spuds, no tea, no sugar, no butter, no bread, no milk, no coffee - one large tin of pilchards. Miserable.

R [*in her final year in the Fashion School; she went on to study fashion at the Royal College of Art*], Roger and Tim came up at eleven to say Holterman's after me for not coming in. My thesis will be on the face. I'm so ugly today.

Sometimes I hate painting, the mess, the physicality of it seems so basic, so crude, it involves mess, turps, muck - but with music and writing... I hate bad, art school painting. I loathe it, it makes me scream, mine particularly.

Today Jo [*Jolyon Ward, graphic artist, ex-Yeovil School of Art*] came to see me. It was a lovely surprise. He played ping-pong and ate other people's sandwiches.

November 1959, Park Street, Taunton

Since I last wrote I've sent off forty poems to the Mitre Press and my book has again been returned. I hate my internal NDD composition but I'm forced to go on with it; the sight, the thought of it, makes me sick.

Sunday 13 December 1959, Park Street, Taunton
Mitre Press have left the offer open but I'll never get £126. They say John Betjeman's the only man to make a profit on poetry this year.
Stanley Spencer died the other day; also Matthew Smith, who I always imagined to be a young hot-blood. Epstein is also dead; soon it will be Picasso, Chaplin, Braque and Schweitzer.
Reading Anne Frank's diary - it's very disturbing.
JPD and I were sick at the Arts Ball and very miserable - so much work and preparation and then it was all over so quickly. But it was a great success.
This last week Roger, Tim, R and I have been painting murals at the Blue Horizon, in Wellington. We've had so many arguments and little success. One evening the Andersons and the Murphies came to play skittles. I hate skittling. It was an odd week.
I don't feel that dreadful loneliness any more. I'm all right since Roger's come. My mind is ticking over again - where have I been?

Thursday 24 December 1959, Yeovil
Tonight my brother gave me a little white lighter. He's very good to me though we argue and lose our tempers so often. No letter from Derek. JPD gave me twenty fags. A card from Brian.
Later - brother quietly drunk, mother at church - I am neither.

Friday 25 December 1959, Yeovil
Christmas Day - raining with heavy, cold drops and running drains. My deepest wish was a letter from Derek but there was nothing for me. There is no merriness in this house. Mother cooking, Peter savouring a morbid hangover. I stay in my room. I'd rather it was like this; I'm very embarrassed by festive drunkenness and gay giggling and toasts and sentiment and over-eating and am completely without religious feeling. I must get into London University, I must.
Today Brian came up and invited me to Peter Keane's [*ex-student, Yeovil School of Art*] party on Saturday. Derek is coming down tomorrow. Brian is the sweetest person on this earth.

Friday 1 January 1960, Yeovil
So now it's 1960. A very important year I feel very strongly, both personally and internationally. There is something special about 1960. It's a crucial date. 1960. Perhaps I'll be in London before next New Year. I hope I am. 1960 - an extraordinary year. I hope a year with a little happiness and a little measure of success. Perhaps it won't be a pointless year; that's the worst feeling in the world, a feeling of pointlessness. 1960!
Beaver, Anne, JPD and Roger. Patches is amazingly straightforward. He doesn't drink or smoke! He's really nice and I'm very fond of him, and JPD and David.

I'm working on my book [*Koolyghin, children's book about a white Alsatian*] which isn't going very well. Writing for children is so difficult. This room is thick with fug. I've decided to go to Bill's party at Taunton tomorrow instead of Pete Keane's because there's no point in being bloody miserable if I can choose whether to be or not.

Sunday 3 January 1960, Yeovil
This morning Derek came up with Jo. He looked fabulous, beautiful clothes like Murphy. He's going back to London with Brian this afternoon.

Tuesday 5 January 1960, Yeovil
Had a letter from Derek asking me to go up to London this week. I've written explaining the situation.

Wednesday 6 January 1960
Trying to work on the book. How I ever wrote 67,000 words on the first one I just don't know. This one bores me. I hate writing for children.

Thursday 7 January 1960, Yeovil
A foggy, cold and dreary day. Last night JPD and R arrived to fetch me to hitch to London but I've no money. Awful dreariness. I wish I was in London. Can't write even. I'll go mad in this room if no one comes. There's no one *to* come.

Sunday 10 January 1960, Yeovil
Back to Taunton tomorrow. What an awful thought. I can't face the next two terms. I hate it so much. God knows what I want to do. Anne has gone back to Leicester. She's dreading it too.

Monday 11 January 1960, Park Street, Taunton
Ugh, each minute of college work is a blinding dragging bore. Totally uninterested. I want only to write. Yet I believe I'd write myself out of words in five years at the most. I have a thesis to write. Tim didn't get in to London either.
A letter, surprisingly, from Derek. He wants me to go for a serious talk. I know exactly how it will be. Nothing will be said - he'll go all vague and I'll be back in the train worse than ever. I expect he's quite pleased to have a slight tangle in his love-life, a bit of mistress trouble.

Friday 14 January 1960, Park Street, Taunton
An awful week of trying to get enthusiasm like blood from a stone. This term seems intolerably long. JPD has been here all week and spent all my money. He's living with R.

Saturday 15 January 1960, Yeovil
Worked mostly on my thesis - so few words, 2000, so much to say. Had another letter from Derek asking me to his party next Saturday in London.

Much later - it's beautiful weather, slashing with rain and very windy; the wind throwing up dustbin lids and calling out. It makes me excited and restless.

I have an idea for my next book - about a woman, leading up to a point almost to suicide, then the world gradually lightens with the development of a unique friendship - the world of these two people - then he dies and she commits suicide because without that person the world was the same as before. I must write as much as I can now - even though I can't possibly have much to draw on for experience at nineteen. At least I'll be learning and gaining experience in writing for reference when I'm older and more able to write.

Must get a William Golding book from the library. They have a Penguin André Gide in the Dragon Bookshop.

February 1960 - I have to finish the kid's book in a few weeks [*to enter for the E.Nesbitt competition*] and my thesis and a painting and a sketch book. I have no interest in them. Sometimes the misery in me wells up and I feel I will go mad - my whole being seems to be breaking up into a million miserable bits.

February 1960, Park Street, Taunton
With the money I'd saved to go to see Derek I bought many books in the Dragon Book Shop sale: Ezra Pound, Ibsen, Arnold Bennett's journals, Barbellion's journals, Byron and a beautifully designed book of poems by a young Oxford graduate, Dom Moraes, which is very interesting. It's his first book and he's only twenty-one. No letter from Derek.
I've worked solidly on my book - it's slow progress, about five pages an evening, that's about 1,400 words a night.

Thursday - a pink letter from Derek. He wrote about painting and asked me to come up this weekend, next weekend or any time I wanted to. Pink envelope - *well.* The day seems a little brighter now; but it will pass.

Monday 29 February 1960, Park Street, Taunton
A pretty terrific party on Friday night. All the old people there; danced with hundreds. Going to London on Friday, God help me. My papers are in the Clearing House - I don't care where I go. Frantically typing the kid's book and now the damned typewriter's gone wrong again so I had to give up at ten o'clock. Rewritten most of the poetry too. Ribbon threadbare but no money for a new one. Need every penny for Friday.

Wednesday 9 March 1960, Taunton
At one o'clock this afternoon I started reading Barbellion's *Journal of a Disappointed Man.* It's now eleven o'clock at night and I'm still reading for I'm convulsed with sympathy, sad at loss and completely engrossed. I can't put the book down. He found to his dismay on

reading Marie Bashkirtseff's *Journal* that it was as though he was reading his own thoughts. When I read *him* I'm partially dismayed but I'm a unique individual, in unique surroundings and cannot be a duplicate. I think perhaps when I eventually read Marie Bashkirtseff I'll feel even more frustration for, as a woman, I suspect the alliance will be that much stronger and even more disturbing.

After all we are merely bound in our symmetry and the circumstance of existence to be subject to the same thought cycles but each pair of eyes must essentially see different forms for the brain to decipher therefore men seek art to expound their individuality. But I have felt strongly the despair at realising another personality has experienced and recorded well an experience common to myself. Perhaps it should be a stimulant, a comfort.

Barbellion voices my emotion to a dot. There's no point in succumbing to the desire to refer to them, record them in my own handwriting for I would have to copy out the whole book for every thought is applicable. At first I thought there's no point in writing anything ever again for he's already said it or someone else has. Marie Bashkirtseff is bound to have! But it's the same in visual art.
If anyone should ever read this, please read Barbellion before you read another line. It must register. Barbellion must be read.

This eternal need to be unique, this urgency of life, this egoism that will always be because we were created to exist as a unique creation. We are not lumps of plasma. We are singular. Unique. Each one. Of course he felt he was a genius, he gets it through this realisation, he was, he was unique. Any creature that realises his uniqueness with such intensity must have the power of genius. He was no more conceited than I am.

Because of this self-analysis, this acute realisation of an existence, he suffered loneliness as I have - not so much loneliness for people, for the world, though this is strong, but a sheer loneliness of existence, of involuntary presence in a form that is inescapable. To stand alone and think, feel, this is not where I am meant to be. I'm from somewhere I can't remember. I have known things I cannot conceive.

I was surprised he used exactly the same words as me in the beginning of one of my poems - 'to be with people, going somewhere, a part of people walking'. Of course, his obsession with himself against his anonymity to other people was terrible but it must be accepted and stepped over - what a game of counter-tensions, counter-illusions life is and how difficult it is with so many of us in the game.
His feelings are mine now, they are my own. I have a great desire to find him, speak to him, haul his body from the grave, claw at it with my hands to find the spirit that thought like that - like me - the heart that made the trembling hand write like that.
Barbellion has affected me a great deal. The name of Barbellion must never be skipped or these words of mine are invalid. I am afraid that to read Marie Bashkirtseff's *Journal* will destroy my desire to record for myself. Barbellion's almost did.

Now that I am tentatively looking into the future I hadn't conceived alone I want never to touch that miserable emotion again. I have no love left. Last weekend Brian and I went to the Van Gogh film in Chelsea. I waited in Brian's room [*the basement of 94 Cromwell Road*] for Derek to come back. He didn't come back until two o'clock from her place in Hampstead and we went to bed where he told me at length that my life was a mess. The Friday night he promised to be back by six. I sat in the flat on my own until gone midnight. I went out for a walk. I went to bed. He came in and said he had been working at the College. By the time it was Saturday I just couldn't hurt any more and the thing I dreaded so much became a reality. He came in with *her*. My spirit broke. It's over. I'll miss the flat and some of his friends. I might go up just to be with them but I don't know yet. I was a creature full of love and now I have none. I had so much to give but it was never asked for. It all went on him and he flung it back and cursed it and now it is gone.

Thursday 10 March 1960, Park Street, Taunton
This morning I looked out of the window at the silent row of houses opposite. They looked weird and totally unreal, like fairy-land château, starkly bright and coloured like in children's books. I was the only soul alive, sitting on a pot with a pain [*cystitis*] in a small room at the top of a bare house. The sky was a rich royal-blue and stiff with white, unblinking stars.

I must get myself right for the exam [*National Diploma in Design*]. I must pass. I must succeed in the paltry, idiotic tests of society, I must earn my living, I must conform. Were I on my own with no mother I could bear things more easily but she can't take things like me - she goes to pieces. I have the nerve-racking experience of getting them together again which is unfair for I'm weak myself and can't bear up for two people.
More scenes, tears, curses, silences, crying. I shall go mad. I live in fear of her having a nervous breakdown for I am so near one myself. Isn't life unbearable?

Beastly, nauseating life-room. I have odd times when I just don't go in for a day or an afternoon. I just sit and watch the clock pass two and stay, knowing that as each hour mounts up there will be trouble, but I have to stay. When I'm in these moods nothing will induce me to go. I must steal these odd hours to read, to write and to think. I must force myself to turn up at break time and get on with that blasted row of houses. I've written and typed my thesis - on aspects of escapism - and this has to be be bound and made into a book.
The children's book has to be submitted by 30 March. The exam is in a few weeks, I have a sketch-book to fill and a painting to submit in a couple of weeks.

Roger has produced some very good paintings. I would like to paint so purely, so well. Thick, pure, tonal shapes, very pale; he is extremely talented for it's not even his specific subject and yet he's far advanced of Tim or me, not in drawing and experience but in attitude. His painting is good.

If I fail NDD, which is not unlikely, I shall go away and get lost. This pain is worrying me - I feel I shall just rot and say nothing. I must finish *Koolyghin* this weekend.
I'd better go and do a drawing from the landing to submit with downcast eyes when I return in fear and trembling. When I have these fits of time stealing I'm not really conscious of my intention to stay away. I just don't move from my chair and faintly wallow in stolen hours and disobedience. I've no cigarettes left so I'll have to go out soon. This pain. Oh, to be nineteen with a father with a million!

I've tried to persuade Roger to read Barbellion but he will not read anything that he does not know is good or proven. To me this is ridiculous. He will read Ezra Pound, T S Eliot and Wilde. It's name value plus a certain knowledge which is very irksome. I'm also subject to it to a certain extent but I'm often exempt through a natural curiosity, perhaps plain nosiness into other people's thoughts, more so than their actual works.

Tonight Roger and I drank beer and he suggested that Derek was being brutal to be kind. Still suffering from this brutality I am not inclined to give him credit for kindness but I know he used to have it. He was a very kind person once. Perhaps Roger is right - perhaps out of kindness he told me what a mess I was in. I had to move on or die. I am breathing again now. I have remembered that I am a free female individual, not a grovelling, vulnerable extension of another.

He had grown to be a lump in me that really hurt and hampered - now it is gone, ripped out by the roots, and the place feels empty and cleaner, but a little sore. Now it's gone and although I feel lost and lonely without it, I'm better as a whole and what is left is free. I've gained and lost and it's past. I'm a person who needs a good shaking from time to time for I become obsessed.

What an ugly creature I am. I would frighten a child and I've done that before now. Twice, perfectly placid dogs have taken one look at me and gone berserk. I'm fast losing my looks. I have no prettiness left and no beauty to take over and no heart to bring out beauty from inside. No heart - what a mess.

This terrible earthquake in Agadir. It's too ghastly a hell to imagine. A vast city reduced to a heap of rubble; parched bones hovered over by vultures, with thousands of humans buried in a hideous grave; jackals and mad dogs with rabies running all over it, trying to tear them out. What a nightmare. The refugees are hoarded up in tents just outside the city heap, overrun by rats which have brought an epidemic. It's like an account in Revelations. The name Agadir has a grim note.

I feel sure I could be helping in some way. I haven't heard from Work Overseas Service - now perhaps I've lost the chance of finding a place. Why must I speak German or be able to build roads, or belong to a stream of charitable societies? I want to go and dig my hands into the stones and be on my own and be ugly and leave everything behind. I want to work hard at something.

I went into college to paint but instead I curled up on the bed behind the screen and read Barbellion. Tim and Roger were painting and Guy [*Belgian student studying graphics*] pottered around muttering to himself, laughing at our jokes in complete ignorance of their content.
In the pub Roger and I were considering that we spend the whole time laughing yet so often we say we've had a miserable day.

My life began again this week. I have been drawing a tiger's skull which is magnificent. I, too, Barbellion, am now, 'a giant that the world walks around'. Yet sometimes I shrink from the very sight of me. I'm so used to being stared at, spoken rudely to - especially amongst strangers in the street - that I'm so gratified when by chance someone smiles instead of sniggering or staring.

One thing I hate, when I'm trying to be normal and pleasant in shops and things so that people won't be horrid to me, I try to say things that bore me to tears to be liked - I'm completely out of touch with other people and distorted beyond even my own awareness.

Friday 11 March 1960, Park Street, Taunton
Damn Tim for making a mess on my new notebook but with such a book, a new spring in my life and a bottle of sepia I can't keep up an ill-humour for long. My other book annoyed me and I couldn't write another word in it. This book will not house any more sentiments for it's the house of another person, one with no sentiment left and hardly any feeling.

Friday 11 March 1960, Park Street, Taunton
Again at three o'clock this morning I woke up in pain and seemed the only person alive. I lay in bed, just a big pain, and it almost drove me mad.

Saturday 12 March 1960, Yeovil
I'm awake, alive and last night the pain didn't wake and torture me but this morning it's back. It's an internal pain like a bruised tube or something to do with the bladder. Weeks of reasonably good health are taken for granted like a terrific lull in an automatic drill.
I'm expecting JPD to come in on their way to a party in Lopen. I want to stay here and write and think and read but I would like to go. I can't bear the thought of missing a party.

Much later tonight. Very tired but more at ease with the pain. Now I have a chronic pain in my back where my kidneys are. It's like an iron grip and really painful. Perhaps it's a severe chill after all.

Sunday *13 March 1960, Yeovil*
This morning I can't move with a gripping pain on the right side of my back that pins me to the bed. I can hardly write and have much to do. I must try and forget by remembering things. The day Beaver and I went looking for a flat a year ago. We went to a huge, grand but derelict house outside Taunton, bare and set back about four hundred yards from the road. It was very dark and damp inside with many closed doors and little furniture. A woman appeared on the ground floor - a small, white, hunched woman of about twenty-five, hair thin and matted on a shiny skull - white, waxy legs, feet in carpet slippers with no bottoms, thin filthy clothes adhering to her frail body. She took us

wearily up long flights of stairs, which were bare, filthy, cobwebbed and dark in shadow.
She seemed glumly to say goodbye - she was a sad, lonely, wretched, grovelling creature. Her husband, she said, was ill with bronchitis and they'd had nothing but trouble since they came there. It was a dark house. But when we walked through a garden with shrubs and bushes and warm sunshine there were several children playing - some were watching us from the bushes and some were laughing; some just stared.

We went to many galleries when we were in London a week ago. I was very disappointed in the Manet in the National Gallery and in a Renoir, girl with basket among umbrellas. I think it was horrible and not much better than a tasteful John Bull cover. The Manet, of a crowd under trees, was pretty nasty - the distance was better. The Manet next to it, of the lady in a white dress, was awful. The dress was a mess of white with no colour - it was large and revolting. The nude lying on her side in the grass with leaves twined round her head by Renoir is pretty terrific. I was amazed by Cézanne's *Gertrude Stein* and the still-life near it, and the same with the other Cézannes. I'm always amazed at their beauty and have never yet been disappointed. We didn't have time for the Rembrandt room.

In the Tate I went downstairs - I fail to see how a painter can progress without constant stimulation from other painters. I liked - what a stupid, inexpressive word - the Braques very much and most of the Picassos, much of Rouault, superb colour, also a beautiful Matisse. Some really hideous Salvador Dalis, terrible. I was disappointed in the Marc Chagall, of the green meadow and the poet lying down and the horse. As always, I loved the Stanley Spencer, of the mauve-pink tones with angels leaning out of windows and remembered going to Cookham with Derek years ago and getting the key to the chapel - wonderful pictures. And on the first floor, to the right of the entrance, *Domes of Venice* by Derrick Greaves, beautiful white colours, huge, full of air, exquisite. I was somewhat disappointed in the Bonnard. The colours didn't have the freshness I imagined they would. Van Gogh, the painting is so guttural, it aches. A beautiful portrait in brown, black and ochre by Modigliani, ruined, particularly so, in reproduction.

The Keith Vaughan exhibition made a terrific impression on me. I thought them very good. Fresh, some brilliant design, colour, perhaps a little irksome in some cases. I think they gained from numbers. A really exquisite male nude and similar to a Cézanne; I would say as good. He's a homosexual and although this is made clear by his constant pre-occupation with the male nude, it's not offensive in company with such mastery of design and colour. In one or two cases he has mastered an almost inharmonious shape with genius.

Italian Art in Britain at the Royal Academy. It was very good but there was too much of it - it became indigestible. Beautiful Rubens and Delacroix, Titian, and Poussin; some simply terrific drawings by Michelangelo, Leonardo, Raphael, some Turners. Surprised at the abstracted simplicity of Paolo Veronese, terrific. The broadness of these huge paintings amazed me. They are extremely elastic, almost to a degree of laxness in some cases.

There was a disgusting exhibition at the Beaux Arts, of Timothy Behens, really nauseating; sloppy, crude, ugly, pointless sloshings on badly stretched canvas, badly framed, badly hung, etc. It was altogether shoddy and we only stayed a couple of minutes. There was a Bratby there, a still life, which diminishes on seeing it. We went round and sat in a Charles Eames chair.

In Chelsea it's the vogue to wear dark glasses at the dead of night and to shave the head bald and the homosexuals wore spring daffodils in their lapels. One of them in the Gilded Cage, could not control himself - but his friend, who also wore a daffodil, seemed more interested in getting his coffee. The juke-box played Acker Bilk without stopping.
There was a person in there, tall, lithe, blond and fascinating. JPD said it was a man because he knew his friend but it might well have been a woman, a masculine young woman in men's clothes. Its blond hair was thick and straight and long in front of the ears. If it was a man it was very attractive and if it was a woman, it still was. It completely fascinated me. Most of the people in these places are absolute bums. When I come across human beings that are distorted and humanity is

violated I get a real sickness in my whole being, or rather, I used to. Now I am surprised at very little.

I remember clearly in Paris, three years ago. I must have been sixteen. We were walking through the Boulevarde St Germain, past the tables, brilliantly lit and buzzing with humanity. Suddenly, I saw a lump of brown clothing jumping about amongst the tables. He was a madman who was supposedly harmless and he was kept by people and more or less used as entertainment, something to look at, an attraction. The poor blighter. The people were laughing and jeering at him and he was jumping about and shaking his fists like Quasimodo. It is said that young people from the jazz club chase him with sticks. I was sick to the soul when I saw him and suddenly very frightened.

Roger has told me of a time in Montmartre, late at night, and he was walking through a very dark street when suddenly, from one of the doorways, scuttled a creature, tiny, shrivelled up, neither old nor young. It ran off into another doorway across the street, where it was black and desolate and there was an empty pram in the shadow of the doorway.

And the maid in the hotel in Paris - she slaved all day running the place. She was ill-dressed, treated like muck and too terrified to speak to us. In the evenings she had to sit next to the proprietress in a lamp-lit, musty room, and listen to her read the newspapers. She had no time off at all, not even on a Sunday. She was exceedingly ugly, scared stiff, miserable, about twenty-seven perhaps, Algerian, and her name was Maria. She had to sweep the rooms with a broom made of twigs. One of the days we made the bed to save her doing it. She didn't seem to understand - she dumbly undid it, stripped off the bedding and turned the heavy mattress. We tried to help her for it was heavy and she was frail but she would have none of it. The thought of not making every bed in the house, according to the rules, frightened her. We left two lipsticks in the drawer for her but I doubt if she got them.

I would love to own a tree. Outside, in someone else's garden, there's an exquisite blossom tree, it's so beautiful. I want it. I want a house. I want children, a tree, a house, a dog.

Much later; this afternoon Beaver and JPD came and we talked for several hours about the state of the world. We laughed a great deal though with a sense of deep fatalism and consequent despair. JPD and I know exactly how each other's mind works and we can communicate humour and seriousness in monosyllables. I miss him. He's very hard to be with for one is never quite sure if he will make an utter fool of you - and he'd do it with a smile. We bear with each other with affection. He's a scoundrel but I'm more fond of him than most people who are my so-called friends.

Monday 14 March 1960, Park Street, Taunton
A bad day. This morning I collapsed in the college and was sick, much to my horror and annoyance. The pain in my back made me sick. I could hardly stand and it was as if the whole of my back was on fire. Murphy, Roger and Tim clucked like hens and I came back to Park Street to wait for the doctor. He was so quiet, strong, efficient, gorgeous - like Leslie Howard - and he had to rub my stomach and back, which was surgical bliss! The landlady stood by. I have inflammation of the kidneys and will be better in a few days. The most wonderful thing happened. A part-timer, a retired woman doctor, came up with some beautiful blue irises. It made me want to cry in the face of such kindness from a stranger. And to think we always ignore them and wish they weren't there. She's so meek and uncertain of herself, with white hair and a very lined face. I had some medicine like cow's diarrhoea and some extraordinary pills the size of mountains. Roger has been very sweet running about buying food.
People rushing in and pulling down my eyes and thrusting ancient thermometers down my throat and grasping my wrists with anxious expressions on their faces.

Tuesday 15 March 1960, Park Street, Taunton
I couldn't stay in bed so I'm up and dressed but the pain in my side is still there. Without a murmer I swallow foul green medicine. I've made

many cigarettes out of various visitors' dogends, a field in which I am supreme.
I had decided not to go home but in a note from my mother she insisted. I may get to college tomorrow. This short break is just what I needed. I wonder if Brian will get his guide to Montacute published? What a rude bunch we are. JPD is living off Jo, who has a studio in Station Road, Yeovil, of all things, the epitome of Stephen Potter's Lifemanship - and he has a wife, called Priscilla, a golden spaniel, called Sukie, a telephone and an office with files! It's too much. I remember him at Yeovil Art School, in his filthy old ginger coat and his beard full of indescribable objects and as he walked down the street the Teddy boys used to yell 'Rembrandt!' after him.

The Andersons have lent me some good records of the monks in Beuron singing plain song - beautiful.
There's a building construction down the street with a vast red crane as high as the steeple of the church. There's a man walking along it. He must be God. It's fantastic against the steeple, bright red, iron filigree and it has a lift.
A woman in a pale green frock, high up in a house making a bed alongside an arched window, reflecting the sun.

Wednesday 16 March 1960, Yeovil
I'm too ill to write. Last evening Tim drove me home. My whole stomach and spine felt as if a steamroller had crushed it. I've never conceived such pain. Last night it was coming on with terrible contractions of the spine, making my whole body jump up. It was really bad. I'm thankful to be alive this morning and somewhat surprised. I'm sure it was an attack on my philosophy of the relativity of pain.

Yesterday, from eleven o'clock till four Roger and I talked about what love does to the brain. He is in love but not very deeply, I feel. He has a fine humour and a keen brain and will be exceedingly attractive at twenty-five. He said there are three people that dominate his thoughts in life and one of them is me. I was a bit upset. It's strange. We talked about this and other things for ages. I think I helped him quite a bit. I had a letter from Brian who seems to be in the same state. I felt it all coming back and began to think of Derek but I kicked it from my mind like the bloody disease that it is - I refuse to succumb to such a beastly negative emotion. Now two men are beginning to rely on me to bring them out of their messes. Both are very sensitive and without friends to help them. I've received no end of help from both.

I have just written at great length to Brian. Mother saw me writing and said I go from one bed to another. How cruel people are with their false assumptions. She clucks with pious sympathy about the constant flow of pregnant girls from her school, that's all right, but she calls me a slut and a tart. Rarely do my friends have children - which is the sin. It's a fact that college people abstain from sexual intercourse far more than is believed. The labourer, the factory girl and the shop girl, they're always doing it, yet she can't see that. To go behind a hedge and then go home is to her better than spending a couple of days of intelligent relationship. This drives me crazy. She gives me no credit for a brain, an understanding of the values of an individual. I have developed into a completely alien being to her. She can't conceive healthy opposite relationships. She could never understand JPD and me sleeping together without sex, just happy and warm. She thinks if a man goes into a bedroom with a woman it results in the sex act. How bloody ridiculous. I spend hours sitting around on beds with JPD, Roger, etc. yet she will not credit me with any discrimination. She, and others like her, believe sex rules behaviour, she doesn't account for anything else. It's infuriating.

I am a bit worried about the exam work and I miss Roger and Tim. I must get the book off and some poetry. I had the information about the NUS workcamps but it isn't refugee work at all, just ordinary construction jobs. I'd like to go to Rouen grape-picking in the south but I can't even afford the fare to Weymouth.

Nerve-gases and brainwashing are in the news. Cartoons are full of it. Disarmament talks in Geneva. Russia proposed total disarmament, not a gradual levelling off of resources. One day they threaten to bury us all, the next they scorn strategy and violence. Through all this the Americans are persecuting coloured people, students are barred from universities, cafés, etc. It's beyond my comprehension, this stupidity. I almost wish I was coloured, there would be so much to work for. A coloured man must be very bitter. He must loathe we grim-faced, skull-like creatures, hollow, pale, bloodless people. Let me learn tolerance and preserve the tolerance of youth.

Thursday 17 March 1960, Yeovil
I felt despair coming again last night so I didn't write. I've been dosing myself with aspirin which helps a little. I've forgotten what it's like to have no pain in the body. I have to watch JPD every second else he'll borrow all my books. I can get even by borrowing his André Gide from Beaver. He's got my *Three Contemporary Plays* and I'll do anything to get my Chekhov back. Tim will not give back my Delacroix *Journal* which really annoys me because he won't read it. I wish I had lots of money to buy books. Library books are just not the same - I must *own* the books.

Friday 18 March 1960, Yeovil
I feel much better today; the pain has gone and there is a stiff soreness instead. I want to be well and get on with my life but seem to be stopped at every turn. Roger must be on the road to Oxford now - I wanted to go with him. I must try again to get into a refugee camp. Everybody else seems to be going to Italy. Anne has applied for a job in a secondary school in Bristol. What a ghastly, inevitable prospect. I want so much - I will get so little. I don't feel I have seen a human being for so long. Strange that it's Friday at the college - Tim and Roger being silly, I expect, or just Tim painting a dreadful study of a tiger's skull and Roger heading for Oxford with a lump in his throat.

Standing at the window just now I saw a small girl skipping along the pavement, laughing and talking to herself. Only she was alive. I was dead, a dead shadow next to the curtain, behind glass. She was free, so alone.
A moment later, a small boy came racing along, letting his coat fly behind him, buttoned only at the neck. He was a great bandit, magnificent on his way home to lunch.

Another small girl out from school, in a world of books and tunes and dreams - dreams that don't frustrate, don't matter if they never work because there are yet more dreams.

I've just read *Anyes* [*second novel*] again and feel I just can't leave it as a second rate work for there are many passages I wouldn't alter. It must be written again and enlarged upon for it has the basis of a good novel, I'm sure. As soon as mother gets in at five o'clock with some paper I'll start rewriting. I may rewrite it as a play. As in the criticism by Robert Sommerville [*publishers*], it hasn't enough to cover three generations which is essential for the whole theme of the book. I realised how short it fell in this respect but I don't want to incorporate 'padding', which I deplore. It's difficult for I've chosen a theme incongruous with my style of writing which is inclined to be tight but the book interests me and I feel sure I can do something with it.

An old tramp outside, walking up the deserted road singing *Apple Blossom Time*. His voice harsh and strong, echoing through the stone-deaf prefabs. I'm ashamed to say I've locked the door. I'm frightened of another human being who is singing in the road, bloody fool that I am. I should ask him in and talk to him. He has returned and is walking briskly down the road, with a stick, muttering to himself.

Sunday 20 March 1960, Yeovil
Last night I had a dream, a subconscious reality and the war we're all dreading began. At last four bombs were dropped and their huge mushrooms billowed into the sky. There were four along what seemed like the coast of northern France, for I was on the edge of England looking across a stretch of water to this land with its four bombs exploding. I remember the terror, and the resignation, but above all the sickening terror.
At the moment the big powers are talking over disarmament but it's against the policy of Communism to compromise.
Had a card from Roger in Oxford, not one word of which I could read.

Monday 20 March 1960, Park Street, Taunton
Back at college; a letter from JPD which said nothing.

Saturday 25 March 1960, Park Street, Taunton
Everything is one mad rush to get things set up for the Ministry [examining body] by Monday. My work seems very shoddy. I've been in my room most of today working in my sketch-book and wanting to get on with my writing. My work seems so bad. A letter from Brian - strange to receive a letter from 94 Cromwell Road and not be from Derek.

Monday 27 March 1960, Park Street, Taunton
I've been drawing in my sketch-book all day. This evening I drew in an empty studio with a class in another room and felt the acute aloneness of life. Then back here alone to read. I'm glad I'm without the typewriter - I need not work on *Anyes* instead of my exam drawing to be submitted tomorrow. But it seems empty. I'm feeling much better and sometimes indescribably free and light.
Odd phrases that I must get down else they stick in my mind like bones in the throat. I want the black lace parasol for two pounds but I just can't have it.

Tuesday 28 March 1960, Park Street, Taunton
Early in the morning, about one o'clock. Many people in here this evening. They're all going chickening [*loading live chickens at a battery farm*] and they use my room as a meeting place, clad in dozens of sweaters and scarves. Tim, Roger and R are all sleeping here about six. This room looks like a jumble sale. A bit depressed today.

Murphy is always on at me, niggling about this blasted sketch-book and always at my side, making me draw until I feel I'll go berserk and run away screaming. I hate drawing. I hate art. I want to break all my brushes and forget it for ever.
I can't seem to fit in anywhere. I'm not even at one with myself. I feel I will fail NDD and then what? Fail, fail, fail!
I must get some sleep. I cannot attempt another drawing. The sheer physical thing of a pencil or foul pen on paper repulses me. I hate it. How words make nice restful shapes on paper.

Wednesday 29 March 1960, Park Street, Taunton

A day of finalities. All the NDD work is in and Tim says that we have quite high marks. I don't care about marks, I just want to pass. A day of chicken sandwiches and strawberries. Now, a moment ago I looked in the glass and my eye is all funny and swollen. Horrors, what an ugly girl. Much fuss and sticking on of labels.

This morning, at six-thirty, R, Tim and Roger arrived and we messed the place up and crawled to college.

Thursday 30 March 1960, Park Street, Taunton

The landlady told me I should have to get out if I couldn't get my 'visitors' out by ten forty-five. What an odd time! I didn't answer. Then tonight she wrote me a note to tell me to get other digs for next term. Well, that's that. I refuse to go into digs again. We guzzled tea and strawberries. B from Bristol came and there's a party on Saturday but I refuse to go with a pig-eye.

Things have been very odd lately. Today it's all over and I'm in my room, on my own and everybody's at their own places, sleeping and things. I want to get some reading done. I'm glad I'm leaving this room; it's barren and hideous but near college. I seem to find myself cut off in so many directions.

Roger and R were in my bed like a shot as soon as I was out of it at six this morning, absolutely alive with chicken fleas and smelling pretty foul.

Now that I've nearly completed my training I feel at a bit of a loss. I honestly don't know what I'm going to do. Teach, I suppose. JPD came down at the weekend. I want to go up to London again.

Friday 1 April 1960, Park Street, Taunton

My landlady has decided to let me stay which I will do till after my exam, then I'm getting out. Tomorrow we go to a party in Bridgwater. JPD saw Derek in London. I can't wait to hear about the snotty blonde he was with.

Saturday 2 April 1960, Park Street, Taunton

I've begun to read *Voss* by Patrick White which won £1000 in a literary competition.

Sunday 3 April 1960, Park Street, Taunton

Went to the party and much happened. First we hung about in the pubs in Bridgwater until ten o'clock, then three cars set off but we waited outside some house in the country - wrong place - then Beaver's car went into a ford and sunk to the seat level and R and JPD shrieked and climbed out into pitch-black water up to their knees. Much chaos in the cold and dark getting tow-ropes - hoots from the men in their underpants, wading about and being silly, their pants and shoes stacked neatly on the banks. Quite a good party, low rambling house, then at four o'clock we had to tow Beaver's car and everybody was still slightly sloshed. Beaver asleep at the wheel and the tow-rope breaking every couple of yards and the police stopped us. By the time we dropped R and JPD off at Wellington it was quite light. Beaver and I drove back really out of it and bought milk and chocolate out of a machine. The girl who gave the party was a bitch. I've done nothing constructive this weekend and although these parties are funny, they are nothing more.

Tuesday 5 April 1960, Park Street, Taunton

An evening on my own for a change. Tomorrow we finish college, thank God. Roger has been moody and hasn't been up lately and we are hardly civil. JPD is sleeping here tonight as R is in hot water and her parents are moving first thing in the morning. She has a caravan in Trull. I may live with them next term. I have to lower some cotton with a fag packet on the end for JPD to tug when he hitches in from Wellington after ten tonight. It's all very complicated. Life drawing all day - ghastly. Beethoven harp, gorgeous.

Thursday 7 April 1960, Yeovil

At last I have stolen something from JPD - this pen! Wednesday was one big rush. We went to the caravan. It's just right and I'll live there for a while. There was a party at college last night but I came home. I spent the whole of today in my room, sticking up pictures, sorting

things out. Reading *Voss* I realise I am, after all, a reader, not a writer. A reader of other people's brilliant writing. I will never write again, I'm sure.
This pen will do me nicely; a bit thin but good value and a personal triumph. So much in this room that it shrieks at me from all sides. Roger is moody and annoying me intensely.

Sunday 10 April 1960, Yeovil
Beaver came for me yesterday afternoon and we ate buns and went to the reservoir where she did a hideous drawing. We went into a wonderful Norman church, without a parish and very fascinating; so lonely, so old, with terrific wall paintings, badly drawn and faded but gorgeous. I would have liked to have stayed there for a long time.

I rang Roger but he was out. My annoyance was overruled by the joyous sound of return coinage.
Most of the day I've been reading *Voss*. This is a great book I am sure; every sentence is poetry and therefore cannot be read through as prose. Full meaning is excluded at the pace of prose reading. It holds the mind every instant; every statement must be checked, digested and appreciated and therefore it is enlightening, amazing, but tough reading.

A white man has shot the South African Prime Minister[17] in the face. He had it coming to him. There was a world row over the massacre of negroes in South Africa as there should be. I get very angry and upset and am no use in an argument on racial discrimination or capital punishment. I can't remain reasonable about these two things. But as I think on I realise I can hardly keep reasonable on any subject for I am angry and bitter about everything but I do nothing, only turn away in despair.

---

[17] Hendrik Vervoyd, [1901-66], politician: South African right-wing Nationalist Party. Became Prime Minister in 1958. Shot in the face in 1960 but survived, only to be assassinated six years later.

Monday 11 April 1960, Yeovil
I'm more or less waiting for Roger to come over. I can't bloody well afford to phone again. I have very upsetting, vivid dreams that stay with me for several hours of consciousness and the remembrance of them sometimes for several days. Other times they vanish with their feelings on opening my eyes. I feel so tired I could sleep for days without waking. I doubt I'll win the E Nesbitt prize. I doubt anything I write is of worth to a living soul.

A wild, bright, blustering day of glitter, light and clouds moving over air which is cold and racing high. I am all life lived. Looking at trees, such grimly contorted speechless growths spewed up from the bowels of the earth, clinging like hard tongues from the throat of clogged earth. Why aren't we horrified? We are conditioned not to be because they have never once reached out to harm us.
The wind is clamping at the doors like hard, bitter gums. I would like to go to sleep for several years and try again to live.

Tuesday 12 April 1960, Yeovil
Roger has gone back. His feelings burden me.

Wednesday 13 April 1960, Yeovil
About an hour ago I was reading *Voss* - books like these are, for me, real, not fictional. I live through the experiences in them. I gain three years in printed time in three hours and I am exhausted and made miserable and exalted and humiliated in turn. Patrick White is a brilliant writer. I wished I could have written like this. It's on the level of Zola, Tolstoy and my God, what a glorious level, what weighty, glorious heights!

The weather is such that it condemns whole families to the emptiness of their crowded houses, leaving the outside to the pelting rain and allowing the wind to lash at random. But kids stand with their noses stuck to glass and mothers bake and clean. There's a host of smells associated with the temperature of the rooms, the closed doors and the sounds, the feelings of these days when it is too bad to go out.

How records revive memories, smells, sicknesses of the mind and feelings, actual minutes lived in otherwise obscurity. I remember I used to live in a haze of memories - now each second is the future being made past and these past memories are almost those of a stranger. This suspended present can't last much longer. I wonder where Derek is.

Without more of *Voss* to read I feel empty. There's no rain now. My hands are a sooty black with paint, the palms showing pink. I wonder if I wish I were black as an incentive to stand up for something really important - as if the task of one's own fight against oneself in an unsympathetic environment isn't enough! Me, who gets so irritable and angry when people stare. Me, who can't set foot in the town unless I have to. Me, who dreads going out in the daylight. And I wish to be *black!*

Tonight on the television there were some young 'toughs' on motor-bikes, leather jackets, etc. and they were unbelievably thick, following the code of heroism in accidents, death, risk. They fixed aerials on their bikes so people thought they had wirelesses or that they were the cops. Incredible mentality. Thick as the hills and totally pathetic.
I still think of Derek quite a lot.

Anne had written something on life at the old art school at Yeovil. An impression of me: '...serious, tall, blue-eyed, long-haired girl that fell into our life straight out of grammar school like a veteran; she would stay quite serious then come out, quite suddenly, with something quite witty'. I don't even remember if I had consciously tried to create a façade. I imagine I was very self-conscious and not at all sensible.

Friday 15 April 1960, Park Street, Taunton
This morning a huge Easter egg from Roger with twenty fags inside and a sad note which worries me a little: *'A novelty Easter egg - good to have some money. To conceal the heaviness and sadness of my heart. I am tired of life. Forgive me for thinking about you so much.'*
How can I eat a boy's heart? So much love in me twisted and gone to waste.

Saturday 16 April 1960, Yeovil

I didn't know until today about the Aldermaston march to London. Thousands of people marching, jazz bands - why aren't I there? Because there's nobody to go there with me. If Taunton wasn't such a bloody awful place it would have some proper people in it. I'm sick to death with everything.

An overcast evening scowling darkly but with the gentleness of some nights; in my room listening to music. I should be out, having fun. All this time cooped up in here alone, getting miserable. It's ridiculous and dangerous to the state of my mind, the stability of which I sometimes doubt. I'd give anything for the party I refused tonight at Taunton. I change my mind at the slightest thing.
I long for London and wonder where Derek is.

Monday 17 April 1960, Yeovil

Men digging their gardens and women sitting on small patches of grass, with aprons on, and dogs and children running for thrown sticks. Babies sleeping in prams, one crying further down. Washing, line upon line, blowing smells of finished dinners; and the rattle of plates and the shadows of women in kitchens, wearing red jumpers and their husbands standing about in gardens. The smells, the sounds of the lunch hour on a council estate. The men prop their bikes against the privet hedges or the peeling aluminium walls. The sun is out and the sky has taken on immense proportions like a vast blue bowl.

In the garden behind this window is a beautiful boy of about sixteen, of a beautiful coffee colour, very tall and lithe with beautiful hands playing with some children. I want to go out and speak to him. But he would probably stare and think me peculiar.

Tuesday 18 April 1960, Yeovil

Last night Brian came and we talked and drank ale and he mended my gramophone. I'm reading Arnold Bennett's *Journals* which doesn't interest me so much as poor Barbellion's.

It's late now and we've had a good time tonight. Roger came over from Taunton this afternoon and we sat and smoked, talking and playing records. At six o'clock Beaver and Anne arrived and we went in high spirits to David Chant's at Martock; a quaint and dated treat we all adore. We went for a drink in the village and generally clowned around. We chased a fire engine for about eight miles into Langford in the old Ford, risking death at every turn, hooting with laughter and singing. We ogled like morons at a chimney on fire and then we all went for a wee on Langport Station. We left Roger ascending a decrepit bus marked *Street* and bought chips in Stoke, having dropped David at Martock.

Wednesday 19 April 1960, Yeovil
Sitting in the sun on the back step, scared of the grass spiders. I hate sitting in the sun. I can't concentrate to read in this light and feel mucky and bitty and irritable. I long for the cool gloom of my room.
The more I read of Arnold Bennett's *Journals* the more I like them. His descriptions of scenes and episodes in London, Paris, concerts, cafés, carriages, please me very much.

Today I felt very unhappy in my tapestry coat which has shrunk miserably in the wash, standing outside the Rendezvous in Yeovil with Brian, waiting for a bus. There were people idly waiting around and suddenly I looked and they were all staring blankly at me and wouldn't stop. I felt like screaming. The sun was out and I felt so wretched I wanted to kick them all - or just run away. I started to stammer and say senseless things to Brian while they just stood there and watched with their awful cows' eyes.

Thursday 20 April 1960, Yeovil
This afternoon Anne and I made spaghetti properly and fussed over the arrival of her 'betrothed', Dan Cake [*a young dentist from Newcastle called David Dewell*]. He's very nice; quite tall, thin, with a bespectacled and gaunt face, shy, funny, and wholely nice.
JPD is with Beaver at Rampisham and is after my blood about an arrangement misled or something. Beaver says she has no hair at all

except a faint green growth on her scalp, shaven at the back - she was shrieking down the phone, hooting with laughter and not saying a thing.

Saturday 25 April 1960, Yeovil
The last two days have been one long joy-ride. A train to Evershot, much fuss and endless wit and humour. David Chant and I fairly sped along the road to Rampisham, he striding ahead, straddled with countless albums and folios [*press-cuttings of his performances in amateur theatricals*] and wearing a hideous yellow blouse and baggy trousers. Searched the horizon for him, he was but a speck and found him by the side of the road, grey and panting. JPD was rude to me. Headed for Weymouth in Beaver's car, shrieking with laughter all the time. The car was a wreck in body but a lion in spirit. It creaked and groaned but carried us all the way to Weymouth.
But there was no dance at all and we all turned on Beaver and cursed her. Sat in a glum ring and drank beer. Then all eight of us returned in the car to Rampisham where we sat around an electric fire, drinking horrible tea and talking and talking; slightly irritable, very tired and too lazy to get up and go to bed. David, of course, thought he saw a body in the spare room at the end of the house that is haunted. He retired under protest, still babbling. Everybody smoking far too much. I feel choked with nicotine but very content in this company.

In the morning David went home, mumbling to himself and we went to West Bay and ate lollies. JPD has been annoying everyone and there is great hostility at Rampisham. I've never known anyone as funny as David. Beaver has no hair rather like the Queen Mother in 1920. I can't bear to go back to Taunton, the very thought of it is grim - the place is so empty.

Sunday 26 April 1960, Yeovil
I cycled up at great peril and considerable discomfort to see Anne. I sat in the garden in a hot sun glare. I'm broke and was rolling fags from dogends again. They went off to Leicester and I was sorry to see them go. They're so lucky to have each other. Anne is a different person, all faithful and quiet and not referring to the past. How I long to get all this bloody art school business behind me. I haven't touched my

brushes - I've ceased to be a painter altogether. I'm not an artist at all as though it has worked out of my system. I've no enthusiasm left and the subject is almost strange to me. People talking about painting bore me. All talk of art bores me. I haven't written any poetry for ages. I'm drained of all creative energy. My life is slowing to a halt. It's a void.

Monday 27 April 1960, Park Street, Taunton
Today I did some really atrocious drawing and Murphy talked about Venice and Florence. I went to a lecture on Berlioz and Ravel until six and came back and felt sick. Then I forced myself to night-school where I found the models posing like lumps of cold suet pudding. I went out again, unable to stay in the face of such horror. I hate the college. My heart sinks as I enter it. The exams begin on 9 May and then I'm off. I don't know where. I'm a curious creature. I love to stay in my room for hours and hours and hate it if anyone comes near me - yet I'm lonely. I half hope someone will come to see me yet when they do I feel annoyed and begrudge the time taken up in stupid chatter.

Tuesday 25 April 1960, Park Street, Taunton
Working at college is grim but less unbearable than I'd imagined it would be. I stayed in its walls all day and went straight back to evening class but at eight o'clock I crept away into the lavatory to read Arnold Bennett. The freshness of reading, the joy of words, the lack of physical nerve and mess was very pronounced and I felt pleased for a small pleasure stolen.

Roger is slumped in misery but no longer confides in me. Tim is sporting his revolting Moses sandals. Liz [*artists' model*] looked like an elongated fish this morning and would not keep still; she knits and reads and writes shopping lists all over the place but is as still as a mouse when Murphy's around.
Tonight we went to the caravan to visit R and JPD whose troubles I'm involved in. We are three, only he lives with her. Murphy came too and we're going to make pigs of ourselves at his house tomorrow lunchtime.

Wednesday 26 April 1960, Park Street, Taunton

Tim, R and JPD and I went to Murphy's house for some lunch and eating at a table at lunchtime seemed strange. Many deliciously funny and highly obscene jokes, all of which we'd heard many times before. JPD has at last got a job - laying tar on the roads. He was allowed thirty bob pre-pay and bought me a penny pancake in the Green Lantern. Someone has lent him a bicycle to get to work - they'll never see *that* again.

Roger has been morose and will hardly speak to me at all and never to anyone else. Something has really upset him. He sits staring at me and I see him fighting not to come when I call and not to do something I ask of him. He's trying hard to hate me. He may succeed. I know how he feels and all the time I'm twisting my spirit about, remembering when it was me. But Derek's no longer a reality; it's the memory of him I still miss.

Thursday 27 April 1960, Park Street, Taunton

It's gone three o'clock and this evening several of the students have been discussing the life-force, ethics, etc until we were all nervous and hysterically depressed. But it's very good for me. I'm on my own in several trains of thought. The nearest to perfection is presumably death but to what degree of perfection, under the handicap of the body, can the mind reach? To me, at the moment, the Buddhist monk has probably achieved perfection, having rejected the body in the search for the absolute limits of the mind.

Endless discussion on Time and, of course, the Bomb. There's so much I want to record but it's all as exactly as thousands of students all over the world are talking and thinking about and common knowledge to so many.

Earlier we played crap at Murphy's house and the player, shaker or banker, or whatever it is, was absolutely surrounded by hundreds of pieces of Woodbine packets, dogends, tins, hair grips, pens, biscuits, etc, as betting stakes.

Friday 28 April 1960, Yeovil
Back home and suffering the aftermath of a flaming row with mother about ideals, learning, knowledge, intellect and, of course, money. I completely lost control of my temper. She mixes sentiment with abstract criticism, condemning anything she doesn't understand. She's completely illogical and contradicts herself over and over and refuses to use her brain or even anticipate any state of which she is oblivious. That she is my mother makes no difference to me. She is just another person not using her intellect.

Tonight Brian came and we went out for some beer and talked over many things. He goes back to London on Sunday and again voiced his admiration of Derek's work.

Saturday 30 April 1960, Yeovil
I'm going to start reading a book on Villon and I'm certain this is the time for me to get into the teachings of Buddha. It's superb having hours to fill, alone, with books and beautiful music, a room much loved and my own wondering mind to savour. For some time JPD has been trying to get his André Gide for me to read. He feels sure I will like him. At Frank Anderson's flat last week I read the first few pages of *If I Die* and he's right.
Murphy told me that at Colin Wilson's lectures at the Royal College he always arrived on his bike with a gas mask slung across his torso.
The character of Villon fascinates me as it was bound to. I've forced myself to sit in the sun but it irritates me and the slightest breeze on my bare flesh makes me shudder and shrink from the outdoors altogether. It's an immense waste of time for I can't read in the glare of the sun.
Strange how millions of Europeans almost kill themselves trying to reach the colour of the negro. White seems to me the most sickly, the meanest of colours for skin. In a cinema or café or after a film full of coloured people, when one looks in the mirror or at another white, one appears very peeky and insipid and almost frightening. I can quite see how a black person would find us a skull-like, tight and nasty race.

I hate the sounds and smells of summer; they reflect the nausea of time past that I'm loathe to remember for reasons I'm uncertain of. I went up to the shop that serves this estate and was stranded in a sea of children, all gazing up the length of me in curiosity. I was blushing and my hands were wet and sticking to the money in my hand.

I was talking to Brian about this last night. In some moods one can go anywhere, be stared at, without minding; another time it drags you down to the depths of discomfort and one just wants to crawl away from the stupid, endless stares. Yet college humour is all about embarrassment. We get endless pleasure from being really rude to each other in a way that some might think cruel. JPD is brilliantly rude and, knowing one's every weakness, goes for the jugular every time. It's a typical student humour, ridiculous and vulgar to anyone not participating. All humour is at the expense of other people's embarrassment. Tim and I can spend hours doing drawings of the Queen, etc, whom we abhor. Members of the royal family are supreme to draw in all their mediocre vileness.

Villon's writing is strange at first reading. I find it hard to imagine fifteenth-century men going to universities and schools or any collective form of learning.

While I was reading *Voss* I felt very disinclined to write anything again for my unexposed intentions in this field were so insipid and pointless in the face of what I could see it could be. Whatever I write now must necessarily be of no consequence, perhaps always. But then, I might just as well write poor prose or poetry as not write at all - either way is negative but the former far less so.

My hair looks good just now, silky and a gorgeous brown, hanging loose and straight, curving my face.
Roger is in love with me.
The days go by so quickly; the night is very quiet. Brian calls the estate 'China Town'. It's tatty, a huddle of shacks that look like rows of match-boxes, once white, now the sheet walls are lined with weather-maps. Row upon row of washing flapping the same way, the same clothes, the same washing powder; the smell of dinners mingling with the sharp voices of children.

As one gets older impressions shift into perspective. I saw a woman on the bus who used to live opposite. I saw her, not as a familiar, unidentified form, but as a human being with a particular, independent shape. Some eleven years have passed since I knew her - a lifetime to me, a measurable distance to her.

So too with teachers. I remember a student teacher from France; she always smelled of chocolate éclairs and didn't seem much interested in any of us. A student teacher, with humour, memories, going through the horrible experience of teacher training and I was so unconscious, cut off, so unseeing; relationships left unmade through difference in development.

Therefore, when I teach on Saturday mornings [*art classes for children at the College*] those children see me only very vaguely and in a distorted and distant way. If they like me it's not a proper, full, lasting liking, not a conscious but a blurred thing. This should make teaching easier, knowing that to the child it's relatively unimportant whatever you do and everything is slightly out of focus.

A teacher isn't a person at all, just a familiar arrangement of shape, sound and smell, plus a name-tag and associations with certain habits and characteristics on view to the child.

A child doesn't realise itself as a person until about fifteen so it can't possibly consider the teacher as anything else. Parents are also merely familiar extensions of one's own unconsciously performing self. Realisation of fallibility comes with realisation of oneself.

As soon as the child develops into a fully conscious mind directing a body independently and at will then the so-called, over-emphasised, family ties are severed. After all, few individuals can live together. In marriage there's the sexual balance and bond and the sharing of views and ideas which is a terrific tie. Whereas the child finds itself living with people who are alien to it with ideas and habits quite adverse to its own.

I remember at Junior School, during lunch rests, lying in dusty classrooms, on scratchy reed mats - no speaking, close your eyes. I can remember writing 1946 with a dip-in pen at the top of the page; the ink-monitor filled the little white porcelain ink bottles each morning with a cup with a spout. I remember learning my tables chalked on coloured paper and listening to stories in the afternoons. I remember learning to read with a woman who is just a vague shape or remembrance.

School meals, having to stand by the table if you spoke. They made us eat great lumps of hideous, yellow fat and gristle. Day after day we had this wretched mutton stew and as we lined up with our plates our eyes would fix on the descending ladle, praying it wouldn't contain much of the vile yellow fat which we knew we would be forced to eat. The wily ones would offer their 'meat' to some poor sucker and push all the fat in with it. We used to sit in misery, almost vomiting over the stuff. When it was cold we'd cut it into tiny bits and try to swallow it with a lump of potato. And it never entered our heads to *refuse* to eat it.

My first feelings of individuality were after the results of the Eleven Plus. The names of those children going to the Grammar School were read out and I felt important because not many got through. We used to sit in double desks [*with heavy wooden flip-lids and cast-iron legs screwed to the floor*] in order of cleverness. I was usually about eighth. How awful this system is, to be read out and literally placed in order of cleverness.

Sunday 1 May 1960, Yeovil
I remember hanging around an empty lobby before school began, swinging on those cold iron bars. I had a cold and my voice had gone and I remember talking a lot, hearing the echoes and feeling important because my voice was temporarily unusual and attracted attention.
I had to wear awful beige, *hand-knitted* stockings with elastic garters and as I was always falling over, the knees were invariably out. I hated wearing home-made things, like wearing cream Vyella blouses instead of the white cotton shop ones. I was very fond of my brother who I felt protected me just by being somewhere in the school but in fact, he ignored me completely.

On the news more and more demonstrations. London is convulsed with great rallies in Trafalgar Square and Hyde Park. Anti-apartheid and anti-nuclear arms, etc. All over the world there are reports of demonstrations with endless shooting of students and party leaders. There's a great surge of democracy sweeping the world, of justice and of rights.

*

I remember how Valerie [*student at Yeovil School of Art; married the painter, Bob Organ*], Anne and I were suspended from the Art School for keeping mice in a condemned room upstairs. They were in a box over an old bath; the tap had overflowed and water had dripped into an office in the Technical School below. There was one hell of a stink which was very childish and unnecessary. We were suspended and sent off in disgrace until a decision was made as to our future by the Board of Governors. And I was told not to return until I cut my hair [*incredibly, considering the freedom enjoyed by students today, my hair was only to my shoulders*]. I remember that was my first instance of personal conflict between my own taste and that of authority. I was furious and felt well and truly victimised. And I didn't cut my hair.

Fanny was the ageing model but a very good one. We teased her all the time, throwing grape pips at her and making rude comments. When she had the curse she wore a hideous flesh-tinted elastic 'object'. She lived with her father, who looked bearded and biblical, in a cottage completely crammed with antiques, photographs, pots, frogs and spiders. They slept on bear-skins and were always making things. She was very eccentric and cynical and she wore funny knitted skirts and weird hats and thick woollen stockings. She would pass us in the street and amid our cries of 'Fan!' she'd remain deadpan and refuse to associate herself with us at all.

It was a fantastic school. For the Common Room we had a revolting underground air-raid shelter, over-ridden with insects and thick with mould, damp clay and sick from parties. The air was disgusting. [*We even had to grind our own lithography stones and boil pots of gum arabic on a camping stove.*] Students' cooking mess was everywhere and the place was littered with stale food. Around the walls were casts -

antique statuary - and a clay bin that looked like a coffin. The roof was held up with concrete pillars and there was a large hole in the wall, jammed full of rubbish. We used the pubic region of the Venus de Milo as an ash-tray. There was one old black leather chair which was Valerie's throne; only Derek or Jo would attempt to sit in it. She was long, tall, cynical, frightening, with long straight hair, beautiful clothes and heavily made-up eyes.

The painting room was forbidden territory but I could hear them talking inside. [*There were only nine full-time students.*] They were dirty and always laughing. They never spoke to us. We were humble in their presence. At break we used to creep down to the modelling room/air raid shelter and stand around watching them. I don't remember how I got in with them. I started to smoke and looked a bit like Valerie which helped. I was taken into the group and so was Beaver and they used to take off her 'county' accent and nervous blink - we went through a great deal of teasing.

Later we began to take lessons in the painting room with Robert Ellis, a small, dapper, thirty-ish, grey-haired man; very attractive and egotistical. Then Brian, Derek and Jo left to do their National Service and only Valerie and Anne remained. The headmaster was a truly legendary character - a north country man of hideous countenance, no bottom, no chin, huge stomach, an absolute scoundrel who kept Afghan hounds. He made people like Derek and Brian work on his wretched caravan instead of painting and was always prying into their affairs.

Then there was Miss Kohler, an amazing amazon of a woman, quite mad with her hair in ear-phones, an ape-like face and a body highly reinforced with corsetry. A stupid, bitter, terrible woman with a wicked tongue and a pitiful adherence to false 'gentility, breeding and the finer things of life'. We were endlessly at war.
Peter Crabtree came to teach for a while; he was thin and nervous and then just disappeared. Then came Bob Organ, a brilliant painter, who was immediately worshipped.

Monday 3 May 1960, Park Street, Taunton

I'm beginning to re-write my thesis. My landlady is in her bed next door reading a love story, badly written, listening to her radio, having watched her television, having eaten her supper, having finished her tea, having reached once more the age of solitude.

JPD is still spreading tar on the roads. He moans continually about the damage to the sensitivity of his mind and the delicacy and length of his finger nails.

I can hear some guitar music somewhere. It's extremely sensual in that it becomes consistent with beautiful feelings. Sometimes I don't want to hear beautiful music because it sets up a longing, a glimpse, an essence of something inconceivably exquisite. A few bars of music can evoke a flood of indescribable feeling. A feeling I can't express. I don't know what it is.

Wednesday 4 May 1960, Park Street, Taunton

This love that Roger has for me weighs heavily. I can transmit myself completely and become him and understand for I have felt the same about someone. But I can't do anything about it except try to avoid doing or saying the things that I know will hurt him. He sits and stares at me until I could scream.

Last night we went drinking in the Compass and he sat staring at me with a pained expression. He behaves very erratically and sometimes goes off to brood, after which he apologises. I can do nothing.

Today I had to walk through the town, something I rarely do. Every man in every car turned to stare and several slowed down treacherously. I wasn't looking freakish at all. I was in one of my nonchalant walk-tall moods and took the attention as my due. Yesterday a man driving a lorry loaded with cars was waving and grinning at me and shot straight across and into the wrong lane of traffic. He was stuck amid an onslaught of speeding traffic and it took great concentration to get the load back on track. I'm not writing these things out of vanity for every reasonably pretty girl gets whistled at and receives endless male attention at every step in public places. Of course, R with her long, flowing blonde hair, gets the treatment even more so. I fail to see how my looks warrant such impromptu and enthusiastic responses but most of the time I like it.

I've been reading about the execution of Chessman[18] and I'm appalled and it's too upsetting to write about.

Princess Mag's marriage to Tony Armstrong Jones on Friday for which great occasion we get a day off. The press is busily scribbling away about his fine background, determined that the woman won't marry an ordinary commoner. What the hell does it matter? £4000 a day will be spent on the honeymoon. I need say no more for my exasperation and contempt can find few words. All this business of plumed soldiers bobbing about on horses and glass coaches is completely unnecessary and uninspiring.

I can see why a crowd might clamour and cheer a great political leader, a great musician or what have you but not this senseless idolisation of a set of rich, rather dull, supposedly untalented but gracious people, usually atrociously dressed and with no interest in the arts. The princess, it is said, simply adores the poems of John Betjeman - to select his work from all poetic output is just ludicrous.

I've just been on the phone to Beaver about the party at the Palace in Bristol and saw my chalking of FREE AFRICA on the wall up the road. Now I'm obsessed by an unwarranted fear that the police are after me for it. I've even thought about creeping out later and rubbing it off. How incredibly weak I am.

I've just heard a whistle and seen Roger walk by, hitching a lift to Bridgwater where he lives.

The sound of church bells - how I hate them.

---

[18] Carl Chessman was hanged after a series of reprieves. He had been on Death Row for eleven years.

Every morning my landlady talks to herself quite loudly, presumably while she's dressing. Strange, I always feel cross and defeated to find her up before me as though my youth has done the dirty on me. She doesn't like me and rarely speaks and only acknowledges me in the street as a tiresome duty.
I looked quite pretty before but don't look so good now. I've had a bath and feel very tired. I wonder what girl is winding herself round Derek's body tonight. She may even love him; even so, I hate her, whoever, whatever, she is.

Friday 6 May 1960, Yeovil
I've been sitting in the sun today and wasted a great deal of time and now have a headache. I've written short, empty letters to Brian and Anne. There's really nothing to write. Mother nags all day and gets on my nerves as much as I get on hers. If ever we're in the same room we row and argue all the time. Her blind, subjective acceptance of things makes me see red. She rejects all learning or any use of intelligence as pomposity. 'Who do you think you are?' is the constant taunt. This, I know, is partly my fault because I get so het up about these important things that I shout at her for her stubbornness and inverted snobbery towards anything she can't grasp and feels it's not her place to question. I lose patience with her; likewise, she has no patience with me but with others she is sweet and reasonable and good-natured.

Saturday 7 May 1960, Yeovil
Sitting in the sun again under a vast blue sky. I can't concentrate and feel messy.
Rows of rumpled nappies and empty gardens; babies lying in blankets like dead things, life suspended for a few hours. But always some dogs yelping, perhaps at the butterflies or stray children that surprise them with a clumsy touch as they doze.
I'm a profusion of red-brown and pinks and rather sore but delighted; the quest for blackness has begun. The normal colour of the European is really revolting, like dirty marble.

Reading Arnold Bennett's *Journals* again. Will they never end? I tire easily and lose interest. I don't much like the way he writes; to me it's dull. My brother has had the television on full blast all afternoon for the Cup Final and the whole estate might well have turned off their sets and listened to ours.

I sat on the step and began to burn to death with a determined smile. I don't want Roger to come over tomorrow so I'll ring and say I'm suffering from severe sun-stroke. He was looking so bloody miserable when I left college on Thursday I said he could come over tomorrow. He may insist on coming in which case I'll be in a foul temper when he arrives and he'll wish he hadn't come. I can be a bitch sometimes.

Monday 10 May 1960, Park Street, Taunton

The start of NDD. I did five frightful drawings, real monsters and that's the truth. I almost went mad sitting there in that stuffy room in dead silence making hideous, irritable marks on paper - bottles of ink and pens and brushes - revolting. At four-thirty I just couldn't stand it any longer and if I'd been flogged with whips I couldn't have touched the paper again. I just sat for the last half hour. Tim wasn't drawing well either.

JPD is still spreading tar on the roads.

All over the world there's fighting, endless fighting and hatred and there's big trouble brewing between Russian and America over spy - planes.

Tuesday 11 May 1960, Park Street, Taunton

In bed and just been reading about Islam - very interesting. We walked out to the caravan last night. I itch all over from insect bites. My life painting isn't too bad but I'm bored with it. Another three and a half days!

Wednesday 12 May 1960, Park Street, Taunton

Continuing under silent protest with the life painting. Murphy seems quite unnaturally pleased with it, thank goodness.

The invigilator is an interesting but pathetic creature - a very frail, painfully thin old lady, very genteel, respectable and timid. She brings with her each day a round tin of sparsely filled sandwiches and a flask

of revolting tea, very weak and without sugar. She sits for all these hours nibbling her crumbs slowly, quietly, her eyes round, like a bird's, no longer bright, dulled yet watery, her gaze cast to the ground or her shoes, which stand side by side, as though she's remembering.
She lives in lodgings and repeatedly thanks me when I offer her a Woodbine. In a quiet and cultured voice she asks me if I've ever tried Dominoes, four for sixpence.
Her face is continually, faintly twisted into the expression of a lone person feeling in the way, one accustomed to sit silently, feeling that she shouldn't be listening to other people's conversation. A flickering, vacant expression, her hands always touching, rubbing or arranging things. She's ultra-polite and walks with conscious precision. Will she die unmissed? I expect so yet she was once a beloved child - once a young woman, now lonely, poor and gently subservient to even young students like us. To me this is incredibly sad. She wears a little nail varnish which is an odd twist of the female nature I've often noticed in these elderly women. It always makes me feel sick.

Started rolling Old Holborn, a really delicious tobacco. Drinking with Roger in the Compass again; as always he weighs on me with his looks and things he does. How cruel it is. Saw some really fabulous Lâncome lipsticks. Mrs Murphy has got *three*.

Thursday 13 May 1960, Park Street, Taunton
More on the life painting; now I'm really fed-up with it and feel like sloshing white paint all over it. Holterman says to leave it and get on with the other work but Tim says it's nowhere near finished. Hell, I can't do any more to it.

Friday 14 May 1960, Yeovil
Back in my room, a familiar stranger. A card from Beaver, alarmingly legible. She must be in great pain. Roger is bitter and morose and awkward to please.
I look rather ugly tonight. Home in Tim's revolting car [*little Austin 7*] at a steady smelly twenty miles an hour, hay-carts and bicycles overtaking us with ease.
Lovely wet, dark rain. Glorious. I hate the sun. I like rain, rain, rain.

Sunday 15 May 1960, Yeovil
A good day of chucking out piles of unnecessary press-cuttings, photographs, knick-knacks and odds and ends. I want no possessions. But I feel uneasy for I shall soon be leaving completely and won't have a room *anywhere.* It's essential for me to have a grounding place, four walls where I am myself, alone. Always staying in other people's hideous places - I can't bear it. My room matters too much and has become essential to the stability of my mind. Some people find it difficult to understand.

I must have a place where I can paint the walls white and have my own things. I begrudge the intrusion of other people's belongings about me. Many files, clipped and bulging with torn-out photographs, press-cuttings and reproductions - all treasures, all of which I need. They need a room, a grounding place, not suitcases or crowded baskets - nowhere to go, nowhere to hide. I must have a room completely my own or I'll up and maybe die.

A third of the letters I've ever had are from Derek. I felt sad looking at them. But I haven't cried since last Christmas at J's party where I literally felt my heart break. I haven't cried tears since then, even when I was ill and in such pain. I wonder if he ever cries. I hope not. I hope he never needs to.

Monday 16 May 1960, Park Street, Taunton
Tonight I went drinking with R and JPD. My eyes ache. Roger has gone spare. JPD and R are about to murder each other after several months of bottled up hatred mingled with a kicking dependence on each other.
The weather is damply depressing and stifling.
A letter from Brian which I can't stop thinking about. Everything is crowding in on me. Another rejection slip from *Poetry Review*.

The days go on, the hours pass impersonally and little seems to be gained.

Tuesday 17 May 1960, Park Street, Taunton

Tonight I'm depressed and worried. This summit conference in Paris between Khrushchev, Macmillan, de Gaulle and Eisenhower is going very badly and tonight in Compass there was a woman about fifty talking as people do in pubs. She said: 'I haven't been so frightened since just before the Second World War.' People were coming in and their first words were: 'Any news?' or 'Heard anything yet?' They are admitting now that those 'exhibitionists' who went on the Aldermaston marches weren't so stupid after all. In fact, they are to be praised for making even a futile protest.

'What right have these four men got to just press a button and get rid of us just like that?' said another woman. How often have I said the same thing. I wanted to have the usual innings, wretched or good, but I doubt that I'll have it now. Is this the echo of every soul, of every decade, of every time? What does it matter if I get the window in my bloody composition right?

Politics seem to have reached a futile and childish level of personal hatred between separate pig-headed, proud individuals, whilst we, the wretched, wait the command to stand up and die. As far as I can see from the press reports Khrushchev has spent the day stamping out of the conference room, muttering oaths and then coming back to insult Eisenhower. I want to grip these maniacs by the shoulders and shout: 'Don't you dare destroy me!' How can I live on probation like this? How can anyone? But we do.

What's the point in these ink marks on paper in the shadow of such turmoil? There is none.

I would rather be a live Communist than a dead nothing. Is the life in Russia that bad? Provided that this extreme socialism can also cater for the individual, which is the crucial point of difference at present, then it seems ideal. I'm reminded of a line in my poem: 'Will I be amongst the ones to leave this Earth en masse or on my own mid-century?'

As I switched on the light tonight I was frightened by a sudden rustle behind the chair. Out fluttered a very thin and frightened starling. It

flapped about the room with glazed eyes. I drew back the curtains and wafted him out, almost sorry to see him go. I'd love an animal. I would be indescribably excited to have a dog.
I'm doing a composition, a row of strange women with children in front of tall houses, the luscious, grotesque Victorian ones across the road from here. I never stop looking at them - the colours, with delicately painted designs all over them, and the arches and patterns and pointed churchy windows are very Piero-esque. Some of them look like the château in children's fairy-tale books, delicate yet sombre.

A friend of Roger's came up earlier this evening and talked endlessly about his drunken escapades. Talk by young men about their drinking habits bore me to tears. I used to think it was clever and sexy and adult to get roaring drunk at parties. I get quietly sozzled now. It's much better, I don't miss so much of the company, am better company, perhaps, and it saves me some moments of embarrassment when the dawn approaches. Roger and I have a pint of beer every night. I hate cider; it reminds me of the old Yeovil Art School days when we were realising we could make the room spin with two pints of rough cider at sixpence a pint from the White Lion during modelling breaks.

Wednesday 18 May 1960, Park Street, Taunton
I've finished the original design exam. Examinations in art are ridiculous and invalid. Roger and I have sat in complete silence for the last five and half hours but we couldn't do without beer so bought some bottles. I felt very amiable towards him tonight. I have no desire to hurt him for I'm very fond of him underneath.

It appears that the Heads of State are returning in angry storms to their countries. The most hoped-for Summit is a complete failure and more than that, a reckoning and a clarification of the terrible gravity of our situation and that of the entire human race. Amazing that if two Heads of State personally dislike each other it can sway the balance between success and failure, understanding and mistrust, for it becomes a personal thing between wary individuals out for their own prestige and power over the other.

Thursday 19 May 1960, Park Street, Taunton
Painting all day. This evening we drank with the Murphys and went to their place afterwards. It's about 1.45 am and I'm full of smoke. Murphy said that Holterman wants me to try for the Royal College. I'm rather pleased and honestly surprised. How useless and untalented I am compared to Derek. The Murphys have a beautiful flat with huge white walls, very high with a carved ceiling, one studio couch, one table and cabinet, a clock, some books and a large midnight blue carpet. Very like the Bates' room, exactly as Derek will have his rooms - Royal College taste, verging on the austere. I liked this evening. When I visit these couples, making gorgeous personal places to live in I feel very envious for I have no such immediate plans of my own.

There was a man in the pub with an exquisite fox cub on a leash. A beautiful, soft creature, unbearably delicate and sensitive. It was lapping beer. I wanted it for my own.
We made fun of the part-timers tonight; the idiots, presumptuous, ludicrous creatures, the source of endless amusement and annoyance.

Friday 20 May 1960, Yeovil
Back in my room, now in bed, enthused and, for the first time, almost ambitious. An illusion, a trick of purpose here as my NDD painting is not going particularly well. The papers are full of the failure of the Summit. The name of Khrushchev has taken on the terror of Hitler and his rally in East Germany was exactly as the Hitlerite ones. Swarms of humanity with right arms adjacent to their eyes. Very impressive. Frightening.

Saturday 21 May 1960, Yeovil
I still feel the weight of Roger very much. We're together nearly all the time. Strangely, I feel jealous mentally if he considers another woman, which is pleasingly rare, though his opinion of me and my mind isn't particularly high. In fact, perhaps he despises women but he is incredibly romantic and touches women with an extremely sensual gentleness as he does flowers and animals. He has pale, tapered hands which are very sensitive to touch, green eyes and long lashes.

Sometimes I feel so incompetent in ordinary living and unable to cope with working with other people. I feel that I can never get away from my screaming self. This screaming self will have to earn money yet it seems incapable of any constancy, any routine, in service to other people for money. I'm afraid it will mutiny. I'm afraid of myself, afraid of my incapabilities.

All the time I'm fighting for normality; I strive for it but it seems impossible. Yet I loathe normality, morons, masses and mediocrity. But if people don't stare at me I feel inconspicuous. It all depends how I feel. Sometimes I feel that if one more person stares at me, man or woman, I'll scream or cower in a doorway. Another time I just ask to be stared at. These are lovely moods but they don't last long.

Sunday 22 May 1960, Yeovil
I've just done my habitual paper reading and mutilation. More precious stones for my files. Reading about Gertrude Stein, Leautard, Gide, Hume, Gerard Manley Hopkins, one of Roger's favourites, Robert Bridges, Paul Potts. I'm still very interested in Lawrence Durrell whom I'm sure is a very good writer. Roger won't recognise this. Now I must start painting. I've been reading a little of Dylan Thomas, Auden, T S Eliot and Wilfred Owen.

Beaver came this afternoon and we talked of men and morals. Sometimes we gossip atrociously and as usual bemoaned our various and innumerable faults, parading mournfully before every available mirror, deploring our looks and bewailing our present singular state and above all, bravely musing on a future similarly indisposed.
But for me it's a very serious thing for I'm afraid I'll never find a person who would fit my personality because I'm so egocentric and think only of myself and not always in relation to others.

Monday 23 May 1960, Park Street, Taunton
Painting on the NDD composition which is going badly. I've borrowed two books by Albert Camus: *The Outsider* and *The Plague*.
This tobacco has started to discolour my front teeth. Much shaken; perhaps it will be my vanity that will overcome my habit.

Tuesday 24 May 1960, Park Street, Taunton
Late but reading Bertrand Russell all evening: *Why I Am Not A Christian, The Uses of Christianity* and *Freedom and The Colleges* - all very interesting. I should have been in college but was too engrossed to go.
Only five cigarettes today. Really upset about my teeth.

Wednesday 25 May 1960, Park Street, Taunton
This morning my mind is jammed, full of Bertrand Russell's thoughts; now I'm waiting to digest and sort them out. It strikes me that in several instances he evades the point, a fault he strongly stamps on in his debating opponents. A brilliant thinker, bringing one into the new sphere of minute objective thought, not general thoughts or assessments based on feelings, nothing more.

This evening Roger said he loved me and wanted to marry me. He was upset but there was nothing I could do. We talked about it for some time. It's a wickedly cruel situation and a parodox.

Thursday 26 May 1960, Park Street, Taunton
The painting is going better. A strange day with this odd thing between Roger and myself. This evening we sat in here as usual and talked about religion.

Sunday 29 May 1960, Yeovil
Just in from a party at the Palace in Bristol. Met a vast and beautiful man, blond, about six foot four, again, an actor at the Bristol Old Vic. He was delicious, egocentric and surprisingly honest.

Now I'm awake and almost happy in a state of aching bones and voices still pitching, movements still shifting. Last night Roger sat piercing his eyes into my head all night. I can do nothing but keep away. I was very popular last night with many assorted men following me about. What a fool I am.
I ache all over and feel restless. I sense trouble. Better then that he didn't write and I see no more of him.

Monday 30 May 1960
Now I'm sitting at an ugly table in the green and cream waiting room at Yeovil Town Station. Each morning I insert a tiny piece of damp cotton wool into the nicotine-stained crevice between my front teeth. I secure its position with a cocktail stick, green nickel plated in the shape of an arrow. A cocktail stick from *HMS Canton*, sailing, I believe, between Hong Kong and Southampton.
Interesting, eh?

Upbringing, unfounded pretensions, condemnations, prejudice, bias and unreasonable and false conclusions. Behaviour should be governed by reason, not circumstantial prejudices, echoes of other people's misconceptions. These murky stumbling blocks are passed on from birth with low rumbling voices eking into our intellects, saturating our channels of individual, precise reasoning, to become our own second-hand stock of reasons for behaviour.

To have been consumed by ethics and ideas for nineteen years only to find that none of it is relevant. Today, now, to be 'immoral' is to have a sexual relationship with someone one isn't legally married to. It's a sexual thing. No matter that immorality can take other forms, less tangible, like gossiping, vanity, sadism, bitterness - these are all far more detrimental to humanity.

Of course, there's the question of children arising from 'trial marriages' but this can be so easily avoided by contraception and this I don't believe to be morally wrong either. I think it's morally *right,* outside an environment essential to the serious upbringing of a child.

To me the milestones of an existence are within. All the important decisions, extensions, additions, discoveries and advancements are in the mind. And then I sometimes wonder if the love of aesthetics isn't merely another distorted disease that once contracted, infects one for life.

Tuesday 31 May 1960, Park Street, Taunton
Made my way to college, looked doubtfully into the painting room, saw my painting and walked out and into the Life Room where I sat for an hour watching people through the window.
An early summer evening in a small country town. A bevy of hard-ridged bums belonging to oldish women in dull colours, urging slowly in unison along pavements, taking their handbags for walks, blending into the general greyness. Corseted, similar, constipated, wanting to relieve themselves, nasty bulges pushed in by bone corsets, shifting on rolling flesh. They waddle, all the energy they have left used up in concentrating on putting one foot before the other, as though carrying great weights.

A wheelchair, in which sat an old woman, on the back of which was grafted another woman, also bespectacled, her image in twenty years time. Strange that this old woman gave birth to that old woman. It came to me urgently that the young should never feel obliged to push the old in wheelchairs. I saw many of these middle-aged women in greys and browns, far older than they have a right to be, stiff and corseted with barrenness, complacent, repulsive, their bodies moulded by years of motherhood and sacrifice, their hands shaking from good works.

I saw a tall woman, youngish, walking awkwardly, her thin, dull skirt flopping uncomfortably against her thin, nondescript legs - awkward beside a small man. They walked a couple of paces apart, she obviously embarrassed by the difference in their height, enforcing a distance between them so they might appear as mere acquaintances.
Then I watched two young people walking slowly, erratically, a yard apart, forever turning this way and that, jerking their legs, savouring every step. Obviously on a first date. They were so young they made me feel old.

Why can't oldish women *walk?* They seem incapable of moving with the smallest degree of grace. They really annoy me, they're so grey and stiff and *unnecessarily* old.

Groups of girls in giggling colours. Two figures, one grey, one mushroom, sat adjacent on a bench for ages without a single word, without lips, and eyes that only shifted slightly from left to right. And their assent to rise from the bench was simultaneous and silently performed. Two individuals sitting on a park bench in silence, the husband in grey, the wife in mushroom, with absolutely nothing to say to each other.

On Saturday I saw a tramp with a charcoal beard chalking a swastika between his feet on a lonely stretch of road near Glastonbury.
Young men strutting with sexual pride swinging the angular arms of young girls in summer frocks. The click of heels.

Friday 3 June 1960, Yeovil
Had to go through a hideous train journey and realised how much I want to get away from here where horribly familiar faces appear like ghosts. I hate it here.

I was in a compartment with three young women, really revolting with fuzzed-up, matted mousy hair, blotchy white skins with red goose - pimples on their arms. They wore horrible sleeveless, see-through, dirty blouses over revolting patterned skirts and they all had great hairy, white legs with bloggy black shoes and dirty feet. And they all smelled hideous [*the pre-deodorant days*] and the sweat was in streams under their arms, soaking in to the mass of hair therein.
They didn't laugh once or say anything except about the weather. They were married and I pitied the men having these smelling cabbages about the house, feeding them chips and never laughing, never looking nice and totally without the charm of their sex.
I didn't see one interesting or good-looking person.

Mother is out and I'm here, part of this endless, familiar bloody estate, with its unbearable sounds, where there is no beauty. I want to go away and lose myself.
A woman in the canteen at Taunton Station refused to sell me cigarettes. She asked me to prove I was sixteen. I was very angry.

The exams are over. Roger has been beastly all week, hardly answering when I speak to him and being rude to me.
My art training is over, thank God.

I think that a relationship of some intimacy is essential though one must expect misery from it. I must have another intense relationship to live through rather than vegetate alone. I wanted to see more of the actor but it seems he's not going to take me on. Charming and terrifically attractive men like him are depressing in that one can never believe in their honesty or fidelity but they are beautiful creatures and I'm instantly attracted to them.

What then of my career? I care nothing for it. My painting is of no importance. I don't particularly want to teach. I have no idea what I want to do. I am good for nothing. All the time I'm getting less and less equipped for a responsible existence in this society. What becomes of creatures like me? Alone, it seems that becoming a social misfit and breaking down is inevitable. I feel on the brink of insanity quite often, only a fear of being unable to climb back into sanity of a sort keeps me on this side.
Sitting in that stinking carriage this evening I felt a great desire to be obscene or go berserk and I had to fight against it by staring hard out of the window or pretending to be interested in their stupid prattle. I try to appear normal but they always sit staring with huge rabbit eyes and nudge each other and giggle.

Saturday 4 June 1960, Yeovil
Today this desire to get away is still strong. I hate to linger. Today, I cycled up to see Anne, passed places, houses, streets I've so often cycled through and it sickened me, the very sight of it, the remembrances, the sounds and, above all, the smells of summer. I hate summer clothes. I lose my identity in brightness. I'm nothing. I hate to go out and like to wear dark colours. I went to the town with Anne; it was terrible. We slunk into Woolworth's the back way, masses of slowly shifting morons, passing rows of greasy faces, wafting smells. Great bunches of odious spotty youths chewing gum, staring at white pimply girls in sloppy thin dresses, exposing their pink spotted backs.

I've decided not to do ATD [*postgraduate course*], but to go to Bristol and look for a job in theatre decor or something. But for an extra year of hell I could get a qualification for fifty years' work if necessary. I don't want to teach but the thought of unqualified jobs for the rest of my life is grim. I have no ambition in the material world.

So much I've wanted to write, fleeting impressions, gone now.

This room, a dead symphony. I've just torn down several photographs and press-cuttings from the walls. I must get it empty and leave. If I get all my thoughts, what I am, in here, in this book, and all my records in carriable things, I can go and be anywhere.

Sunday 5 June 1960, Yeovil
It's late afternoon and I've been reading Salinger's *Catcher in the Rye* - an interesting book. Happier today because it's been raining hard and the sun has gone in. With Salinger, some stylised, gimmicky stuff, the kind one winces at, but somehow it works and it's only boring, and the slang becomes irritating and unnecessary, in a few places.

I've just stripped off more paper. It looks desolate. I washed the walls but they still look shabby. Another argument with Mother. She believes I'm doing all this to annoy her by making the room even more shabby. She doesn't realise that I'm pruning my life down to nothing ready for flight. One more wall of pictures and I'm ready. These four walls are no longer important.
I shall come home hardly at all. This room is my home, falling apart as I pack things into folders, eliminating small treasures. To her, I'm just being awkward by removing some cuttings, showing the bare walls underneath.

Monday 6 June 1960, Yeovil
I am guilty though I feel no remorse. I hate mothers who break down and cry. I think it's a revolting sight. My eyes were as dry as stones. Now a day or two of tight lips, awkward silences, blowing of noses in other rooms. I'm just tired. She refuses to question anything. That's how it started this time. I was arguing with my brother about using

Giotto's frescoes to illustrate crumby sentimental religious commentaries. I was bursting with anger. But in this house one must never argue about 'high' things - to do so after ten o'clock is an affront to decency - and it's the height of wickedness to *question* anything at all. To question anything is to be presumptuous. To mention religion with the slightest mistrust is the cue for hours of tight-lipped coldness. It might as well be the Middle Ages.

Much later: borrowed Huxley's *The Doors of Perception* from Anne and find reflections that are echoes of so many thoughts written here. The more I read the less I write for it's already written. But the solitary confinement of the human state, time, a split-second continuous vision, everything in the first twenty pages are echoes of my own thoughts. This happens so often and is both reassuring and yet exasperating at one and the same time. The drug Mescalin creates the power and vision of an artist. I have been reading so much that excites me.

Anne's mother was telling me about her poverty-stricken childhood in London. Her father was a policeman and her mother would line the children up each day and run a lighted candle along the seams of their second-hand clothes to kill off the sleeping bugs. They all had shaven heads to get rid of the lice.

Tuesday 7 June 1960, Yeovil

In a brighter humour today and less aggressive. Beaver may come and take me to St Ives but I want to stay here and read and listen to my music. A lovely day, cool sunlight, occasionally yawning into slight warmth. My mother is better, almost cheerful. I was talking to Anne and her mother weeps and moans in the same way; so does R's mother. It seems to me an unnecessary and unfair trick to stop argument by tears, an effective escape for those who have nothing to say.

Thursday 9 June 1960, Park Street, Taunton

Back in Taunton with a feeling of desperate boredom. Beaver and I went to St Ives on Tuesday. I've never been to Cornwall before and loved it. We picked up a philosophy student on his way to Exeter. He philosophically slept the whole way being most uncomfortable on the top of primus stoves, bags, baskets, tents, and anxious not to start up a dreary conversation with us.

We arrived in St Ives about nine o'clock and saw a club-type place full of interesting-looking people but we looked so revolting we were too shy to go in. The rain was pelting down. We had a tent but no tent pegs so we hired a caravan for 7/6d a night and sat talking and drinking tea until all hours. The place is alive with beatniks and bohemians.

We went to the Labour Exchange and I was surprised by their hostility. I've never come across such pure aversion to artists in my life. They were very rude and told us to get out of St Ives. They said that artists had defiled St Ives but I pointed out that without them their holiday trade would go.

That morning we'd ventured into the coffee-house and met a terrific woman who owns it. Sitting outside was an oldish man dressed like a clean fisherman; he looked rather like Picasso, his hair thick and white. The room was beautifully laid out - white stone walls, black wood furniture, very sparse and plain, and the coffee was served in thick pottery on round wooden tables. Sitting near her, and only occasionally speaking, was a younger man, a bit shabby, with a kind face. He was asking to clean the floor for a few shillings. He said he'd show us the way to the Exchange. He walked ahead most of the way and said he was a painter and did odd jobs. He said that the 'Picasso' man and the woman were married and got on very well but rarely spoke. He lived on the pier and she lived in the coffee-house.

At the steps of the Labour Exchange he said goodbye and disappeared and yet the man said vile things about 'that creature you come up here with'. I asked if he knew him. He said no, but they were all the same and we'd picked him up, didn't care who we stayed with, etc. I hated him. The pompous bloody sterile toad. He's the sort that are really lecherous. Bloody hypocrite.

We went back to the coffee-house and met an American - he was there to write ballads. I wish men wouldn't wear shorts. He sat in all his vastness eating sausage, bacon and eggs - in shorts. Nothing could be ruder. He was very excited, in a cool way, and thought St Ives was quaint. It's full of drunken beatniks. Worse by far though are those pretentious old bats that spend days painting hideous water-colours of boats and narrow streets. I detest them.

Friday 10 June 1960, Park Street, Taunton

Yesterday Holterman brought me some luscious pink roses from his garden. They're so beautiful. I don't think I can bear to come back here next week. It's such a wicked waste of time.

Friday 11 June 1960, Yeovil

Beaver came over to Taunton and drove me home early. Now in my room, a feeling of personal quiet and peace with my music once more. This Beethoven Quartet on a two-shilling 78 is exquisite. It scratches and I dread it will wear out.

The estate is television quiet; the doors are shut, the curtains drawn and the dogs are in. Even the cats seem to have deserted the gardens. I want to dance. I want to have fun. I want to have an affair. Roger has cut himself off completely from me. This is extremely annoying but I give him credit for considerable strength. He is growing to dislike me intensely.

Saturday 12 June 1960, Yeovil

Brian and I went on the scooter to Glebe Farm to see Beaver. I loathe and detest scooters. My hair lashes against my face and clears off all my eye-make-up and to get a comb through it afterwards is impossible. My legs ache and are cold. I remember the hours and hours of discomfort and jolliness Beaver and I spent on hers, careering around the countryside like mad things.

We all went to the cinema in Sherborne and saw a ridiculously unfunny film about the Navy and then a Western, which didn't help me forget my aching back and bum. People in the audience muttered, booed,

sighed and shifted in their seats in utter boredom. Whatever induced us to go?
Gobbled fish and chips on the way home. I stood in the fish shop and it was full of Teds and they all stared in silence. They always do. I'm always a target for quips, shoves, giggles, stares and silly remarks. It's a situation I both loathe and avoid yet I'll probably miss it when I'm older and plain and uninteresting and people don't bother to stare or even make silly remarks. To walk about unnoticed would be awful. To have never been noticed, terrible. But my world is a great sea of faces, in my mind's eye at least, all facing towards me with hostility.

Monday 13 June 1960, Park Street, Taunton
I went to Bristol with Beaver today. Now I'm in this beastly barren room, feeling lonely and empty and depressed. I dreaded coming back and wished the car would break down as it continually threatened to do. But we got here, the inevitable reality. I feel like a stranger all over again. I loved being in Bristol. Dozens of art students looking alike and sitting around on steps. I get sick of them but at least they're alive. Here there's nothing, not even *phonies*. I hate the place. The Palace stank to high heaven, a real hovel but I like it. The ash-trays were full on the floor and the washing-up high in both respects. The actor's door was tightly shut. I didn't want to see him. It's too late now, things have lapsed.

Bristol is brimming with gorgeous women which is both disconcerting and humiliating. I feel so hideous sometimes. But I'd rather be a nonentity in a place like that than a freak in this bloody sewer. I want to finish, I want to go, get away from here. As I climbed the stairs tonight I realised I'd never had any happy times here and on the whole it's been a miserable two years. I've learned a bit about loneliness, about love and about living on my own, being responsible for my own existence.
My relationship with Roger has been important. So many things have centred on this town and yet they've been flat, unhappy years despite the humour. I don't think I can stay till the end of term. I want nothing more to do with paint. I want to find something else not so messy and without the memories of the past four years.

Tuesday 14 June 1960, Park Street, Taunton
Had a long talk with Murphy. He agrees that I must either really regain some enthusiasm for painting or leave it alone but he thinks I'd be stupid not to take ATD. He wants me to work for the last month on painting for the Royal College entrance exam. He says they choose the men for their talent first and then pick good-looking girls to keep them happy! But I'll try for a place as there's nothing to lose. If I can muster up some enthusiasm. It's terrible having to do something creative all day and hating every second of it. It's almost impossible.
Painting with me today was a young boy who works in a shoe factory in Street. He lives on his own in a caravan because his parents are separated and neither want him. He's about sixteen and a half and very awkward, but sensitive and somehow older than his years.
I handed over the Chekhov plays to JPD with due ceremony.

Wednesday 15 June 1960, Park Street, Taunton
I've just woken up from another timeless, terrible sleep but it's only just nine in the evening. Again these fits, so frantically trying to regain consciousness or at least the consciousness I know, for these turmoils take place, not in sleep, but just below the surface, terrifying in a peculiar way. They follow a pattern, in itself split up but recognisable as a whole. Looking down at my body from a point just above my right shoulder, trying to will my mind to wake up.

When I eventually woke I felt really strange as though I was suddenly in the world for the first time. I barely recognised myself or the houses outside or the traffic nor did the noises register or the feel of the texture of things. I felt dizzy as I looked down to the street far below and the air felt cold and strange to my face. A dread yet a desire to see someone I knew.

I went downstairs in strange shoes and made a cup of tea to re-establish myself. Half an hour later I still feel strange. What is it? Is it fear? Maybe I'm run down. I've got into similar states before. All these things I've been 'dreaming' are easily analysed, this sequence of terror and sickness which envelopes and terrifies me. I can't remember when I was last there besides this evening. Last night, I believe, and the night before. Even as I'm writing these words they seem far away. I can't remember what I did today or the day before or at St Ives. I ought never to live alone. But I have company all day. What is the matter with me? I need a distraction or I'll go mad. I'm afraid to sleep; I reach this place, this feeling, this fear in my subconscious and try with all my bridled mental strength, in sleep, to get free, in fact to wake. It's this awful fight for consciousness when I watch this raw point of fear of something. If only I could decipher this fear perhaps these awful things will end.

At the moment I'm sitting on the end of the bed, a timeless existing lump of living matter.
Someone is giving Anne a black and white billy goat for a wedding present. I've started rolling my own fags again. It saves about ten bob a week.

R and I hope to hitch to London next weekend. This afternoon Tim and I had to retreat to the library because a part-timer talked solidly for hours and hours.

Roger has disappeared this afternoon. It annoys me intensely when he won't bother to answer when I speak to him.

Thursday 16 June 1960, Park Street, Taunton
Five o'clock in the morning. It's light and there are a few lorries on the wet tacky roads and a milk-woman doing her rounds. I'm so happy to be breathing freely again for I've slept without that terror screaming around my head. I can hear birds. I wonder if birds have nightmares and if they dream? They seem excessively happy and rather relieved in the mornings. This morning I feel like a bird, part of the human race now that I'm not possessed of this demon, at least for a while.

I've just heard my landlady going downstairs. It's only five minutes to six. I wonder what she's doing? I immediately thought she was going to rush in and kill me. I didn't realise she got up so early. It's the best time.

A long day. I've tried to put some enthusiasm into my painting but without success. This evening Roger and I posed for Murphy. I fainted. I felt awful and was as white as a sheet. I don't know why. My head was buzzing and my stomach hurt. Afterwards we went up to Murphy's flat for spaghetti. Then someone sat in Murphy's brand-new Charles Eames chair and broke it. It was only delivered today and he'd waited eleven months for it. Poor Murphy was angry but all the same we laughed a lot. He told us about the time he was marking June [*a very prim nude model*] who was lying down and as he leaned over his tie tickled her 'modesty spot' as she called it and she shot up, very indignant, clutching her bosom, eyes wide and mouth open. She should be so lucky. Most of the jokes were about people we know, models, part-timers and painters mainly.

Both the Murphys think that childbirth is most inelegant, altogether revolting and obviously have no intention of having any children. She is afraid to risk her elegance - she's very beautiful - and he honestly can't stand small babies, they make him retch. Roger missed his last bus and is now probably fast asleep on their elegant studio couch.

JPD had a telegram from Richmond about a theatre job. I hope he gets it then I can live in the caravan.

Friday 17 June 1960, Park Street, Taunton

Another night without the horror. Last night I dreamed ordinary gentle dreams of taking unhappy children around the garden of my house which had a pale red brick wall all around it and all the time I was saying 'we must have more trees, more trees'. Then a tiny ginger and white kitten walked into the fire. I gradually put out the fire but it had crawled to safety into the recess at the back. It changed and then in the mirror I was trying to hook the kitten out of my throat with my fingers. I'm so relieved to be dreaming again. Lack of sleep, nerves and no food made me faint yesterday.

All over the world there is fighting, demonstrations, rallies, mainly students.

Each day, more news of students being shot, killed, imprisoned. Not that I'm a great student fan but it seems a hell of a waste of brain power having to fight with sticks against politicians in embassies for the simple right for peace. On the other hand it provides a certain incentive for constructive thinking but this of course is no mere dabbling in politics in a cloister at Oxford or in a punt in Cambridge. They're getting shot for their views.

In Paris recently, when Khrushchev went there to see de Gaulle, most of the students were anti-Communist and made no bones about it.

The Reg Butler sculpture, *The Unknown Political Prisoner*, that was to have been set on a hill in West Berlin, has been cancelled for political reasons. West Berlin's mayor, Willy Brandt, seems a superb individual.

Tonight I put my poems into a polythene bag that once contained onions and shall carry them from place to bloody place with me. I ripped up five; they were no good.

I also watched a press conference on nuclear weapons. It's all very depressing and makes me desperate to understand men's love of fighting. I feel outraged that I must be destroyed by bloody men quarrelling.

Saturday 18 June 1960, Yeovil

Awake to the joy of having time, time to sit, time to listen. Last night only ordinary dreams, gentle wanderings through Flemish paintings, landscapes of birds and flowers and painted feelings, mellowed.

The trees are in full leaf outside the window. Behind them, white sheets, very still. No wind. Even the children are silent.

I'm making a very short tight skirt this morning, in pink and white cotton check. It sounds revolting.

Sunday 19 June 1960, Yeovil
Sewing most of the day. What a waste of precious time. Beaver came for a few minutes; how lucky she is to be able to buy fags, scarves and lipsticks when she wants to. To me, five shillings is the absolute limit on anything.
I wish I had more confidence. I wish in some ways I were a more superficial person. I'm dark, I shudder at light, exposure, flamboyance, superficiality, effects. I would wither and die if I had to put my hair up. I would have to become a different person. Perhaps I have a slovenly personality. I like to be comfortable in dark clothes, in shadow. I like heaviness, sombreness. I cannot be frilly. My hair hangs quite long and around my face. If my hair was scraped back where would there be any shadow?
My obsessions are out of proportion - as if any such physical thing should matter, should detract from my personality. Is it laziness, slovenliness? My hair is very clean. I get quite desperate when these idiots deplore long clean healthy hair yet they have dirty, thin, frizzled, scurvy, greasy, uncombed bits of nesting on their heads, topped by lumps of shitty felt with imitation pearls, i.e hats. They're not hats, they're grease-soakers and fuzz stabilisers.

This morning I read the entire *Sunday Times* from a review on the *Journals of Benjamin Haydon* to the treaty between America and Japan. The thing on B.Haydon really depressed me. I have always thought that the writers of journals must be egocentrics to a considerable degree for it's obvious that any written word, no matter how personal, is meant to be read. Words can be a vehicle for expressing emotion which is of no use once expressed but to keep these written words must mean they are meant to be read. But this need not detract from their sincerity.

Most people I know who keep journals, like myself, heartily object to people reading them. The words in them are naked. I've never read a single line of these people's journals and no one has ever read, to my knowledge, a word of mine.

Much later - it's cool now and the ink is flowing. Even the children are awake, their voices echoing. Birds singing. Thinking as always about the term 'normal behaviour'. I was struck by this situation. In the college there are two high-backed, wooden chairs and I want them. Now if Murphy at the end of term were to give me one I would have the problem of getting it from Taunton to Yeovil. I take it on the train and people might well consider this in itself rather odd but it's the only way open to me. Now if I get it as far as the bus station at Yeovil and stand next to it while I wait for the bus, that is reasonable and acceptable. Now if I have to wait twenty minutes for the bus and I'm tired, the obvious thing to do is to sit on the chair. *Not* to sit on it would be illogical.

Yet, were I to sit on my chair at the bus stop, my behaviour, though logical and practical, would be considered decidedly abnormal. The illogical action of standing in the sun, with aching legs, would be considered normal.

In fact, despite my reasoning, I would stand by my chair, if necessary till I dropped.

Perhaps it would be more acceptable if one tried to disguise the chair before sitting on it - say, with a few spirals of wrapping paper secured with string and a label. Then, perhaps, to tentatively perch on the edge would be acceptable. A chair should be in a room, in a house, says this illogical law of normal behaviour, and not at a bus stop.

*

A poet I like a lot is Dom Moraes, the Indian Oxford graduate. His poetry is very pictorial but very good. I think I read his work more than anybody's. His book of verse, *A Beginning,* is a gem in my bookshelf. Tim has just given back my Delacroix *Journal*, another precious stone. I feel a great affinity with Delacroix as I do with Cézanne, Van Gogh and Zola.

When I'm opposed in argument I feel my temper snap as a physical thing. I feel outraged and often lose control of my flow of words. Sometimes the slightest thing makes me flare up and I feel sick and shake with anger and frustration. I realise now that I'm more and more irritable and intolerant and in some ways I'm sorry, in others, I'm

anxious. For the less tolerant I become the more unhappy and frustrated I must be.
I want to be happy but it seems that more is wrong than is right. More is unsightly than is beautiful. More is wretched than happily bestowed. I seem to see more misery than I see happiness. Some are healthier in that they are less diseased. Some warmer in that they have more clothes. Some are happier because they have enough to eat and take small luxuries regularly but we are all wretched simply because we're alive and because some are hungry and some are full.
I feel so much but never manage to write clearly: and how little I achieve towards maintaining the ideals which I mentally adher to.
Taunton tomorrow and another weekend over and it's as though I've passed a familiar stranger in the street. I seem not to have visited this room.

Monday 20 June 1960, Park Street, Taunton
Today, a landmark, in that I wore a summer dress without a macintosh, quite openly. I feel wrong in light clothes. I lose my identity. I sat in a small park for about an hour watching the cars go by and a bird on the grass. The sun was very hot today. I wanted to be in it and get brown but I knew I would hate it given the chance.
I wish so much I wasn't here in Taunton, this place that depresses me so much.
I want, I want, what do I want?
I get so tired I can't even answer myself.

At lunchtimes the parks are buttered with people roasting. Some run about and shriek and get sexually excited about it. Others rub other person's stomachs and backs along hedges and under trees and when they have to go back to the office or shop they get up and the woman looks round and then smooths down her cotton skirt and the man does his hair, looks around and then hoists at his trousers to continue his lunchtime feelings.

Tuesday 21 June 1960, Caravan, Trull
Sitting on a bed in a caravan in a field beside a stream. An evening of posing and supper at the Murphys. Endless stories of the RCA. Bratby

was notorious for pinching everyone's paints - Peter Blake carrying all his stuff, paints, brushes, canvases, the lot, home every night so he couldn't get his hands on them. And Bratby's wife used to put the baby in a locker and sometimes forget all about it. Memories of Minton screeching round South Kensington on frantic pub crawls in a taxi full of sailors and buying everyone drinks.

Thursday 23 June 1960, Caravan, Trull

Yesterday I walked six miles in the heat, out to Trull for this blasted notebook and then I didn't write in it. This afternoon I've been posing for photos for next year's prospectus, my face plastered with foreign make-up. I felt a bit of an idiot. Tomorrow we hitch to London and this evening we paid ninepence each for a bath. R's water was filthy, mine crystal clear. I had no soap. I shall miss my room this weekend.

I must go to see Brian who has sent me another disturbing letter. Roger actually removed his trousers in my sweet presence in the painting room this morning - most unlike Roger. What a paradox of conflicting feelings. I thought I was the only one burdened with hidden loves. Feelings are cruel.

Monday 27 June 1960, Caravan, Trull

I'm living here in the caravan where the urge to write or even record is slight and easily put aside. I wonder if I'm doing the right thing by throwing away the last few weeks of solitude.

On Friday we hitched up to London and arrived after seven cars and two lorries at Regents Park; we stayed in a flat with four girls - strange young women of acquired finesse and they touched their luxury in a self-conscious manner. The list of names of enviable associates flowed from their conversation and they went hungry at lunchtimes to pay for the phone. Heavily gilded mirrors and Ryvita biscuits; dark wood chairs, embroidered upholstery and Nescafé from a milk bottle.

I was amused by the obvious packet of Rothman's King Size cigarettes. The good conversation in early morning dressing-gowns and curlers. The languor of movement. One was a public relations officer, a sharp, peculiarly interesting person, very small, limping, shifting from one foot to the other. The place was lined with her books - she'd been at Oxford - and the others sang her praises and nestled under her brightness. We slept in a bed and woke to be confronted with another female of reserved glances who slid from her cocoon and made for the bathroom, never to be seen again. This flat costs *eighteen* bloody guineas a week!

In the afternoon we wandered into the Portal Gallery, off Bond Street, a place we'd never seen before though I imagined I'd been there with Derek. Inside were works by several painters, including Peter Graham. We got talking to the owners, Lionel and Eric, two highly amusing and surprisingly nice characters. We hung around, waiting for some painter to bring a painting for the next exhibition but he didn't come and we went off in their cars to Hyde Park.
Got caught in a thunderstorm and made for the Portobello Road. We walked the road and then went for some tea in a place full of assorted beatniks and foreigners. I loved it.

Then we went to the home of Peter Graham whose wife, Katey, we'd seen earlier in the gallery. She had a vivid cockney personality - bright, loud and plain-speaking. She wore old trousers and had blonde hair and Grecian features. They lived at the top of a huge house in front of a large, rambling garden. The rooms were stacked with his paintings. He was a huge young man, intensely quiet and good-natured and he made no attempt to impress or sell himself.

They had a small son, a beautiful two-year-old boy called Adam. Katey was very efficient and drove and was a gem of a wife for him. They rushed off to look at some 'primitive' paintings by some Polish refugee. She really impressed me which in a woman is rare. She was always doing something, always helping someone. Their family was great. Their mate in the next room, an African, absolutely adored Adam; it was expressed in every movement of his face. They played and exchanged hats. I was sorry to leave.

We made for Richmond and sat through a lousy play in the Richmond Rep., waiting in vain for JPD to appear. The actual theatre was marvellous, gilded, ornate, exciting. They also kept a theatre pianist for the intervals - a young lad in a Teddy-boy outfit. The audience reflected the play, corny, loving the sauciness. We went in the standing gallery but sat down later on stone seats with rails in front.

We waited for nearly two hours outside Earls Court Station on Sunday morning. There are so many good-looking, fascinating people, male and female, in London. I look and see everything.
Afterwards I went to No 94 to see Brian but he wasn't there and John Selway [*painter at the RCA*] gave me some tea. I like him very much. He said Derek had disappeared after a party last night and he didn't know where he was. Unfortunately, he rolled in just as we were about to go - with a beautiful Spanish girl, who looked exquisite. So did he. He was dressed all in faded navy.

There were tramps curled up on the benches at Regent's Park Station. I saw a fight between two Irishmen in Richmond. I felt sick with pity and some other emotion for a young man being forced into a police van. They couldn't get him in; he was struggling and yelling and they dragged him up the road while people stood and watched. I wanted to push the police away. So much has happened. We had a good hitch, in a Yankee car driven by an Englishman with a ridiculously exaggerated Oxford accent, right to Trull. I may hitch up with JPD to London on Sunday to see them at No 94 before they break up.
Derek is off to Morocco and Brian to France.

Friday 1 July 1960, Caravan, Trull
At last a chance to resume a futile breach between mind and paper.
A week now, living in this caravan in a quiet Trull. I haven't done much reading, little writing, but we've had some verbal discussion of many things. Last night we thrashed out relationships between two individuals, spiritual bodies. At some point it becomes difficult to reconstruct what honesty smashes and the point of honesty is difficult, where honesty is honesty, not self-deception, perverted pride or self-evasiveness.

We talked at some length about the relationship between men and women. I would consider that for all our superficial fuss and shows of false pride, we women are far more deceitful in our wiles and equally as fickle as men. It may well be that it's the steam of our own deceits reversed that stings our eyes, and each day I become deeper in this mire of self-deception, of intolerance of other egoists. Yet, strangely, R is as large, as extreme an egoist as I, but we have a remarkable tolerance. For her part it may be that she is such an egoist she believes my presence subordinate and of no consequence. As for me I cannot fathom how I can so easily tolerate someone equally egocentric. I feel less fickle than her; I doubt that I am.

We had supper again with the Murphys. We aim to eat out free twice a week, in doing so we can cut food costs to ten shillings a week each which is reasonable. Each morning I clean the van out pretty thoroughly while R works in Taunton at the college. I wander up into the fields and half-heartedly paint because I am obliged to.
Yesterday we ran in the fields, shouting and laughing like school kids. There are three wild kittens in the barn. In the prospectus I look like a bloodhound or an eighteenth-century tragedienne.

Saturday 2 July 1960, Yeovil
Beaver and Anne have just been. They seemed like strangers and they were annoyed by the strangeness they felt was in me. All this seems removed from me now. I belong nowhere, only in myself, to no one.
I'm wearing the dress that R made for me, a beautiful, dark-striped thing, like a 1920s drape. I like it as much as I like any clothes and it's in keeping with the way I am, what I am.

I feel strangely free, unbound by any physical emotion. I've been offered a job as a chambermaid; it sounds awful but I must earn some money and try to get to France or Italy later in the summer.
I've been re-reading some Bertrand Russell this morning. Someone has my Balzac's *M Grandet* and I mean to find out who and get it back.
I feel restless.
I've just been up to see Anne. It's torture being lumped on a bike along roads where familiar faces stare and known views of houses and trees

around them glare. My skull is tight with nerves. She was out. I can't explain how depressed Yeovil makes me nor how much I hate and how ill at ease I feel. The faces I know, the faces that I like, aren't here, all that is the least important to me I can't find here. Even the memories of the two years at the art school here I don't associate with this place. To me it's dead and the sight, the feel, the smell of it is uncomfortable. I won't come home much more; when I'm here I'm depressed, isolated and find no ease, no peace.

I can't think why they don't print more than one of Russell's books in paperback. There is one of his at 3/6d - *Common Sense and Nuclear Arms* - which I shall get next week. I want a wireless so much but I will never be able to afford one. I want at least a hundred classical records and approximately five hundred essential books! I don't crave for clothes half as much but not being able to afford books and music aggravates me and makes me miserable.
This room that I've loved so well has a stagnant, temporary atmosphere. I believe R and I will be hitching up to London on 13 August. I want to live there for a while.

Monday 4 July 1960, Yeovil
A wandering day touching on the old familiarity of my room, my belongings, but only for a few hours and then I go back. I must leave my music behind. I love it so much. I listened to it all day. I've cut up the last fortnight's papers and filed a few things. Tomorrow I buy some books. But what about the day after and the week and the year following? What will happen to me then?

*

Caravan, Trull - Roger, Tim and R have gone 'chickening', loading bloody broilers into vans for thirty shillings for a night's work..
Anne is mad at me for some reason. She's off to the job in Sidmouth on Sunday. I've turned down that particular job but feel obliged to continue looking for employment there as we had arranged to work together. She has photos of Bob and Valerie [*Organ*] and the baby. She had her second child a few days ago. I believe she has got what I want in life. If I had the security of faith I would pray for so much else but

my reason leaves me in the hands of circumstance and the consequent wisdom or stupidity of my own actions and the effects of other individuals.

Tuesday 5 July 1960, Caravan, Trull
A chicken curry smelling as it cooks on an electric fire turned tail; R bending over it. Today Roger gave me a book, *The Wings of Death* - Tagore's last poems. He'd spent his 'chicken' money on it. I was surprised and unable to say anything. I'm always overcome with remorse when people give me things.

Friday 8 July 1960, Yeovil
A mixture of feelings today. This afternoon Roger's presence really irritated me and I knew he was about to start again. He said: 'Are you interested to know I still love you?' I said, 'No, not in the least', which was a foolish lie but I was so aggravated, the way he feels for me really weighs me down. All love is cruel and its joyous complexity is an illusion. I jumped up and went into the kitchen part of the van and started to wash up and the noises of the water and the dishes cut the heavy silence. Then I heard the door slam and he went off, slumped and wretched and it was raining steadily.

Usually I am patient and sympathetic with him and I'm worried now for his safety. One night last week he came to the van and lay on the bed for three hours staring at me, unable to speak. He said but three sentences.
Yesterday in front of the others he said: 'You never stop talking about yourself'. I hadn't realised this but it's quite true. But he also accuses me of talking solidly about other people. One must necessarily talk about one or the other, surely? I said, of course, and wasn't annoyed or embarrassed but listened to the others who talked constantly about themselves. He tries to hurt and humiliate me whenever possible.

It's strange. I miss R and what is stranger is that people seem astonished and slightly suspicious when I say that we sleep together; although we have to in the van, which is tiny, we like sleeping together.

We know each other as much as we find necessary and cuddle together like puppies without the slightest embarrassment or reserve.
R once said that she would be likely to accept a form of love-making from a lesbian whom she found not intolerable and I believe her. Thirst for experience in all forms and at all costs will lead her to this but our relationship is without sexual content, as far as any relationship can be. I certainly don't condemn her for her possible homosexual traits if she does indeed harbour them. But the idea of it just doesn't appeal to me. I have too much reserve and am far less self-confident.

Today I bought three books for 9/6d - Gerard Manley Hopkins, D H Lawrence and Descartes, *A Discourse on Method*. I hid them in my bag in the van so that Roger couldn't find them for I felt I might well have bought him one instead of three for myself. It's just that I'm desperate for books but hate to be thought mean.

I'm not fully decided whether to try for the Royal College in November. Always this endless pestering from the staff to get me to work. All day they follow me round and nag me to paint when I'm almost in tears of hatred for paint. I've painted for a few hours tonight which is very unusual. I felt like painting for once in months of indifference and distaste but the enthusiasm soon died.

Holterman caught me yesterday and flew into a rage and threatened to strip me and beat me. I didn't answer and he went out fuming and shaking his head. I refuse to be badgered and pushed around and made to create hideous things in paint. I have no fear whatsoever of college authority and will not be bullied.
I feel to the fullest extent the importance of the last few months, weeks, even days. At last I am becoming free.

In London I must be selective and keep my mind and reason clear and unclogged by experiences and illusions which are bound to crowd in and suffocate me. I wish I had real ambition, an enthusiasm to adhere to. This is what I need or else I shall sink into a useless, inferior person so easily. A student might be able to work through a course without much ambition but once 'out' he must exist for definite reasons. I have no reason for living, no reason not to. I want to get married and have children as a serious occupation and thousands of females waddle through this period I'm in with the very same aim but I feel circumstances are such that in my environment, this aim may well be overlooked and considered of lesser importance - thus frustrated I may become demoralised This may already have begun. The other ten thousand females mix with such males that require the same and therefore they are more likely to succeed. Of course I am not as stupid to insinuate or even suspect that my sort of people all lead promiscuous lives governed by contraceptives and variation. This is not so. But we may be less easily satisfied with each other. We may be more selective, thoroughly so, mentally and physically.

Perhaps I am wrong in imagining that I have less chance of acquiring such a partner from within my creatures. I may be so right in realising that I'm likely to be incompatible with another individual.

Circumstances are such that I am nineteen, trained as an artist of sorts, attractive, supposedly, egotistical - and a hell of a lot of other things - and without ambition in any field of career or creative intention. Then what must I do now? I must work at something I mind about, that is essential. I can never leave the realm of artists, of that I am sure. Without them I am nothing, they provide me with a backcloth and I'm completely at home with them.

Now I'm about to crawl from my cocoon of studentship with no pass into the other region except my personality. I feel it won't get me far. It's nothing. It's a thing cut loose and intimately personal and hardly any use to society. I have nothing to offer.

Saturday 9 July 1960, Yeovil

This morning I read many of D H Lawrence's letters. A good introduction, though unusually long, by Aldous Huxley, who knew him. My thirst for letters and the thoughts of these men is immense, but as I saturate myself with more and more of their inward cryings I feel the hopelessness of writing them. For even my sympathetic and fervent interest is second hand and Artic cold unless I can participate wholely

in an experience. But of course I can argue with my own feelings and answer my own questions. Present time is the point of existence and the past is to help, stimulate and correct the present, and there is no past with the living. Dead material creates the past.
I also read some Gerard Manley Hopkins. I love my books. I like to feel them and touch them. The sky is dark and it's raining heavy wet rain.

This afternoon I've reached a semblance of enthusiasm and I've been painting two canvases. I decided I couldn't afford the time to go to London but I will. A wretched nightmare last night in this room. I dream miserably whenever I come home.

*

I remember nothing of Jerusalem, Egypt or being carted across the sea from South Africa in the war, nor life-jackets and crowded evacuation camps. I remember nothing. I didn't realise that when I was becoming more conscious, that is about 1946 or 1947, when there were ration books and a quarter of sweets between us each week, that the war had only just ended. When sweets first came off the ration there were stories of people who bought several pounds of sweets at one go. This seemed a gross gluttony and we still only had a quarter a week, not having the money to buy more. We used to have two Sharp's toffees a day at a quarter to seven in the evening, just when *The Archers* started on the wireless. We used to fight over the peppermint ones and by the end of the week there were only orange-papered ones which weren't very nice.

*

Deliciously sexy Elvis Presley records. [*I remember racing to the record shop after school in 1956 to listen to Heartbreak Hotel.*] I love them, they really excite me but now they remind me of my room in Park Street. That barren dark wood room under the eaves where I wrote my poems, my two books, where so much was fought out, made. The thought of the room sickens me. It saw too much but it never participated. I've left a candlestick and a mat there but I dread to go back. It seems an age since I was there but it's only two weeeks. I so quickly forget and adapt to new surroundings like a small child.

I realise of course that my book *Anyes* was of no literary worth; it was not writing, it was merely a fervent creative vehicle for my overwhelming emotion at the time. It's somewhere in this room but I have no desire to look at it nor do I ever read my poems. Once my writing has been read and rejected, I lose interest in it, I feel it's worthless. You see then how little vocation, how little confidence I have.

*

Late now - Brian came unexpectedly and we went drinking beer in the White Lion. I felt depressed because he reminds me so acutely of the desperation in Derek's character. He is greatly influenced by him and constantly talks about him.

I realise I hadn't really thought objectively of my future existence. Now it's but a few days away, waiting to begin. I will have to work for a society that I hate for the most part. I will have to conform. I will have to come out of myself, take notice of people who don't interest me. Serve food or coffee to people who make me sick - tie up my hair so that it won't run the hundred to one risk of dropping out on to some slob's spaghetti. I dread it. I feel like a weak plant on the edge of a thrusting plantation.
I must then imagine my strength for I feel in me a fortress that is my knowledge of my own personality which I know to be worth keeping and progressing with. I will despise the buggers who will take time from me because I have to work for hours to feed myself. Wasted hours of pointless labour that leaves no morsel of pure time for thought and only a little for fleeting reflections. I become nothing when I work. They don't know nor want to know that I do strange paintings, that I envy a past friend with a husband who perhaps I might have loved, who has two babies, rabbits and dogs and a goat.
That I had a room that was an extension of myself and has now disintegrated and is lost. I will have a nose, eyes, mouth, body not unlike many other young women. That is it, I will be just a young woman.

Why do I feel I have some significance now? At college I have friends who like me and find me interesting, above all they know certain facets of my personality which I have shown them and they have liked some and some they have disliked. In fact, they know me and still like me.

It's raining and the drains are clanking throatily. I felt affection for Anne tonight and I'm sorry she's going. I feel inclined to take the job in Sidmouth and put off what must be. It would be much easier, another provincial delay from the city of my fate. It's so easy to cling to rooms, friends, places, but I must get away and face what will happen to me and find out how my life will continue.

Sunday 10 July 1960, Yeovil
Brian tells me that a girl at 94 Cromwell Road works in a coffee bar in Earls Court for six pounds a week and she tops six pounds in tips. If I could get a job and start on Monday and get a room at two pounds five shillings R might share with me. She doesn't want to stay with JPD in the houseboat at Richmond.
I'm beginning to worry about my lack of will to work for I feel I may have thrown away the key to a better life by not taking the Royal College entrance more seriously. I may have got in and my life veered another way. Three more canvases for entrance in November. In London they just won't get done. I missed by my foolish laziness the chance of getting them done these last three weeks. I have no patience with painting. My ideas overtake my technical skill. I'm not happy at it and therefore I do as little as I can, with a feeling of regret at my own unwanted idleness.

I found Roger's *Buddhist Scriptures* in my stack of newspapers and am loathe to give it back. I want a sea of books to drown in and I want a forest of wood and books to lose myself in.

*

Derek's coolness seems to attract but this is not the thing that consciously attracts me. I must see him before he goes to Morocco. The rain's lashing down. I shall go into Brian's room at 94, feeling the room beyond the wall even though he won't be there. I remember the first time I went there, with a feeling of adventure and the strangeness of seeing him there, in London, in new surroundings, vague, cool. I loved the room straight away. Even now I feel as if I'm going home, everything is so familiar. Now other women must feel the same.

Evening now and I realise it's the last evening in this room. This music will remain unheard now until my next room, somewhere, perhaps in London, but the sounds will be strange and some of their beauty will waft into the traffic and I won't hear it or love it half so well.
I'll go and forever be lost, so there's no trace of me. None of me left and these walls will be papered over, the air changed, my records and my books sealed off in cupboards to die for I may never find my resting place. My beautiful chair might end up in someone else's hideous place, if I find none. My cushions cut up, my gramophone silent, the plug dismantled, my music silenced. My dread is to find no resting place. I must have time to listen, to sit, to meet myself. If I keep writing here as I love to do I may not lose myself. When I have nothing to write but incidents that happen outside myself then I'm lost. When I no longer feel, nor sit, nor listen, nor write what is inside, then I am lost.

Much later, in my bed in a much barer room. I've been stacking away papers, endless files and folders, my cut-out scrap books, my records, now silent in quiet piles, my books stacked. I've been doing it all with great calm and almost cheerfulness.
I will have to work for two months. Then that blasted ATD Course. Lately I've been accused of insincerity in my promises and Anne said seriously that I make promises which I don't keep and I lie too much. Also that I exaggerate so much it all becomes lies. Often this is so but in some cases I plan these things and get excited about them but it wears off and I'm left with a situation where people I've convinced are rallied and ready and waiting and I'm off mentally and physically on some other scheme. This must be insincerity but at the point of enthusiasm I am sincere.

A while ago I was dead set on working in St Ives. I really loved it and wanted to work there this summer. Then Anne arranged a job in Sidmouth by which time I'd lost interest and now she's on her own in

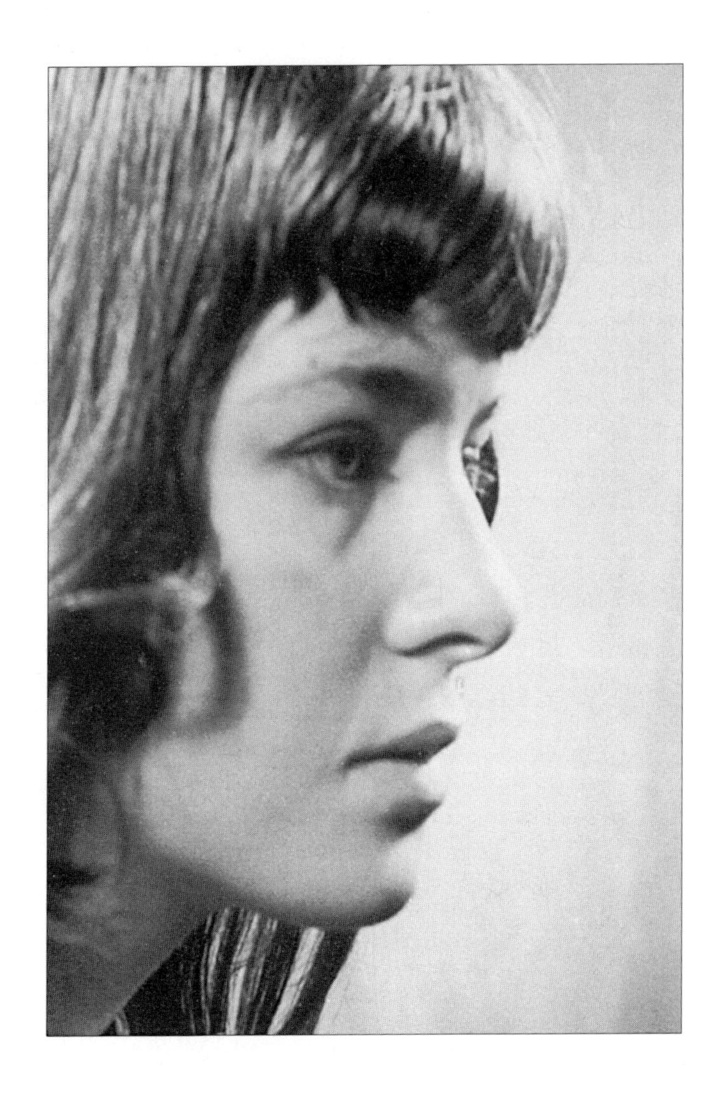

Kate Paul, shortly before the beginning of the Journal

Derek Boshier photograph ©Tony Evans

Derek Boshier, photograph ©Tony Evans

Derek Boshier and his dog, Rynty

Anne Dewell, née Cornelius

Kate Beaver being dramatic in one of her designs

Valerie Buxton
and Jolyon Ward

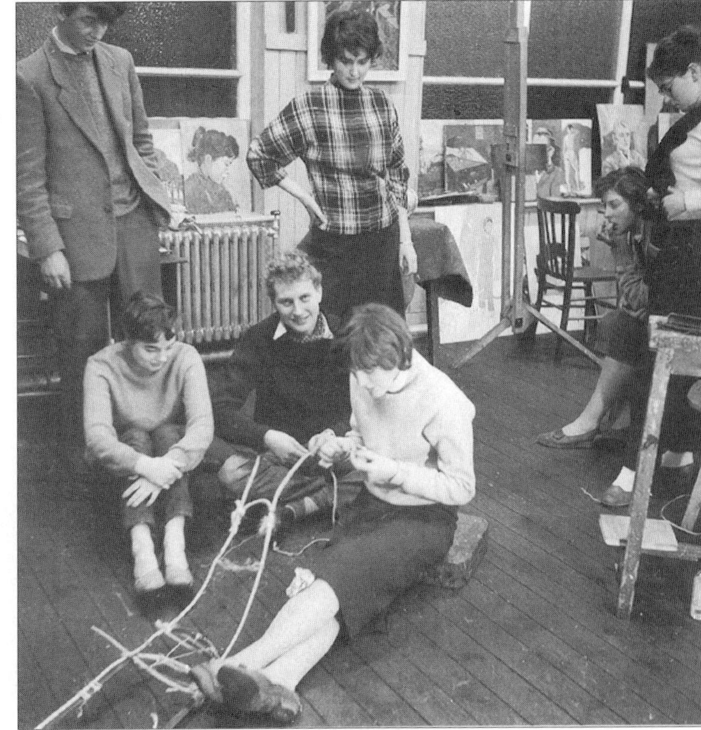

Yeovil Art School,
1958.
Left to Right:
Tim Spilsbury
(standing),
Anne Cornelius,
Derek Boshier,
Biddy Penrose,
(standing),
Valerie Buxton,
Kate Beaver
(seated)

Left: Bob Organ
Above: Valerie Buxton shortly before marriage to Bob Organ

Left: John Porter Davison
Above: Terry Murphy and Roger Tarr

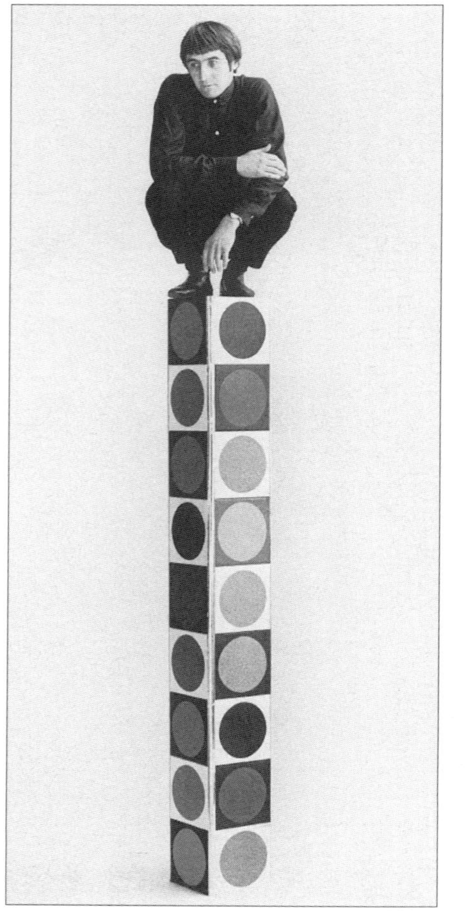

Left: Brian Rice on geometric construction Photograph © Tony Evans
Above: Josh Kirby
Opposite: Brian Rice with geometric paintings Photograph © Tony Evans

H-BOMB PROTEST MEETING. A section of the large crowd which gathered in Trafalgar Square yesterday for the mass meeting held at the end of the four-day march from Aldermaston by anti-H-bomb demonstrators.

LEFT: Miss Ruth Singer, 16, of Hampstead, smoking a pipe when she stopped at the Albert Memorial, where the marchers had a lunch break before completing the 53-mile trek.

MARCHERS HOME WITH A RALLY & TRAFFIC JAM

20,000 IN TRAFALGAR SQUARE

DAILY TELEGRAPH REPORTER

ANTI-HYDROGEN-BOMB marchers, who left the Atomic Weapons Research Establishment at Aldermaston, Berks, on Good Friday, arrived at Trafalgar Square yesterday afternoon. Their numbers had swollen from 4,500 to an estimated 15,000.

The head of the motley procession reached the square at 3 p.m. Its tail, which arrived at 5 p.m., was still at the Albert Hall when the leaders had finished marching.

The Aldermaston March: *The Daily Telegraph:* 4 April 1961

Laurie Fricker

Bernard Taylor

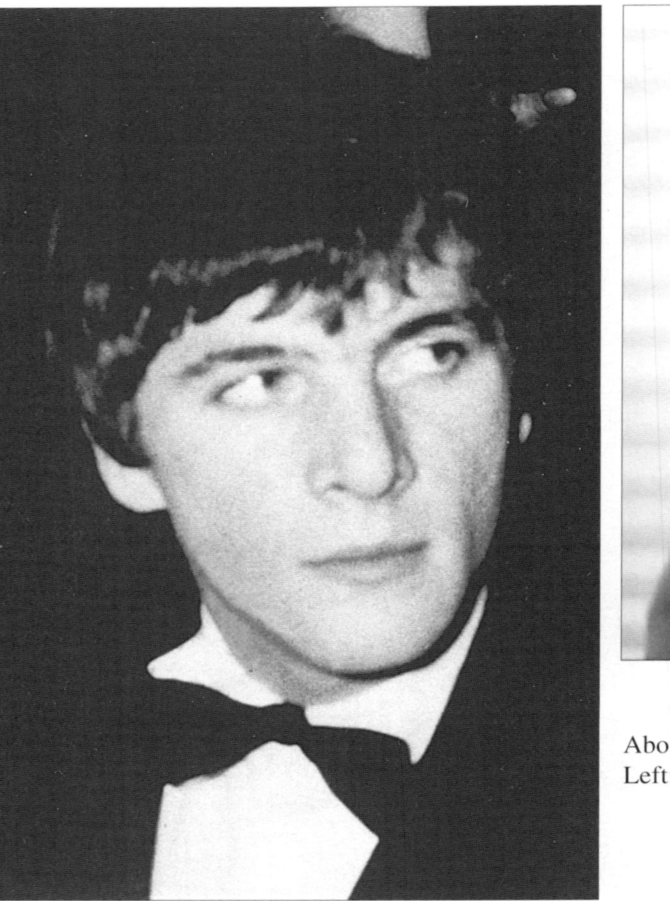

Above: Kate Paul Photograph © Tony Evans
Left: Roger Tarr

Eni Faers at the flat in Coleherne Road, Earls Court
Photographs © Tom Watt

Tom Watt Photograph © Michael Capinaros

Derek Boshier and David Hockney in the RCA Painting School, 1961
Photograph © Geoffrey Reeve

David Hockney and Derek Boshier in the RCA Painting School, 1961
Photograph © Geoffrey Reeve

Painting School, RCA, 1961. From left to right:
Peter Crutch [reclining], Peter Phillips, David Hockney
Photograph © Geoffrey Reeve

Nick Jensen

Kate Paul

Photograph © Tony Evans

Above: The Troubadour, Earls Court
Right: The flat [second floor] at 13 Coleherne Road, Earls Court
Photographs © Tom Watt

Kate Paul [about four years after the end of the Journal]
Left photograph © Tony Evans / Right photograph © Tom Watt

that beastly place doing a lousy underpaid job. Now I'm obsessed with the idea of working in London. The odds are that I won't get a job, or get a hateful one and simply loathe living in London, where I will be wretched and lonely - but I must take the chance.

Friday 15 July 1960, Caravan, Trull
My last day as an official student of art and this produces a series of feelings, few it seems of regret. So much has happened since I last wrote. And the finish of my time here has been overshadowed completely.
It's raining and the long grass outside has been cut and there's a ginger and brown cat stalking mice in the bits that are left. There are rats here.

*

On Monday afternoon R and I hitched to London with good lifts, the last one straight to Richmond Green where JPD was waiting outside the theatre. I couldn't face going into town to 94 Cromwell Road so I stayed in the houseboat with R and JPD. On the Tuesday I went to Evansky's in Bond Street, for R to have her hair done which took over *three and a half hours* and I sat watching beautiful and ugly women having themselves flattered and fussed over. The hairdressers were very young, Italian-looking men and I feel they must either really like women or loathe them for the majority of women look both ludicrous and revolting with thin wet hair off the face and in rollers.

On Tuesday evening we went to the Richmond Theatre and watched another corny play. I slept in a sleeping bag on a bunk while they copulated all night. I didn't mind in the least and slept soundly. A huge houseboat [*a converted torpedo-boat moored under Richmond Bridge*], old and shabby with five rooms, including a long kitchen.

*

After much arguing and tears R went back to Taunton on an early train to be on time for the Fashion Show which was very important to her. I went with JPD to the theatre and spent an interesting morning back stage. JPD and I had a terrible time hitching back here yesterday afternoon, arriving too late for the fashion show. We left the theatre at noon and got here about eight-thirty which was ridiculous. The theatre there is full of neurotic characters but I can't write of them in this filthy caravan. I've just spent two hours scrubbing it out and it's still filthy and upsets my stomach. It never seems clean.

When I was in the theatre Derek rang JPD about his flat and I spoke to him on the phone and he was very friendly and insisted I came over to Earls Court straight away. I declined and he asked me to stay at Basingstoke on Monday before he goes to Spain.
I'm hitching up with R to Richmond on Sunday and from there I'll go to Basingstoke.
There was a party at the Murphys' flat last night and a row with R over JPD. We came here and cooked, we hadn't eaten for two days, literally, and felt ill - we'd hitched from London without a penny between us.

*

The rain is pelting down and I must somehow get to Taunton. R is madly posing in front of the County Hall this morning. Tonight we have a booze-up. I feel exhausted and haven't a moment to write, to read, to think. This is my fear of London, to be swamped by events and people. Everything is such a crowded rush of actions and faces with no resting place nor time to think into myself again and again which I must do. It may seem stupid of me to go to Basingstoke but I think not. I may be wrong to think he can't hurt me anymore but I don't think he can.

Saturday 16 July 1960, Yeovil
I'm home again after a revolting and dirty train journey through the West Country. The train stopped at every cow and five porters told me different versions of its destiny and whether it would reach Yeovil by mid-August or next year. I was very irritable. I'm planning my move tomorrow. Everything is happening at once and all is a great muddle. Last night we went to the Andersons' flat and I saw them all and Murphy for the last time. The latter I felt sadly over and he was quiet. I wore my new vamp dress and R did my hair and they all said I looked

smashing. I felt sad. I've left all my work at college. I don't want any of it.

Yesterday afternoon I was really drunk. Everybody was, except Holterman, who can't drink again yet. Tim was a scream, tight as hell and got a parking ticket. Roger didn't say goodbye. I went to say goodbye to Holterman and was so drunk I fell into his arms and apologised, laughing.

Now I am no longer a student but a human being who is in a muddle and no money and nowhere to go. We hitch to London again tomorrow. And then I go to Basingstoke. I'll not see Tim again nor Guy for he's off to Belgium to do his National Service in the Congo. The college was littered with drunk students and staff. Tim becomes unusually agile and hilarious when drunk and we samba-d like crazy. I was half dead with laughing. I'll miss him, I think.

Wednesday 27 July 1960, Yeovil
Now I'm back here in this room amongst the things that are no longer quite so necessary to my completeness. So much and yet so little has happened. I miss Richmond. Even the habit of writing, the badge of personality, is weakening. I go back on Friday. I couldn't get a job with anything near enough pay so I hitched back yesterday with R who had to come to see her photographer. We'll spend the weekend in Richmond and then go to work in Brighton on Monday.

This last week and a half seemed incredibly long on reflection, but first I was in Basingstoke with Derek for three days. He's in Barcelona now. He told me that he was equally cruel to all his girl-friends and it was a calculated defence. He was, as always, and more so, extremely rude and bitchy but we laughed a great deal. He's now the secretary of *The Young Contemporaries.*

The habit of this room has weakened and even my records echo slightly and my books stand back, just a bit. I've been painting since I came back but achieve nothing with alarming consistency. Again, in this room, I have violent dreams and wake up wringing with sweat and very nervous. I was very depressed hitching back and slept in sulky silence while a sporty man made conversation of the highest stupidity with R, who was in a temper too. We are beginning to annoy each other a lot. I went to Kew on Saturday and spent three hours watching people, not trees. It felt like I imagine India to be.

*

Much later - I've been painting most of the afternoon and evening. It never works in the slightest degree. I have to cover up and annihilate all the time. Now the idea of RCA entrance has begun to matter to me but to be honest my work is not good enough.
It's so exasperating to wonder whether, with some will-power and enthusiasm I could perhaps have three years in London which would change my life so much. Or else I'll be away in some suburban town which is horrible to think of. A few weeks back I thought I'd never paint again, the touch and smell of paint and brushes, the thought of it made me sick and the thought of three more years as a student was pretty grim - now I must get some canvases done but time is short and everything is a chance with great possibilities, more of disappointment than success. I get so impatient with my shortcomings.

Thursday 28 July 1960, Yeovil
Painting all day. I was almost happily enthusiastic. I've written to Anne, Roger and the registrar of the Royal College. Anne writes often and is genuinely sweet and concerned. She and Dan have offered me a resting place in their house when they marry in September.

I've just rung R and we hitch to London at three o'clock. My painting stares me in the face. R has been posing on penny-farthings on the streets of Taunton. She admits she has really enjoyed acting the sophisticate before crowds of goggling typists and workmen.
Tomorrow I must hitch to some outlandish crossroads miles from anywhere, sit on my grip and wait for God knows how long for her to hitch in from the other direction. Then London at last.

*

LONDON

Tuesday 2 August 1960, Buckingham Hotel, Cromwell Road, London
Walked round all the hotels asking for work; got this job, eight pounds a week, living in. It's three o'clock now and I've done my allotted chores for the day. Chambermaiding is chambermaiding and in any place, anywhere, it's the same. I live in a room in the basement where the night porter remarked: 'There's more atmosphere down 'ere than ever there is up there.' Up there is the placidity, the quiet, the air of money and good living. Below scuttle the mice of this vast building, those who serve. There are six Irish chambermaids. I'm the seventh and a foreigner. Not being Irish I might as well be blue. As always the hotel business takes on a small surplus of socially and emotionally inadequate oddballs.

I feel misplaced, an idealist. I may seem extraordinarily naïve but I'm not. I know what I want is difficult to attain and I may not have the right qualities. What do I want? I want a relationship that I know is possible. The Bateses achieved it without living with dozens of people and having abortions or babies all over the place.

The house I stayed in on Friday was full of French people. I'm glad to be away from R and JPD - living on the boat was like Sartre's *In Camera*. I want to forget the time spent in Richmond and could never go back to Somerset. London still appeals to me although this evening, walking along Old Brompton Road, I felt hideous and the men were whistling and my feet were aching. I felt so sick of it all and don't know where I wanted to be. If I can bear to stay in this job I'll get my paints up and paint in the afternoons. A good opportunity to get some work done for the Royal College entrance. I can't wait to start buying books.

A man in a sports car with a peculiar battered look about him followed me along the kerb all the way down Old Brompton Road and then sat by me for about two hours in the Troubadour.[19] There's a tiny Indian working there who's very sweet. This evening Mike yelled at him that he was fired but he didn't seem to notice. Eric [*Lister*] has a minute Picasso drawing in his gallery [*the Portal Gallery, Grafton Street*] which I swear he's done himself.

Wednesday 3 August 1960, Buckingham Hotel, London

I must be quick and get to sleep to be up at 6.30 am. It's hard work but I don't hate it. I went again to the Troubadour but Mike glared at me. I was given a shilling by one of the hotel guests for a cardboard box left in a waste paper basket by another guest - crazy.

Thursday 4 August 1960, Buckingham Hotel, London

Sitting here in this cellar smoking fags with my feet up. On another floor today. There's an antique shop round the corner, next to Gloucester Road tube station, simply loaded with things I want. On my floor there's a man in a double bed who refuses to get up. I've barged in with the hoover in one hand and the Vim in the other several times but he stays firm. At one point he demanded 'one glass of milk, one fresh apple and the *Daily Express*'.
The housekeeper and I, both on the same floor today, have carefully avoided each other. I dislike her and the manager and this morning I cleaned his sink out with his own flannel.

I haven't been to the Troubadour today. It's too far to walk the length of Old Brompton Road before seven when I start the night shift and I have no money left. I'm hoping to get a letter with a ten shilling note inside from my mother. The rest of the people here have begun to

---

[19] The Troubadour; a coffee-bar in Earls Court, run by an eccentric character called Mike; despite, or because of his abrasive attitude to many of his customers, the Troubadour was a favourite meeting place of artists, philosophers and oddballs. The whitewashed walls were hung with cast-iron implements and Sammy Davis, Jnr, Ginger Baker, Rambling Jack Elliott, Marcel Marceau and Dudley Moore all performed there..

accept me. Jack, the chef, cooks breakfast with his blond hair in a hair-net and talks to his reflection in a hand-mirror. He swears I worked in the same hotel as him in Euston.

One o'clock on Thursday night and I feel contented, almost happy. This is both unusual and delightful. This evening I had to wear a black skirt and a borrowed cardigan and a little frilly white apron and go through all six floors turning down the bedlinen. In one of the rooms there was a young Dutchman who looked very like Yves St Laurent. He's very sweet and I like him. We went first for some beer and then to the Troubadour. We talked all the time and he told me about his wife and child in Holland. He wanted me to go up and sleep with him but it's impossible in this hotel. I would be seen for sure and get the sack. But he is very sweet and goes to Rotterdam tomorrow. I wish he were here for longer, we could have such fun. I felt good this evening, my constant apathy had gone - probably because I was with someone who interests me and who liked being with me.

When I came in I had some tea and talked to Jack who is gloriously funny. He's so vain; he's forever declaring how beautiful he is - he's not - and how much his boyfriends adore him. He's very effeminate with a sloppy, North Country voice and bleached blond hair. The dancer, Tommy, less so. They seem to like me and I like them very much. I soon become attached to people like this and will be sad to leave. I'm dreading to leave London. I *must* try to get into the Royal College.
I was pleased that the Dutchman liked me because he was so unpretentious and interesting. Quiet, superbly fluent in the English language, using the most obscure and sophisticated phraseology. He attracts me very much.

I had a talk with the night porter about painting tonight or rather, he told me about painting. Surprisingly, he did know quite a bit for a layman and more surprisingly, some of his ideas were sound and constructive and, above all, sincere. I had to borrow four shillings from Bridie with the jet black hair; she's very pretty and I wonder how she sees life and what will happen to her.

The staff hall is a heaven/hell for me with a kettle on for tea every hour of the day. The room is very unhealthy, almost as bad as the Common Room at Yeovil Art School. It creates a nausea in the stomach and a continual slight headache and pain behind the eyes. We are like blind mice, blowing our noses which stream with watery phlegm. The women have hollow chests, tiny eyes and tight mouths painted a dull red. As it happens my skin has improved, I don't know why but it has and my hair is growing very long and shines very much. The air in this room is revolting and I feel just like a subterranean animal. [*Whilst the hotel itself was well-appointed, luxurious even, in 1960, when these Journal entries were made, conditions in the basement, where the staff lived, were far from congenial. Staff accommodation has no doubt improved since then.*]

Saturday 6 August 1960, Buckingham Hotel, London
I'm sitting in this room with a mug of tea and a fag and the noises of the crazy kitchen staff. Under my door was a note from the Dutchman and a telephone number for me to ring before he leaves for Holland.
In two days I'm twenty. I'm quite at home here.

I had the 'apple, milk and *Daily Express*' room to clean this morning. It was a hell of a mess. His clothes were filthy and thrown all over the floor. There was food and lots of loose money all over the bed and floor. The trousers of his pyjamas were folded over the wash-basin and his socks were in the bed. He had Japanese bank notes screwed up under his pillow and his passport was on the floor, barely recognisable it was so worn and battered. He himself has an air of bizarre, rich madness. Foreign guests keep asking me to accompany them to the 'feelms'.

The night porter showed me some of his 'abstracts' which, in fact, were not as bad as expected. At least he's industrious. He's taken to drawing me aside for talks about art which may well get a bit hard to bear.
I phoned the Dutchman. He wants to stay another night in England. I'm meeting him at Waterloo. I feel a great desire to get on with some painting.

Sunday 7 August 1960, Buckingham Hotel, London
I can hardly write for the steam from the kettle badly burned the fingers and thumb of my right hand. I'm depressed and miserable and these bandages on my hand are driving me mad. Yesterday, when I had the accident, the pain was almost unbearable. This morning there were great yellow blisters and to do the work was agony. I can't do the heavy work with one hand. I feel ill, alone, depressed and strange to myself. Totally disconnected from anything, past or present, and the future doesn't exist.

Yesterday I spent the evening with the Dutchman. Then, very late, we went to a hotel in West Cromwell Road where the porter was Russian and very drunk. The night was strange and not me. My hand was agony. Now he's gone and I can still hear his voice and see his face but I'm glad he's gone. I can't breathe down here. To have to wash with one hand is enough to make anyone crazy.

Monday 8 August 1960, Buckingham Hotel, London
[*It was my twentieth birthday but I didn't mention it in the Journal*]
I feel better today but there was a terrific storm and the whole basement is flooded up to two feet in water. It's really unbelievable; filthy water all over the place; people wading through the dark and smelling corridors to salvage their things. These people are so funny but the place is so dirty it makes me feel sick.

No wonder I was feeling strange yesterday - I had no food at all on Friday, made love all night and then rushed back to the hotel to start work at 6.30 am. with no sleep, no food and the feeling that my womb had slipped two feet and my right hand had dropped off. By the end of the day I was seeing things, literally, and the rooms were spinning and the beds like lead.
As to what I feel about my short affair? Very little, which is strange. I have no regrets nor one single unpleasant or sad thought.

When the basement flooded there was a grim contrast between upstairs and downstairs - the calamity, the laughter, the moans, the filth, the great catastrophe downstairs where it was so cold and dark and then I

went up in the lift, through all the floors, turning down the linen, wearing my frilly apron, my feet still wet and the smells of the basement still in my nose. And upstairs all was plushy and warm and easy and clean and silent and it seemed so incongruous that we were all human yet so unequal.
The guests knew nothing of the flood nor the wretchedness of living like this. They only saw the rain sliding down their tightly-shut windows or occasionally heard it amid their dreadful prattle.
I feel so much for my constant companions down here - the basement people, the working class proper. I receive the same snubs and coolness and condescension from the rich as they do. I'm a chambermaid and I clear up after people who pay to have it done.
I arrange and dust the bottles and jars of expensive make-up belonging to stupid horse-faced women with no grace, no manners and no charm. I am their servant, and intellect has no consequence. It doesn't make me angry because it won't always be so. I'm a temporary slave and that makes a hell of a difference. But I feel anger against this treatment for these people who will never escape from it and can never hit back.

I haven't been in the Troubadour lately, partly because I've got a few spots and my hand looks revolting encased in filthy wet bandages. A young nurse at the hospital did it and very badly for she had hands like a cowman and kept jabbing the raw flesh with the scissors as she cut away the still living-skin. She was herself in some doubt as to the legitimacy of her treatment for she kept anxiously reassuring herself that her superiors weren't looking. It was very, very painful and my fingers look like raw sausages.

I can't stand this lack of light down here, not to speak of air; it really gets on my nerves. I must write to Anne and to R but I've become so detached from them. They seem like strangers. It's since I burnt my hand that my mind has gone peculiar or is it this place? I was reasonably intact before. I'm losing my critical powers, my reasoning and my perception. I must get to the Picasso Exhibition. To have my gramophone here would help - my music might re-establish me.

Tuesday 9 August 1960, Buckingham Hotel, London
Another day. Today a letter from the Dutchman. I was very surprised; I want no contact. It's over, gone and should be left and remembered, not drawn out. He wants to buy me things but I don't want anything from him. He thinks he may be in London again next month. I hope he doesn't come. Even to me, this seems hard and unfeeling. I like him but he's married and no relationship can follow.

Tonight I went to the Troubadour and J sat next to me but said very little. A friend of Derek's took me to a French film at the Paris Pullman, about a green horse or something.

Today I took off the bandages and all my nails are broken. I feel revolting with short nails, it really upsets my morale.
What will happen to me? Time goes, my life is going so quickly and everything is dark and not right and all illusions are shattered and there's no place for feelings. Love is as intangible as it is terrible. Even now, even now in a room full of these men I find attractive, mentally and physically, it's still Derek that I really care for. It's intangible because I'm no more attracted to him physically than the others, nor mentally. Love is neither of these things - it's magic, a supernatural force that plays havoc with people's lives.

Wednesday 10 August 1960, Buckingham Hotel. London
On Friday I went to a nightclub with one of the waiters. I think, despite the language difficulties, he's a bit stupid. I've come to a decision that I will have none of this. I am becoming unselective and going downhill. I must gain some maturity and reassess attraction. I am stupid. I won't have sex with these attractive and pleasant young men because it's unnecessary and I'll gain nothing from it. It's all so complex and depressing and vital.

Thursday 11 August 1960, Buckingham Hotel, London
Now there's a flap on as to whether there's a party or not. Ferdi, one of the Italian waiters, is going around like a lost sheep and Tommy, the dancing queen, is drinking beer in the staff hall, bless him. I must write of some awful urges I have when I'm in Judy's flat. When I'm carrying

her baby around I have a dreadful urge to throw it out of the window, which is about seventy feet above the street [*Lexham Gardens*]. It's totally irrational and now I dare not go near it for fear of what I might do. Deep in my subconscious it may be founded in envy and frustration but it seems ungrounded in reality. I have no desire to injure any children. She's a lovely and very happy child and I wouldn't dream of hurting her. It's something to do with the weight of her and the yawning gap of the open window and the space below - almost like an equation that needs completion.

In one of the rooms today I was hurrying with the vacuum cleaner and tripped over the cord and fell flat on my back onto the bed, knocking the cleaner as I went so that it landed across my knees and then we both slipped with some force onto the floor in a heap. I was convulsed with laughter and laughed alone, loud and long.

Much later and Tommy, Mario, Pepé and I went to this woman's house in Notting Hill Gate and to the Number One Club. It was deserted. Pepé was glum tonight and has gone back to beat up Mario or something. I like to go out and talk and, above all, to laugh.

Monday 15 August 1960, Buckingham Hotel, London
Tonight I supervised the cutting of Tommy's hair. I had to tell Toni to get out and he went cursing in Italian.

Tuesday 16 August 1960, Buckingham Hotel, London
I don't get to sleep till about two in the morning and get up at 6.30 am. The same routine, the same smells and the hollow sounds and ill, ghost-like figures of servants not yet talking, in pink or navy overalls that hang limply yet cling, like damp flax, passing slowly through the dismal, darkened corridors like dutiful mice. Upstairs, above ground, the corridors breathe quietness and a sickly protective warmth. Yet we laugh all the time - everything is funny, a desperate joke.

Now I'm in bed and it's only eleven o'clock. I feel ill with a stiff cough in my chest. The hotel feels deserted. I felt lonely after nine o'clock because Tommy is at his ballet lesson and all the chambermaids are out. When he came back we made tea but he was in a peculiar mood. Ferdi follows me around and is annoying. The work is getting me down.

Thursday 18 August 1960, Buckingham Hotel, London
So much to write. My existence is dominated by work and the attention of men. Toni goes all hot and dramatic and likewise all the waiters in different ways. They think of nothing else. But I must write about Hal [*artist, South African, one of many young people in conflict with the apartheid system in their country*]. Last night we made love but I care for him so it will end in unhappiness. Now he's gone to an all-night party and I feel wretched. Men never make me happy, yet the play goes on and the stage gets more crowded until it becomes suffocating and the lines get mixed and cues are wrongly taken and the lines that lead nowhere litter the whole area of the play, the theme of which evades me and the end is nowhere in sight and it's becoming a nightmare.

Saturday 20 August 1960, Buckingham Hotel, London
Today has been a very conscious one. Tonight I went to the Troubadour more or less expecting to sleep at Hal's but he wasn't there. Everyone is talking about the South African boycott [a*nti-apartheid movement; everyone stopped buying South African goods, Philip Morris cigarettes, etc*.]. Came back here smitten with this depression, feeling sick and hating life for when I do care for someone it matters so much it overules my existence.

So many days pass and there's Hal and there's J and there's so much to be gained, days to live rather than merely contain oneself in, but this urgency of life doesn't seem to be in them. These people don't feel, they calculate and succumb to physical sensations but there is no urgency in the real sense; there's a quickness but the difference is wide.
Tonight at the Troubadour it was crowded and I had no one to talk to. All was darkness and faces and eyes and music and J was somewhere else and the streets were empty of Hal. Eyes across rooms and urgency only in mine.

Sunday 20 August 1960, Buckingham Hotel, London
This morning I'm only numbed by last night's depression. Hal can bugger off and there's no urgency now. Bridie brought me some breakfast this morning, wasting ten minutes of her precious free time. These people are so simple and marvellous, with none of the bitter nonchalance, this guile.
It's dark in here this morning. I must read. Now Hal is simply a bruised patch in my surroundings but tonight his mere existence will make me despair.

There's a church and a convent of Spanish nuns behind the hotel. They sit outside like cloaked penguins; austere creatures and they sew washing-up cloths. To me, they're incomplete.
On the tube I saw a woman who was very pregnant and she was shining with what was pure radiance, a word not often required. She really glowed in an inhuman way. And she was reading the Bible. She had no shopping bag and no coat and she wore thin sandals on her feet. I asked her a question about the direction of the tube so that she would look up from her reading and I could see her eyes - they *shone.*
To have a child is to enter a range of complex emotions way above the simple scufflings of which I know a little. This is a new realm, glimpses of which I see occasionally.
I feel in a void with no personality.

It's now three o'clock and the hotel is silent, the lift still and the staff hall empty but with the television still on and the naked gas still burning away and the filth and debris of stale food and cups and fag-ends everywhere.

I've been reading some of Tagore's poetry. I wish I could understand *all* languages so I could love all the literature of every country. What a waste of beauty, restricted in this way. My hands are hot and dry from the cleaning powders. I've plastered them with olive oil but they remain dry. It's so bad for my eyes being underground like this. I don't like to go out on my own. What a foolish person I am - here in London and there are dozens of Picassos in the Tate and I don't bother to go and see them. I always think I'll go tomorrow.

Mike was much annoyed with me for just sitting in the Troubadour last night. I'm a parasite on other people's personalities. I don't add anything and it's my own fault that people don't want to know me. Who chooses to know introverted drips?

The strongest friendship I have is with Tommy, who is homosexual, and we talk for hours in Jack's room and sometimes Jack is there, too, in bed with his curlers in. He makes us scream with laughter. I like them both so much. I come out of myself when I'm with these so-called misfits. They have wonderful natures and their humour is marvellous.

Ferdi says he loves me and it's very annoying when he's in the room. Of course, I'm in my element in this underground world where I'm the prettiest and most unusual inmate at present - not difficult to achieve, I must say - and all the Italians are woman-mad, yet forever men staring and talking and pawing me gets on my nerves.
It's all life, it's everything and I get so tired of it all.

Tuesday 23 August 1960, Buckingham Hotel, London
Today my mother came up and she looked well and less irritable. She seems anxious for me to return to a clean bed and some fresh air but I like it here. She got upset when I said I thought doing the Art Teachers' Diploma would be a pointless and wasted year. Few people seriously consider it. I dread to leave here. I don't think I can; I need these people.

Tonight I was happier for I was talking for several hours in the Troubadour with Josh Kirby[20], a weird and crazy painter with a marvellous sense of humour.

---

[20] Josh Kirby: painter. Studied at Liverpool City School of Art. His science fiction paintings are used as paperback fiction covers to bypass the commercial gallery system, notably on the Discworld books of Terry Prachett. His major work, *The Voyage of the Ayeguy*, is a latter-day series of altar pieces in the science fiction mode.

Tuesday 24 August 1960, Buckingham Hotel, London
This evening I went as usual to the Troubadour but at the door I suddenly couldn't go in. There were no more people in there than usual but I couldn't go in. I saw Josh over in the corner but I didn't see Hal. I must see him soon. I think I'll leave a note in his basement tomorrow.

Walking back from the Troubadour I met R with a middle-aged man. We went for some coffee and she smoked many of his cigarettes which really annoyed me because she doesn't really smoke. It was all very superficial and I was so bored and ill at ease that I left them and came back to the staff-hall to watch Bertrand Russell on the television. One good thing is that when there's something I want to watch the rest loathe it and go out, therefore I have peace when I most need it.

As I came in the manager said he was going to move me into another room with another chambermaid. The idea put me in a bad mood. I prefer to be on my own. I haven't touched my paints yet. The time goes quickly and each day I become more attached to this place and the people.

In the last few days, thinking so realistically about it, I fully realised the immensity of having a child and the idea is fantastically exciting. It's terrible having to wait when it's only moral convention and personal reasoning that prevents me. I wonder if I would be prepared to live on National Assistance as Judy does? I think I would do it, but it's a great responsibility. I feel a certain relief that the possibility has again been removed so I can take yet another step towards my line of duty, my training, though I'm crawling along this last lap with some sadness. But what is the point of becoming a qualified teacher and then having a baby? Abortion would be a terrible thing for me - I could never do it.
Strange, the instinct to make an extension of oneself to further complicate matters just when one has reached the stage of finding oneself. As though one has found oneself and been disappointed.

A letter from the Education Office to tell me I've passed NDD. I have no feelings on the matter. A letter from Brian in the South of France and another from Anne bemoaning the drift of her friends.

On the first floor today which is the worst. An American woman gave me sixpence when I took her early morning tea - small things like this are really exhilarating.

Five o'clock and I'm beside myself. I have to move from this horrible room first thing in the morning and move in with two other chambermaids, both very nice but this book alone knows how terrible this is for me. I feel I can't stay more than a week. But I *must* stay in London. I can't go yet.
There's a great muddle over rooms and when I said I wouldn't mind sharing with Jack they were really shocked. I can't understand this. Their code of convention is illogical. The one reason why a female may not share a room with a male is because of the supposedly overwhelming instinct for copulation. Now if the man is virtually female then the problem doesn't arise. They can't see this. There isn't a morsel of clear reason in their taboos and I lose patience with them.

Once again I'm a refugee. Utopia for me is simply a room of my own. It's amazing how elusive this can be. Now I'm faced with a difficult decision - either I stay in misery and at the same time earn some money and see the people who interest me outside. Or else, I do what I should do and return to Somerset and paint for the Royal College Entrance. I can't do it here. The time goes so quickly and so much is left undone.

Three o'clock in the morning. I went dancing at a continental club in Notting Hill Gate with Mario, an Italian from Egypt - a very cynical and ageless person with common sense. I had intended to go to the Troubadour to see Hal but each day goes and so our relationship is starved and will soon be extinguished as all such relationships.

Thursday 25 August 1960, Buckingham Hotel, London
Now I'm in Room 8 and as it happens I like it very much. It has peace, a table to work on and above all, air and light. I'm living in a bed-space, literally six feet by three, but I have only my make-up and six books.

Friday 26 August 1960, Buckingham Hotel, London
Still haven't done any painting and I realise I'm throwing away chances for the sake of the immediate urgency of the present which will soon be nothing. Last night I was with Hal. It's raining now and I'm thinking of our next night together but nothing was said. Time is too short for vagueness. I only have a couple of weeks left.

Eight o'clock and a very hard day's work more or less done. A Japanese man left me five shillings and eight pence and a halfpenny which pleased me very much. This evening I was turning down beds and opened one of the rooms with my key, after knocking, of course, and there was a couple fucking like crazy. I stood and laughed but they didn't even look up.

To give an example of my insincerity - I had promised to go the the Two IIs club in Kensington with Tommy, the dancer, last night at ten so while he was shaving and getting ready I went to leave a message at Hal's but he was there and we went off and I just didn't have the decency to phone Tommy or go back to the hotel or the club as planned - it went from my mind altogether. This is very bad and I feel ashamed but when I'm with Hal I don't really think about anybody else.

Saturday 26 August 1960, Buckingham Hotel, London
Last night I was with Hal again and he's becoming a habit which I must avoid for I leave here soon. I don't want to miss anybody to any great extent. It'll be bad enough missing everybody, everything. He drove me back here at six-thirty this morning. Again it was impossible to arrange to meet. I couldn't ask; I never can. I'm not going in tonight, at the same time I feel empty and it seems such a terrible waste of time. Everything's so temporary and circumstantial.

Last night I sat talking to Josh Kirby, a truly remarkable character, and there was a great battle of words between Mike and a drunken, middle-aged man. I was shaking but the others sat enjoying the spectacle for a full hour. I loathe and fear violence, even in words. I seem to be a basement creature, an underground rat, a basement and boat creature, an animal that lives underneath buildings or in rigged-up torpedo boats.

Josh Kirby is mad and we sit having conversations of such obscurity and absurdity that we are overcome with our own brilliance and wit. Anneka, the pretty blonde girl who works there [*later married the actor, Michael Gough*] has painted her bicycle purple with flowers all over it. I'm losing my looks, if I ever had any. I look haggard and unhealthy. Hal's a good lover and his humour is great. He's testing my intelligence all the time but I cannot divulge any of myself. And to physically touch a man of my own accord, just to touch his arm with my hand, takes a lot for me to do. I'm terrified of indifference or causing annoyance. This arises from those years with Derek. He taught me, by his intolerable coldness, never to show my feelings, to appear to have none. Now I'm mentally screwed tight within myself and nothing, it seems, will unwind me, for all is so temporary that it never seems worth letting it go and therefore to him, and to others, I seem stupid, with nothing to say. But I *think* my conversations without voicing them, therefore I'm a dull conversationalist. Only humour is uninhibited with me.

People are always saying I never speak and it annoys some of them. I'm sure it does but if I do say something they stop, or go quiet but it's not an inferiority complex that silences me : this reticence stems from a love of my own thoughts undiluted by other people's. Also, so much that is said is so utterly worthless and very irritating. I find myself listening to what is said, sum it up in my head and converse with myself; in this way I cover the ground from every single angle and have my say without saying a word.
But with humour it's different. Humour glows with rubbing and even the most personal humour can find an audience and lose nothing. My silence, my wariness, is a form of vanity because whereas before my words had been heard with at least some degree of interest - here, they're but a bleep in a great whirr of voiced thought and my vanity makes me keep my precious thoughts to myself. It's nothing but a pitiful, laughable sense of superiority.
Hal was talking loudly about me in the Troubadour last night. He said I suffered from an immense superiority complex which I veiled by means of an appalling inferiority complex. He's right.

Much later and I've been asleep. I felt terrible when I woke up, as if I'd just been born - this size, in this place, with no familiar surroundings, with no past thought and with no memory with which to re-establish my identity.
More raging nightmares - back in a space in my existence, back in a familiar chasm where reason can't follow. Quite often, and it's a most terrifying experience, my body sleeps and is immovable and my mind is still awake, whirling and raging inside my inert body, fighting for consciousness, until I'm fighting a bodily death and my head feels it will burst with my being pressing the sides to get out. Then suddenly my mind, my spirit, seems to make sudden contact that sets the construction that I know as 'myself' into motion again and I resume my human identity and realise life again. This happens about every two weeks and leaves me sick with fright and sometimes too scared to sleep.

Eleven-thirty gone and I've been reading and thinking. Being here produces a constant enforced sensuality and the capacity for sudden strong attractions and idyllic illusions. Cold, soulful glances that last two seconds, that's London.

Monday 29 August 1960, Buckingham Hotel, London
Last night I was in the Troubadour and sat talking with a group I know by sight, ordinarily interesting. I thought I saw Hal come in and go out again, probably when he saw me. I hope this isn't so because it means he feels whenever I'm there he's obliged to take me back with him, which is ridiculous. But I may have imagined I saw him as I'm always thinking I see people who aren't there.

I feel I'm caught up in a web of what I am and its consequences, for women want security and, to a certain extent, to feel dependent. I'm basically not promiscuous but I like some men. I'm an empty female person who will continue a path put before her and become a teacher. I would rather have worn my fingers to the bone and given up fags and had a child than this barren year ahead of me, cut-off and on my own. I'm sick of everything. I've given up thinking of applying to the Royal College. I haven't enough enthusiasm.

There was another accident outside the hotel this morning. Two cars smacked together with a great pool of blood so deep it reflected the people passing by. It makes me realise the destructibility of this case in which we are hidden.

Tuesday 30 August 1960, Buckingham Hotel, London
R and I went to the Troubadour and I was driven quietly crazy by all those fucking women kissing Hal in front of me. I sat with Josh Kirby who likes me, he really does. I get so bloody miserable. I feel like drifting from one to the other, beat them at their own game but I can't. He must think I'm stupid. Perhaps I am. Perhaps I *am* a nonentity and yet Josh thinks otherwise and many others.

Last night I was remembering the art school parties. I always wore black and no shoes and wandered from room to room, often in tears and usually went off in a corner to sleep. I was always morbidly drunk. I remember the men used to clutch at me as I passed and asked why I never stayed still for one minute and the intrusion of their questions made me cry all the more. The whole business of development has been a nightmare. The trouble has always been inside me. I don't know what is tormenting me. I realise I'm in the grip of a destructive self-obsession, agitated and fed by this habit of self-expression, completely uninhibited, on paper. This has become my solitary conversation, my only real social exchange.

I'm sitting here on my day off, tired and unhappy. I have a pot of tea and two weeks left in London. I wish for a miracle, that I'll get a place in a London college, but I know I won't, they're already full. I can't leave. What will happen to me? What *has* happened to me?

One of the maids in this room asked what I was writing and if I 'got it from a book'. They never think to read for themselves. How can they exist each day without the need to sort things out on paper; without the need to think over a day's existence, to think over a quarter of what one remembers experiencing and going over just a few of the hundreds of thoughts that pass through their minds in the course of the day?

Ten o'clock in the evening now. Feeling depressed stuck in this hotel, this hell underground. I've been in the Troubadour this afternoon with R. I don't want to hang about there too much. I know they think I'm dull and stupid. Must I gush over people and put on a pretence of gaiety and hug anything in trousers and call everyone 'darling'? Must I forever be widening my eyes and pouting or being catty about people? What the hell's wrong with being *quiet?*

I had thought that I was extremely individual for people have never disregarded me even if they've positively disliked me. Where is there a place for me? Or am I expecting people to fit around me? In Taunton I didn't care what people thought of me for they had nothing I needed and I had no interest in them but now I really have to face the problem, perhaps for the first time, for I really want these people to like me.
Where have I gone that nobody can find me?

Thursday 1 September 1960, Buckingham Hotel, London
The basement is flooded again but this time it's not funny. I'm stuck here without fags. I have hardly any money left until Monday. I was talking to one of the cleaners about royalty and we agree entirely. She looks at life honestly.

Saturday 3 September 1960, Buckingham Hotel, London
Today I'm glad enough to be living. I've worked all day and I'm on again at seven this evening. Tonight my brother and I go to the Ronnie Scott's. In one of the rooms I clean there's a copy of *Dr Zhivago* which I'm reading in two-minute sessions. There's so much I want to write; not nonsense like this. The television is on all the time in the staff hall for the Olympic Games. No peace, no solitude.

Monday 4 September 1960, Buckingham Hotel, London
I dread going home, in that house, in that town, snuffed out and miserable. Once again to appear an oddity fills me with dread. To be stared at again, to be alone again, to be dead. Although I'm not happy here I'm not utterly miserable which is wonderful. If only I could get into Hornsey or Goldsmiths. I *must* stay in London.

The weather is wonderful; dull and the rain dripping down all day. I love the rain but people see a raindrop and they moan. It's a habit, nothing more, for rain is lovely.

Wednesday 7 September 1960, Buckingham Hotel, London
I met MT in Oxford Street and we had coffee and gossiped. He tells me that Roger is in London looking for me. I would be pleased to see him. I wonder if he still loves me. R and JPD have a room in West Cromwell Road, not far from Derek's place. I must see the Picasso Exhibition in the next few days in case I have to go away at very short notice.

Wednesday 14 September 1960, Buckingham Hotel, London
I went to meet Anne at Gloucester Road Station but she didn't come and I got drunk with the porter.
Tomorrow I move on to Leicester. Now I shall have to go without seeing Hal. I hate everybody. I'm sick of everything, life.

YEOVIL

Saturday 17 September 1960, Yeovil
I came back to the West Country in a crawling dirty train in a doom - stricken atmosphere. The sky was black and very low and there was a mist and where there wasn't mist there was rain. The countryside seemed suddenly like a great garden and the trees seemed like grotesque herbacious structures rising from the ground, large and heavy.

I had no great feeling of sadness as I expected but certainly no pleasure at the thought of going home. I dreaded coming but I seem to have no aversion left for sudden changes in environment and go through them without even scraping my sides.
My room is no longer. It's an impersonal place I couldn't begin to describe. I have my few belongings laid out ready to pack again. But I don't mind. My resting place is a long way off and the postponement of it no longer frustrates me. The fact that I have no room anywhere in the world no longer matters.

I went for an interview at Leicester and the Principal said I wouldn't make the kind of teacher they wanted - I lacked enthusiasm. I was momentarily very relieved. It was a depressingly awful place and the students gave the impression of being amazingly colourless and dull.
I don't belong there and must get back to London.

On Wednesday I have to go to Birmingham for an interview. Unless I teach I have to face a future as an unqualified person. I haven't the talent, self-possession or will to concentrate on painting as a profession and I would be unable to sell myself in a field which is overcrowded with people far more competent than myself and with far more saleable personalities.

The man at Leicester said he had the impression I was far too dedicated to my own art to make a successful all-round teacher. He didn't realise I was nothing half so commendable. I am neither dedicated to the idea of teaching or my own painting. At the hotel I was offered a job as a nanny to a Canadian family in Belgrave Square but the thought of being permanently 'in service' appals me. I want so much to stay in London but I know that if I get a chance to get into Birmingham I must take it.

I suppose I have made progress in a small ways. I've continued to be myself in the unsympathetic surroundings of a hotel basement. One of the guests was amazed when she heard I was a painter and said I must be a very adaptable person - me, *adaptable!*
I have learned a lot about relationships with intolerable people - like that bitch of a housekeeper and the manager who threw me out when I had nowhere to go - and met some wonderful characters.
I've been worried and appalled by the pattern of the lives of the people I'd joined and have worked very hard. I was accepted as a friend by a collection of people as removed from me as a tribe of Eskimos. I've learned to live and work in an environment where personal feelings, education and intelligence counted for nothing and was given no consideration.

Today I went to see Beaver at Rampisham but things have changed; we're all at a crossroads and it's a bit desolate and things aren't quite so funny. I've written to Judy in Lexham Gardens. I must keep in touch with her and Hal and Josh Kirby. Hal was in the Troubadour on Thursday night but I felt shy and minded too much to say goodbye to him. [*I never saw him again. He married, went back to Johannesburg and became an entertainer.*]

Sunday 18 September 1960, Yeovil
Mother has been blindly insulting to myself and my friends, whom she has not met. She can't grasp values other than her own, but in two days I'll be away again. My records smile like old friends.

Monday 19 September 1960, Yeovil
Tonight life is itching through me and I'm very strung up inside. Every sound, every touch, every single sight is the epitome of life, of being alive. I was with Anne and we began to talk of this disease of art culture which has slyly bitten us for four years, leaving us itching carcasses of self-criticism, watching other untouched bodies drinking the water of not-knowing and eating the food of oblivion. Oblivion of beauty, the love of which is endless frustration and little solace.

I had a letter from Roger which I couldn't understand. I think he's still pining.

Tuesday 20 September 1960, Yeovil.
Today I had an awful shock. I looked for my first two journal notebooks and they were gone. I was frantic. It was as if a great chunk of my life was missing. I was boiling with rage and when my mother came in I demanded to know what she had done with them. She had packed them away because she said they were 'disgusting and atrocious'. I was appalled. She has no right to touch, to read, to remove my property and *her* action is the atrocity. She actually said that if I died she would burn my books, all my things. To her it's atrocious to write the truth. She has no right to read this truth but if she trespasses upon it she must accept it. It is as though within these covers I have confessed to ten deadly murders. I have confessed love, hate, loneliness,

boredom, ambition, disillusionment, crimes we all commit but may never confess, nor find it necessary to, but to act in this way is intolerable. I had dreaded the worst - that she had destroyed them. She destroyed one of Derek's letters which made me rage inside. This audacity with other people's things is intolerable. I am taking all my books with me. She's horrified, afraid they will be lost and someone will read them. They *will* be read but not by chance readers.

*

BIRMINGHAM

Thursday 21 September 1960, Birmingham
Now I am a wanderer in Birmingham. Yesterday I came and was accepted on the postgraduate course. The environment within the college is ideal and I was pleasantly surprised.

Today I have been in a primary school, suddenly drawn down to the level of a child again - the smell, the remembrance of school. Now I must prove to myself I can suppress my erratic nature - that I can go through with it. This is going to be an immense struggle for control. This morning I lay awake dreading it to be light when I would have to begin this alien course. I may move into a shared flat on Wednesday.
At present I'm in typical digs with another student teacher and we eat our meals down the road. Dark wood, mossy memories in halls and walls with faces.

Birmingham seems like one long, nasty suburb. I want to be in London again where there's crispness and no cloud. A man on the course lives in Lexham Gardens so we can hitch down most weekends.[21]

Monday 26 September 1960, Birmingham
I'm moving into a flat with another ATD student in Varna Road, Balsall Heath, a really rough area. At four o'clock this afternoon the prostitutes were propping up the gate-posts, no gates, just posts.

---

[21] Bernard Taylor; Studied at Chelsea School of Art and Birmingham University Teacher Training. Worked as a graphic artist before going to USA to teach in 1963; worked there as a professional actor until 1969. Returning to England he continued to act and also began his writing career. He has had several works performed on stage and television and a number of novels and non-fiction books published. Collaborated with the author of this journal on *Murder At The Priory: The Mysterious Poisoning of Charles Bravo.*

I'm waiting to be able to hitch to London to see Derek. Living through, not in, this world of teaching and all that goes with it. I long to escape but have nowhere to go - except to sordid basements to rot away.

Tuesday 27 September 1960, Varna Road, Balsall Heath
The course [*at Priory Road, Edgbaston*] continues and I with it, not hating it, just existing through it. I think of the people I left behind. I want to go back to a place I know where I can find my bearings and feel again.
Now I'm in the flat in the notorious Varna Road, street of tarts and unsavoury stabbings. It's a coloured quarter and it fascinates me. The flat is quaint, ultra-Victorian. I'm going to like it here.
A day of reading bits of child psychology - there's so much to learn.

Friday 30 September 1960, Varna Road, Birmingham
An evening in this quaint flat. It's a short resting place. I've written many letters; have little money left and my grant hasn't come. I am missing my people in London.

Sunday 2 October 1960, Varna Road, Birmingham
The people on this street live on their sexual instincts and fear. It's a street of brothels and men hanging about on corners. To be white is exceptional. I have just been out for cigarettes. The street was scattered with Jamaicans and Indians, standing in small groups, or wandering in and out of the houses. A few old women, no longer of any interest, walk slowly up the street carrying shopping bags.
There is suspicion and fear, eyes shift from one face to another, black, bloodshot ones and pale shifting ones.

Men in cars kerb-crawl and raise their fingers, leaning forward, eager, their faces drawn with lust. I hate these, not the street-walkers.
As for them, I think they're mad to be in such a losing business. It's really terrible in the street. They have cock-fights and stabbings and the police come up here in twos or on motor bikes.
At night it's really grim, men melting into doorways, beckoning. The endless crawl of cars, the slamming of doors, the women's shrill voices. Old men being insulted by young tarts.

There is one over the road who stands outside in her best blue suit. She stood in the rain from about two o'clock to four yesterday afternoon, twirling her large red umbrella, yelling across to her familiars, refusing old men, walking up and down in front of her house. To me, this one, who is young, is the epitome of her trade, the eternal prostitute but she should be in Paris, in London or Tangier, where it's more exciting, not in this filthy, ugly, frightening street. Her friend on the opposite side of the road, who is older and very buxom, wears tight elastic trews and nothing on top but a purple mohair stole which she continually fiddles with and throws across her chest.
The old couple upstairs, us and two of the tarts are the only whites. The old people, Leopold and his wife, are ancient, amazingly kind and straight from a Balzac novel.

Tomorrow, another slum clearance school, but a very enterprising place. I speak the ideals of education like a parrot, knowing them to be true, but the enthusiasm is false. My whole existence is a new experience - studying psychology which I like very much and living in this street, and this great crawling slum which is the Birmingham I see.

I'm sending twenty-eight poems to the Mitre Press for their Spring Anthology 1961. They might accept a couple, seeing as they were prepared to publish a whole book last year.

Last night C [*flatmate, art student*] and I went to see a simply wonderful film - *Jazz on a Summer's Day.*

I've just been to the front room. The street is alive with prostitutes and pimps in spivvy suits, spilling out of doorways. I daren't let them catch me watching. One avoids other people's eyes. It's grim.

Friday 8 October 1960, Varna Road, Birmingham
I have been teaching all day and my voice has gone. God, a day of these kids is a week of manual work. Every minute, every second of the day saps one's mental and physical energy.

James Haggerty, the course psychologist, came round and was pleased with my teaching. And the headmaster has almost offered me a job; he's very pleased and admitted he was surprised. To me this is a terrific personal buck because only these pages can know how difficult it is to settle into any society, to be accepted - it's been hard. I have achieved what I hardly thought possible. He said I was mature, which is what I've striven so hard for, to be accepted as a person, not a student, but a human being on my own and they *have* accepted me without cutting my hair, without putting away my pointed shoes, without wearing lipstick. With all these I can teach and they have seen this. I've refused to sacrifice much of myself but I am prepared to compromise a little.

I've had a letter from R and was surprised how pleased I was to get it and how it brought back old feelings of friendship and London. And I remember happy days in Taunton - I forget the long days of boredom, frustration and utter loneliness. And I remember the old art school at Yeovil and those days of happiness. I miss London. I can't wait to get back.

Wednesday 12 October 1960, Varna Road, Birmingham
Today a visit from Anne and her husband, Dan, and a wealth of new thoughts, new feelings, for the 'old' people stimulate my mind and I become myself again - seeing them, talking to them brings the old humour back.

The junior school I'm in is very perceptive - it concentrates on the important values in life not forms and ticks on paper. It aims to develop humane human beings accustomed to oral and visual beauty before academic brilliance, which is, after all, only available to a few - but beauty is for all people, all children, a gift they have the right to unwrap but which they're rarely given.

Sunday 16 October 1960, Varna Road, Birmingham
Derek sent his address and I have just written with a new perspective. Now he is almost like an old friend and I enjoy writing to him. Yesterday we went to a Beatnik Ball at the Technical College.

Late, sitting alone in this flat with all the vice going on outside. I am crouched in front of a one-bar electric fire, reading *Wuthering Heights* again, fascinated by Heathcliff.

Thursday 17 October 1960, Varna Road, Birmingham
I've stolen this afternoon under the pretext of making a mosaic plate. I'm sitting here ill and unhappy in this chair, filled with beer to no effect, my tongue sore with nicotine, my feet throbbing with past music and a great heaviness for I remember a love I can't get rid of. It's always there, immovable, as inevitable as being alive. I have sudden impulses to put my head in the oven, anything to stop this ache. I dance, I laugh, I smoke, drink but inwardly I am desperate. I have been miserable enough to write in all honesty that I wish I were dead but now I consciously, coldly, wish that I was.

Saturday 19 October 1960, Varna Road, Birmingham
A multitude of new experiences. Yesterday C and I went to Leicester with a guitar and blues singer, Spencer Davies,[22] in a bus with a band. A great jive session in a cellar with a fabulous trio of folk singers from London. The leader, Keith Bennett, was a brilliant banjo player; they were all marvellous musicians and there was a Californian who never spoke and the girl singer was very shy and pale as if she came from a convent yet she was bumming around with these free-men quite naturally. She had a marvellous blues voice.

They played at this dance, bursting with beatniks, and Spence played solo, very good. Then we were asked back to a flat for an all-night guitar session - it was marvellous. The flat was owned by a nice man about twenty-five with a bulldog called Butch. Everyone sitting around with their guitars; we had no coffee, no fags and no drink left. At about four o'clock we went on to a mews flat and listened to jazz records.

---

[22] Spencer Davies: musician. He was studying Modern Languages at the University of Birmingham. Founded The Spencer Davies Band in 1961 and had several records in the Top Ten Charts, including: *Keep On Running* and *Gimme Some Lovin'*.

We didn't sleep all night and this morning I felt really ill. We went to the University and played the tapes from last night and then Spence came back here and played the guitar some more.

The last two days have been one long music session. The flat is invaded with nice strangers. Spence has just gone back to his room in Moseley for some sleep. He's a very good guitarist and really sweet.
Alone now. I'm filthy. Haven't washed since Friday morning. I could so do with a bath instead of a bowl of water in a cold room.

Sunday 20 October 1960, Varna Road, Birmingham
A dreary day sitting around and feeling sick listening to gay [*jolly*] people and smoking cigarettes. Now C is fucking in the other room and I'm doing some washing. I'm fed-up and drained of feelings.

Monday 21 October 1960, Varna Road, Birmingham
Went to a doctor in Balsall Heath this morning. He fiddled with my stomach and gave me some medicine. On the way a young West Indian walked along with me, arm around my shoulders and being friendly. He knows I live in Varna so probably thought I was an early bird! I didn't mind a bit and we walked together, laughing. The doctor's nurse was appalled when I told her my address.

When I left the doctor I went into a Catholic shop and collected nine leaflets - most of them absolute crap on suicide, Communism and diverse religions. Then I went into a coffee bar and bought some Philip Morris cigarettes. I felt deliciously free and place-less, timeless, without the company of even my own personality.

A lech in a car followed me along the kerb along Varna Road and gawped excitedly. I made a face at him and slammed the door.
I found C in, stealing a day like me. We've spent all day sitting - coffee, fags, reading and getting irritable. She has a romance on her hands. I can't conceive romance.
C can make her ear crack in the most revolting way.

Tuesday 22 October 1960, Varna Road, Birmingham
I will stay in again today. I ache all over and have pains in my kidneys. I feel dislocated and peculiar as though without memory or feeling. I feel without humour or seriousness yet still feel the need to write. This record can't stop and won't end as long as I'm alive.

I'm sitting here wishing Spence would come round and play his guitar. Don't say I'm resorting to platonic relationships with young men who play guitars. All my relationships are without physical contact. But the mental force of them has much more intrigue and complexity than any physical alliance.
Sitting here watching the bell system, old and made of iron, and absolutely still.
Tonight I feel like giving up the teaching course. I can't bear this place anymore or this secondary preoccupation. It's like being in an empty chasm unable even to scream.

Wednesday 23 October 1960, Varna Road, Birmingham
Tried to read Martin Buber but can't follow all of it. James Haggerty has marked my essay B+ which is good and he was pleased and I was too for I wrote fragments of my own philosophy for what it's worth. At the bottom he wrote: 'There are some of your arguments I can't follow for there is an element of mysticism which is foreign to me!'

I feel like a closed room - I have the key, intelligence, imagination, youth, feelings, emotions, longings, aspirations - there are many jewels inside this casket. But I have a memory, a knowledge of one object that isn't there. I can't find it. I remember it. I must have it. Each morning, when I wake up, I return to this room I know so well, turn things over but this object eludes me, taking on the appearance of other things. When I think I have it it's merely an illusion.

Tuesday 24 October 1960, Varna Road, Birmingham
Working today in the clayroom at Priory Road. I made a huge weird plate, a jug and a mug. Talking with Bernie and playing records in his flat. Most of the students are going to the Dodo Shuffle where the Mouldy Figs are playing. Bernie laughs with me but makes no

advances. So many people pass and go - none adhere to me, I adhere to none and my life ges on. I am gentle and kind and loving and horrid and a bitch. Or is it just a vague memory, this loving me? I know I'm considered a strange, cold girl.

Bernie did a terrific cartoon of me in his flat this evening. He is always being rude to me which I love - we insult each other for hours.

Twelve o'clock midnight - feeling depressed, place-less, segregated, ageing alone. I've concentrated till it hurts making a pot which is ridiculous and the clay is cold and I hate the feel of it on my hands, in my nails, everywhere. The pot, moreover, is a failure, an irritating shape to start with. It sits meekly in the hearth, apologising. So it should.

Friday 25 October 1960, Varna Road, Birmingham
A feeling of deadlock with people. I'm finding that people don't like me, rather they find me too peculiar to bother about. C is fucking in the other room with her new boy-friend, T, a sculptor. Rain lashing outside, cold and beautifully clean. A feeling of involuntary isolation. Spence has gone to London without me. Bernie has also gone knowing I'm dying for someone to hitch with. I want to go to bed, I can't. I want to go to London, I can't. They say I look ill. I am considered dull. I must be, except to myself and I'm pretty bored as well. I wish, I want, I need - who cares? A place to belong perhaps. The thought of a relationship makes me feel tired, sapped of the usual reflexes, like an awkward machine. How free I was four years ago. This cage. I've just been into the bedroom and they're asleep. He's staying the night - bloody hell. Now I haven't even got a bed.

Derek has written and says yes, of course, come and use the flat at weekends. So many books I must read. What am I feeling? What am I now? I'm losing track of myself. I'm no longer lost within myself. The Mitre Press are to publish In a Mirror in their new Spring Anthology - the bastards, I have to buy five copies at eight shillings and four pence each. I'm appalled at this business but I can no longer refuse. I'm disgusted with having to hoard my poems in a drawer because I have no money to allow people to read them. I will pay the two pounds but am appalled at having to do it. It's not even my best poem.

I've made friends with T, the sculptor - I like his humour. Next weekend I'm hitching down to London and will stay in Derek's flat.
A letter from Beaver, dear soul that she is. I have no loneliness now. I'm happier now than perhaps I've ever been. Certainly far happier than in any proverbial hour of love for I see no happiness in that mean intruder.
A man banging on the door, shouting incoherently. It's past midnight and C is still out. I spend pounds a week on cigarettes [*living on three pounds a week*]. I can't stop smoking. I buy at least thirty a day - a dummy for the neurotic.

Thursday 27 October 1960, Varna Road, Birmingham
What can I write? My life is one long essence of vanity. Every day people flatter me and tell me I'm beautiful. But I'm an ugly creature and not a very happy one. Tomorrow night I will be in West Kensington in Derek's flat - once more the person I really am - not hard, not beautiful, nor funny or fascinating, but a snivelling, hollow-eyed, miserable young woman in an earthly hell and there of my own accord.

Life goes on, I teach. My life otherwise is a mere undercurrent of vanity, of this beating music and seeing men smile. Tomorrow I will set my eyes on Derek again, breathe the same air, see some of his women and his paintings.

I am still in a void over religion. I have none. I joke and blaspheme seriously. I cannot believe in a life after death but the existence of a master mind beyond comprehension cannot be denied. Sometimes life seems like a terrible screaming nightmare from which I will awake and remember my identity. I sometimes have this feeling that I can remember what I am really, at another time, when I was not a human being.

Monday 31 October 1960, Varna Road, Birmingham
My whole existence is re-strung, shattered, miserable again. In a state of chronic madness because I've been there again. Stumbled down the narrow steps to the basement, dark passage ways and the smell of paint, the place empty of him but he was everywhere. Why am I nothing to him? It disproves all the laws of being, the balance of things.

Thursday 3 November 1960, Varna Road, Birmingham
Another of those blank days when I suddenly decide not to go into college. I need this day for reading, for being on my own. This is my stolen day. C and I are friendly, in a bored sort of way, and make a constant joke of our spinsterhood.

I'm reading the life of Rousseau, Oscar Wilde, A J Ayer and Plato.
So what? I get so absorbed in the past, their intense existences, for all life is one life, living being the same moment of existence in all.
I'm tired of being here, of writing essays on education, of teaching children - I want to move on, go somewhere else. I belong in basement flats - the smell, the voices, the bodies, the minds.

The whole sky has become a great dark scowl and the rain, like me, is lashing, throwing itself to the ground. Lights go on in houses and there is electric in the air. I love this weather - the bitterness, the sad brutality of winter when we humans cower in its path. The country is being laid waste by floods which have swept through main streets carrying with it shop fronts, buses, lorries and people and there are great gales and earthquakes abroad.

The D H Lawrence case is over and he has won.[23] A few people have at last decided his book is not obscene.

---

[23] In 1960 Penguin Books published the unexpurgated edition of D H Lawrence's novel *Lady Chatterley's Lover* and were taken to court charged with publishing 'obscene' literature. The trial was held at the Old Bailey, London, and the jury returned a verdict of Not Guilty - a judgement which vindicated Penguin's reputation.

I was teaching yesterday - it comes naturally. When I think that these children are unknowing and ill-conceive the person they see, who is such a mess and longs to be in London in the basements of strange people. Derek couldn't imagine me in such conventional surroundings. He thinks I'm unstable but he's odd himself. His paintings are good. He really paints and is a painter.

Saturday 5 November 1960, Varna Road, Birmingham
Reading a lot of the time.
This morning I went on a Nuclear Warfare Disarmament protest march through the city. It was organised by a group at the University. The world would disarm sensibly if there was some degree of trust. There were barely fifty people on the march. I handed out leaflets to Teddy boys and young mothers. I felt I was participating in a funeral. It was a serious affair and there was no exhibitionism. I was thankful for this and had expected the contrary and would have been embarrassed and ashamed.
I bought a super Bix Beiderbecke record and an equally superb Gerry Mulligan.

C has gone out on a bonfire crawl with Montgomery, a bright young man heading for London with an empty head, a sheltered, but broad background and rather a lot of charm.

I am glad to be alone, writing, reading, smoking. I sit and *look* at my records as I have no gramophone. I also bought Boris Pasternak's *The Last Summer* and Doris Lessing's *The Habit of Loving*.

I have heard from Roger in Oxford; and from Judy, the girl with the baby in London. Must a child have a father? I didn't have one - is this why I am as I am? My re-ignited fever of madness has burned itself out - now it's merely love, not a mad, grim, agonising obsession. Has this love, which I first felt at just sixteen, created this madness that haunts me and has become an integral part of my personality?

Late in the night and I've just read *Clea* by Lawrence Durrell. What a tremendous writer. I feel like crying at the endless tragedy of human beings devouring each other so hopelessly.

Sunday 6 November 1960, Varna Road, Birmingham
Sitting here by the fire on a Sunday afternoon, bored; outside bright dusk and the street crawling with the pathos of vice; and the smell of Sortilège on my wrists. I've just read Doris Lessing's *The Habit of Loving*. What a poignant description of the eternal malady.
C sorting through her files. The fire moans and clucks like a third person. I lose my identity in half-light.

Saturday 12 November 1960, Varna Road, Birmingham
A day on my own, thank God, in this dull, barren flat of flower prints and tiles. I've done bags of washing, read the papers and written an essay on 'The Education of The Whole Person'.

Last Tuesday, Richard Hoggart's[24] lecture, Wednesday, Humphrey Lyttelton, on Thursday, Nuclear Disarmament lecture, Friday, jazz session, and so on.

R and JPD are still living together in Redcliffe Gardens and getting ready for a Fashion Show. Gouche Street yesterday was wonderful. The prostitutes enthral me - the people, the people. I saw a beautiful West Indian, strikingly like Hal.
A University man with a wit like a gem was here on Friday night; an evening of intense humour, beyond laughter. I have captured one more heart - that of a painter, who is, needless to say, mad. Oskar Kokoschka in Bond Street.

Now the tarts are in the gateways and there's a weird sixteenth century play on the wireless.

---

[24] Richard Hoggart; writer. His book *The Uses of Literacy*, published in 1957, was a highly influential work of social commentary in the early Sixties.

Thursday 1 December 1960, Varna Road, Birmingham
A letter from Derek. I'm going to London tomorrow.
Also a letter from R who is going berserk with despair and disillusionment. JPD is on tour for three weeks - she thinks she is pregnant and wants me to give her a gin bath. I will do nothing of the sort but a child in this environment would be a crime.
I've stopped making pots.

Sunday 4 December 1960, Varna Road, Birmingham
I went to London in a car with a long, lean, bearded and pleasant young man. He had nowhere to stay so we went to the Henry Moore Exhibition at the Whitechapel and then to R's flat in Redcliffe Gardens - then on to a party at the Royal College. I saw *her* and felt sickened but said nothing. Derek wasn't there. Someone said he was moping in his flat.

Went with some College men to one of their classy homes - chicken, Chris Barber records, two dogs, antique furniture and a spotless, well-stocked kitchen with chinzty plastic seats and an Aga cooker. R flirted madly on a chinzty sofa, nibbling a piece of chicken (we were starving) between her fingers. I slept with my mac on in a huge, tall-sided chair and tried not to think. Back in Redcliffe Gardens we talked for hours about the past and JPD and people.

In the morning I went to see Derek. He was, as usual, fiddling around getting ready to go into College. He told me about her. He's almost breaking down and has stopped painting. I can't bear to see him like this. When he had gone I sat in his room, smelling of paint, of him, of five years. I looked through his paintings. He hadn't kept a single letter of mine. I was obliterated from his world. I threw his magazines around, quite calmly. I ate an apple and then left. His name will be obliterated from this journal, the last entry of him, wretched, stripped, not creating. We are controlled by the devil.

Monday *5 December 1960, Varna Road, Birmingham*
R wants me to go down on Friday and do the gin bath. Sunday afternoon in the Natural History Museum overlooking the Royal

College Common Rooms. Two lights on the top floor. R is looking fabulous but in a hell of a mess.

Tuesday 6 December 1960, Varna Road, Birmingham.
Another ATD day, trying to read Hume and Leibniz. The stone carving I was doing is thrown away because I put it in the clamp and the legs fell off and all my pots have cracked. There's a fog outside; it makes me want to cry or something. I never feel lonely anymore as though I've become resigned to solitude. I feel completely, coldly self-sufficient, not liking or hating it.

As we went through this great sprawling suburb which is Birmingham on Friday morning I saw a world of prosperous people living in hideous successful houses - the houses had rich personalities, smiling with their garages and jeering with their drives and lawns. Lives that know there is food in the larder and a greenhouse and china and some money somewhere.

As a child we had food in the larder and a clean kitchen, even a refrigerator, but we lived in a prefab and only had a small corrugated - iron shed and a bicycle and there was no man in the house; to me, a father, the man who comes in and has loose money in his pocket is a luxury, a strangely luxurious secure thing. I have never called a man father. Once, I was curious about this man and looked for photographs or evidence of him when my mother was out. I felt an overwhelming loss of this man in whose face I would never look.

Wednesday 8 December 1960, Varna Road, Birmingham
This morning I bought several books which I will treasure. *The Life of Oscar Wilde*, Rousseau's *Confessions*, Faber's *Modern Verse*, T S Eliot, *Selected Prose*, Arnold Wesker's *Jerusalem* and for one and six the memoirs of an old colonial bod.

Friday 10 December 1960, Varna Road, Birmingham
Stolen a gramophone for the weekend. I'm going to buy a mouse in Somerset. I've made a food and drinking bowl for him and he will be called David. I couldn't get down to London this weekend as no one

was going. But Bernie, the bugger, slunk off slyly, terrified I would force him to take me with him. I will take my mouse everywhere.

It's snowing now, quite thickly and the tarts look smashing, parading jauntily under their coloured umbrellas against the cold.
Snow and frost bring a deep nostalgia and a hatred of other memories of snow, of childhood winters and Christmas, which I hate, making me shiver. I don't quite know why.

Reading Rousseau's *Confessions*. I don't know why I started my own journal all that time ago. It was certainly without any attempt at imitation for I had never read any journal nor did I know such things existed. I believe that Delacroix's *Journal* was the first I ever read.
I can't bear reading in libraries - I prefer to take my small portion away to an empty corner to chew, like a hound. C is out. I have Mugsy Spanier and Big Bill Broonzy for company.

Saturday 11 December 1960, Varna Road, Birmingham
Late now and I've been drinking a lot of beer in Nuneaton with T and C and a typical North Country chap with a huge heart and humour, who has a typical family whom he loves - they live in a row of terraced houses with pottery wall brackets and lace mats and an outside bog. How I delight in these people. It's the middle classes I loathe. These and artists are the people I care about.

Back in the flat and C and T are in there now. I've had enough of sleeping with fucking couples. I'm giving them two hours. When I see them together, in love, as indeed they are, I feel I'm seeing it for the first time. I have forgotten people fall in love, care about each other and things like that. I seem to have lived in a bitter sadistic nightmare for the last four years.

Again, driving through the bourgeois suburbs of Birmingham, curled up in a rug in the back with two people in love in the front, I saw these houses with cars in the garages and lights in the hallways and I felt a great longing to belong to a family. Yet, in all honesty, such a prospect

would be deplorable and nothing would depress or revolt me more. It's just at night when I feel restless, lonely and having no place in this great expanse of earth where I can rest.
My own home depressed me, so small and temporary, like a Nissen hut and there was no place to hide, no warm corner, just a square prefabricated box with a tin roof.

I was thinking of Roger on the way back and of how I would like to see him and talk to him again. I'm almost in love with his mind. I saw a beautiful man, aged about twenty-three, in the shop this afternoon, all smiling and perky and fabulously handsome. Seeing so many of these Jamaicans I see over and over again a striking resemblance to Hal and go weak at the knees.

The weather is still very cold. I fear I shall have to conform and wear black stockings this winter - I shall look like a bloody beatnik or first-year art student. I can remember when it was thought outrageous, when we were students at Yeovil, to wear coloured stockings. We used to buy old ladies' beige lyle ones from Denners and dye them in bowls in the common room. We used to dye everything. Once we dyed a pair of Derek's brand new Y fronts bright pink and he got really annoyed. Now every other bloody typist wears them and the same with short skirts. But last year that witch at the bus station café in Taunton threw me out because my skirt was too short!

Sunday 11 December 1960, Varna Road, Birmingham
C and T off for the day cutting holly. I've cleaned the flat, scrubbed the kitchen clean - the place was filthy.

Late now and this evening the flat was full of people. I won't go to Somerset until Wednesday so I can go to the party on Tuesday night. But I have no money - I've sold my ticket and can't afford another one. It will be a social flop for me, a pointless drifting time, but I love to jive, go mad, drink, smoke.

*

YEOVIL

Wednesday 14 December 1960, Yeovil
I feel a different person since I've been in Birmingham. In a small room looking through my other books of writing, begun in December 1958, barely two years ago. Before, I loved my journals, now I hate them. They are nothing and I can't bear to read them. I was sick and I hate myself as I was, but they helped me - words were a necessary oil to my thinking, no longer so necessary. All this morbid self-obsession. Much as I was impressed by Barbellion's *Journal* when I read it, ages ago it seems, I felt moments of exasperation at his morbid self-revelations in that they revealed an inconclusive theme. It's an underwater occupation and I feel I have surfaced just a little.

Saturday 17 December 1960, Yeovil
A letter from Anne and a note from Josh Kirby. A sentimental letter from Brian.
A dreary, foggy day, everything so quiet and one never sees a coloured person. It would seem pretentious to say that I miss them but I do. One thing I can't understand, why the beauty of coloured people isn't recognised by the majority of Europeans. Still bourgeois minds consider the black races somehow unrefined and less worthy than the white. Racial prejudice makes me sick.

On a train to Exmouth and being watched by two men so that I could scream. I can't stand the sort of lustful looking that goes on and on. One in each corner - one, a sailor, the other, a workman. The train is late, hanging about in cold smelly stations. A hideous bourgeois wedding group on the station - an embarrassed, excited couple.
We passed near Rampisham with all its wonderful memories. The train rolls like a ship as do the workman's eyes while the sailor sleeps. It will be dark when I get to Exmouth.

Late in the night now and I'm sitting on a chaise-longue before a good fire with twenty fags and some fruit to eat and hearing the noises of Anne and Dan getting ready for bed. This is a fabulous flat; five large, high rooms, barely furnished and the smell of paint and smoke. They're happy but I don't feel an outsider. They've given me Dom Moraes's poems which I shall read tonight.

Sunday 18 December 1960, Exmouth

We walked along the sea shore collecting long shells with exquisite colours but I hate shells in houses. One should always put them back amongst the other millions, equally beautiful, untouched, yet to be discovered. For even in a box or on a tray they are just things, other people's discoveries. The beauty of shells is finding them.
And this town is full of people who stuffily walk the sea in cars and fur collars, having no pleasure.

Monday 19 December 1960, Exmouth

A day of cooking and eating and smoking and drinking and laughing.
More Royal College stories passed down by Terry Murphy. About John Minton[25], who was a fabulous character, mad, miserable, sponged on by many of his associates - always gushing and taking his queenies on pub crawls in a taxi. Drinking all day in the Hoop and Toy and when Murphy paid him back some money he'd borrowed he broke down and cried. The great parties he would give, spending £500 on drink. Some people are such parasites and despicable.

And of John Bratby, who lived with the Bateses; they often saved him from starving. And Peter Blake[26], who only did about three paintings a

---

[25] John Minton [1917-57]: painter. An eccentric and colourful character. Worked in fairly traditional style; though an outspoken critic, he was a well-liked and inspirational teacher. Part-time tutor, Painting School at the Royal College of Art 1951-5. Recurrent bouts of severe depression and alcoholic excess led to an early death.

[26] Peter Blake: painter. Studied at the Royal College of Art 1953 -56. A familiar figure, usually associated, rightly or wrongly, with the early British Pop Art movement, whose highly detailed paintings of music hall acts, wrestlers, etc., are instantly recognisable. In 1967, in collaboration with Jann Haworth, he produced the photo-montage for the cover of the Beatles'

year, in fantastic, intricate detail, every stone, every vein and spot on the model, the writing on the Woodbine packet in the gutter. His paintings were of the gawdy floor shows he used to go to in the evenings and some of them had real sequins stuck on to the canvas. He was always getting travelling scholarships. Terry Murphy modelling Ivy League suits and working in films as an extra and the old pub in Hammersmith where Ruskin Spear[27] can always be found with his friend, the butcher.

Sometimes I really long to be at the College but at other times the pace and the illusion of it all, the temporary glitter, makes me tired. The incidental colours in this room are marvellous - a brilliant check cloth, a mauve chair, celery sticks in a blue and white jug, deep blue-green curtains, burning chrysanthemums, oranges, apples, grapes and wine bottles.

I'm reading a grave book on hanging by Arthur Koestler[28] which makes one realise we're a brutal, barbaric race hiding under a self-righteous cloak of justice and goodwill - like hypocrites shading our evil eyes against our supposed barbaric fellows who live on the rest of the globe. Our past is atrocious and future atrocity is assured as long as people like Goddard make the rules.

Wednesday 21 December 1960, Yeovil

Watching a film about a group of missionaries in Africa, I see in them a love of humanity which I so often feel yet without the bridle of religion. So much I see affects me, strikes me speechless with compassion, indignation or despair. Is teaching my limit, my end? I

Sergeant Pepper Album. At 51, Retrospective at the Tate Gallery. Associate Artist at the National Gallery in 1994.

[27] Ruskin Spear [1911-90]: painter of the Euston Road School of Painting. Tutor at the Royal College of Art, 1948-76.

[28] *Hanged By The Neck*: by Arthur Koestler & C.H.Rolph. Penguin Books. Sequel to Koestler's book, *Reflections on Hanging*, published in 1956.

want to be a good writer, wife, mother, person but the future is bleak. I want an incentive, a basis, an axis. I wrote my first book in pencil in school exercise books, some 67,000 words, called *Suspected Vendetta.* It was appalling in many respects for I knew nothing about horse doping but at least I planned and completed it and even sent it to a publisher. I was fourteen when I started it and fifteen when I sent it off.

Beaver came over with a message from Roger to phone him. She seems like a stranger - clean and well-dressed. She has a marvellous sense of humour. Christ, none of the humour that is such an integral part of my existence ever creeps into this journal. I would seem a dismal creature but this is not so. True, I have a rather dismal expression but I laugh a great deal. We laugh at the stupidity of people, especially those who are pretentious. And we laugh at our own pretensions more than anybody's. We love to put each other in situations that would be appallingly embarrassing for other people. No holds are barred. We ridicule and loathe royalty; we're classless and critical of everyone. We hate snobbery, injustice, superficiality and bourgeois complacency.

Thursday 22 December 1960, Yeovil

A dull day in which I bought some wool and Durrell's *Mountolive*. It's late now and my mother is having a minor crying fit, getting worked up and neurotic about the place being untidy.

As the days go by I realise how much I thought of Hal and even loved him in a small degree compared to the love I had for Derek. I'm remembering our short affair, its independance and its happiness. Then we just didn't get together any more and it was finished. I feel no guilt whatsoever. As long as I'm sincere and happy I don't worry. It's my mind that's harmed when it's fooled. Seduction of my mind is this virgin's horror. To be intellectually hoodwinked is my shame. I suspect that Hal was insincere but we had some laughs and it was good, short, enclosed and clean without strings. It's only that sometimes I see a face like his, or a mannerism and I realise just how much I absorbed of him and how much I cared for him. I can see now too that my love for Derek was merely a mis-conceived alliance, a love that was misplaced. When I heard him say he was in love with her I finally lost all hope.

Yet even now, in my heart I still find it somehow inconceivable that he should love a woman other than me, the girl he walked with in the lime fields of Basingstoke all that time ago, long before London began.

Friday 23 December 1960, Yeovil
I'm knitting a sweater which wastes precious time and annoys me intensely. JPD and R came over and we went to the pub; he'd been to Rampisham and had the door slammed in his face. We sat, three socially misplaced persons, repeating old jokes into our beer.

This afternoon was hideous. The town was full of foul young boys, full of beer and trying to be blasé like men. Familiar faces getting older like a nightmare. I hate homes and families and home towns. I want to be in London or Birmingham where I am cut off. The whole business of Christmas is intolerable. This great hatred of people weighs on me for it's not really my nature to hate - sometimes I'm overwhelmed with compassion.

Reading Dom Moraes I realise he uses rhyme throughout. He must have had money to get the first lot published. Perhaps it's just as well I didn't get my book because my poems aren't mature yet. 'In A Mirror' is not the best of them; some of the lines are weak, unfulfilled, superfluous. I'm sorry they chose to publish that one but having no reputation to break it doesn't really matter.
T S Eliot is a beautiful writer.

Saturday 24 December 1960, Yeovil
I sit, an unbeliever at midnight playing jazz records that make me think of other days. My mother is at church, my brother out drinking somewhere with his friends. Out of duty I need not feel I pass Christmas here, reluctantly. Even my gramophone won't work properly. I wonder what Derek is doing, alone in his basement flat. I wish I was there. I would like to see Roger, not twenty miles away, but it might just as well be a thousand. I really hate Christmas.

A programme on the Holy Land and I felt an urgent desire to go there, to the place where I was born, to the place where the man that made me is buried. Where my father is a skeleton under a Service mound of earth with a number, near a hedge. There used to be a photograph of it in the bedroom cupboard under a pile of old papers and when the house was empty I'd bring it out and look at it. There was a time when I'd search for any photographs, letters or any reference to him but there's very little and my mother never mentions him.

A day of tension; three people - for one it's a religious affair. A young man, misplaced in his work for which he has no enthusiasm - and me, ill at ease, filled with my own problems. I won't spend another Christmas here. I don't paint any more. I was never a painter. This awful midnight silence. Records that remind me of parties, of times past, so that I could scream.
Two o'clock, no drinks, no people, nothing. An everlasting nothingness.

Sunday 25 December 1960, Yeovil
We are a wretched trio. Harbouring my own problems I can't apply my mind sympathetically to my mother's situation. Losing her husband after only four years, when he was twenty-eight, times of danger during the war, journeys of evacuation in the Middle East, stranded in Africa with two young children, always working and struggling for money - she's done very well, in fact, but if she came in now and disturbed me I should be rude. Had I been the victim of so much misfortune I would have moaned continually and written thirty volumes about it - well, *wouldn't* I?

Wednesday 28 December 1960, Yeovil
A whole day spent copying out a file of psychology notes. I rang Roger and he gallantly paid for the call.
A few days and I'll be in Birmingham again. I'm going to ask Bernie to start hitching round the world with me. He may well come but he's a slippery fish. He will come forward and be friendly and then dart off as though he's angry. Perhaps he's very shy. He interests me because he doesn't behave in the usual way. Next term I will investigate.

Thursday 29 December 1960, Yeovil
Still reading Rousseau's *Confessions*, little by little at night when I should be sleeping.
Roger came over today and I was glad. He hates the school atmosphere of Oxford and finds the work lacking in real interest. I must get down to see him next term. I believe he still loves me but it doesn't obsess him as it did and I'm glad - but I should hate him to stop caring.

I have become so hardened and used to hiding my feelings that they are now deeply buried. I certainly can't imagine myself in a love affair - I just don't see how it could come about. I really care for Roger, which isn't surprising for we were together constantly for a whole year. We went everywhere together, we sat for hours, countless hours in pubs over half a pint and ten fags for we were very poor. The last few months were very tense and we both got ratty and uneasy.

How distorted things become when we care about someone. Our eyes deceive, our ears believe the most appalling and pitiful lies and nothing is as it is. Love is a form of madness, the most harsh of all masters, the cruellest of all disorders, and yet most of our songs call it a joyous thing.

I was fascinated by the relationship between Rousseau and Madame de Warens. Again, in Rousseau, his physical weakness, or rather his hypochondria, like Barbellion and to an extent, Delacroix and Cézanne. All journal writers are essentially egocentric and therefore care excessively for the state of their health.
I started writing a journal as an instrument for developing a philosophy and this I don't object to for it's constructive but later I became preoccupied with emotion, not philosophy, and the journal has deteriorated. But it's essential that I write it.

I was obliged to give back to Roger three stolen books, much to my annoyance. Two of them I had begun to consider my own property to the extent of writing my name in them but he was adamant.

Friday 30 December 1960, Yeovil

My natural responses are, as it were, to past stimuli and without them my personality hasn't full rein, as though I've learned a role I no longer need to play and there's a void and no other part forthcoming.

I remember the time, recorded here in the journal last year when I was in lodgings with Mrs S, a witchlike creature with no husband, no money and a backward daughter. I almost had a nervous breakdown. I lay in terror at night, staring at spirits jumping on my pillow. In darkness my spirit seems to have no binding to my body, it becomes a real spirit, set loose, fantastic and with a terrible vulnerability as though it has no armour, no shell, no eyes to cover, no hands to ward off things, no legs to run and above all, no voice, suspended without the anchorage of reason. The void is beyond description.

I have some black leather boots with heels and pointed toes which I refuse to take off.

As I read Rousseau's *Confessions* I'm reminded of JPD, the sensual wanderer without profession, just a huge lust for being alive.

I'm reading journals because I'm writing one, not the other way round. But it's a disjointed journey. It hasn't the flow of recorded memory and contains much that is irrelevant but it is a living proof. But to whom do I feel this need to prove myself? Besides which no person may ever read a word of it. I'm writing to prove I'm alive, that I was alive and in doing so I am like the man who wrote, 'I am alive, I feel sick, the year is 1404.' Life is continuous. And being mortal I must believe I shall always be alive. Show me Rousseau's grave; but he is still alive for I'm *reading* his living and he's alive to me.

It will be 1961 on Monday. Tomorrow night I shall be miserable and fed-up with everything because I won't be at a party, like a caged animal.

Sunday 31 December 1960, Yeovil

I'm wearing a black lace garment like one of those seventeenth-century things, laced up tight so the figure is delicious and the bust high. All my undercothes are black lace. I want to be alive again when the clothes were fabulous and intriguing.

In the town hideous people with eyes that are dull, like old hens.
Brian came to take me to a jazz club but I just couldn't go; a room full of familiar faces.
I have a frenzied admiration for Big Bill Broonzy. At his recent concert the whole audience was deadly quiet and enthralled by his artistry, warmth and humour. I wish I'd seen him.

I still have horrible scars on my fingers from last summer. I loved those underground people; I even liked the sheer drudgery of the work. Those chambermaids, plain, unmarried women, with their complaining, their chips and resentments, their peculiarities, their Irish tongue, their laughter, wonderful, pathetic people. I wrote to them but they didn't answer. And wonderful Jack, 'Jacqueline', his one desire to be a lady. The way he danced and flirted with the waiters - I loved him. And Tommy, the dancer, his friend and mine. I just hope he's left that place and gone on tour, happy at last.
I'm going to be writing as 1961 begins. It begins in seven minutes.

*

BIRMINGHAM

Tuesday 2 January 1961, Varna Road, Birmingham
Yesterday I came back to Birmingham and was glad - back to Varna Road and the squalour my eyes saw again with pleasure. This morning an essay lasting two hours but I left out many points and digressed sadly from the main one.

Later, in a lecture, Rousseau was mentioned and I felt they spoke of a dear friend. As I read of his handing over his five children to the State I was disappointed and felt an infinite sympathy for Thérèse for no woman would do that without obligation.
Again, a man of high intelligence and sensitivity coupling with an ignorant woman. Perhaps there's hope for me yet?

I've looked round but I don't see Bernie here today. The bugger is rarely in attendance. Probably prostrate in one of those basements in Earls Court. He may even be dead. Even so, he might at least come in on the first day back.

Wednesday 3 January 1961, Varna Road, Birmingham
Another boring day at college. An eternal seminar on co-education in secondary schools. I haven't said one word in seminars and only one sentence spoken under force during a tutorial. There's nothing to say that isn't obvious and it'll be said by someone else anyway. I start teaching in a girls' secondary school next week. People talking, cups of tea, timetables and note-books, that's the life here. Someone playing a clarinet rather badly, two playing chess, a few working; an institution with a task - to release teachers. I long for the end of all this though I don't loathe it here. I just feel vaguely misplaced and long to get it over with and be - be what? A teacher, endless school atmosphere, I can't bear it.

Last night C going to pieces. And though I remembered all the misery of love gone wrong while she was sobbing I was cynical and did nothing to comfort her for there is none. I grit my teeth and carried on reading, as though the sound of crying was an abstraction. No tears in my eyes.

The constant stream of jokes referring to the *Lady Chatterley* case makes me sick. People behave like children with curious, obscene, starved minds.

Sunday 7 January 1961, Varna Road, Birmingham
All the students are bored and beginning to hate the idea of teaching. I can't wait to get out of this flat. All week I've tried to get on with some craft work but I haven't the smallest atom of enthusiasm. I watch the others making endless things, creating all the time and I feel desperate but visual art is not my vocation. I'm the youngest on the course by many months and will be qualified, if I qualify, at twenty.

Bernie still hasn't rejoined the course and the guy who shares his flat thinks he may be in America or something as he said he wanted to go at the end of last term. I have never come across such a self-sufficient man. His control and self-reserve is incredible and his humour is wonderful. From what I know of him I think he's a really good character and above all, mature, without pretensions and prejudices - and he's not an exhibitionist. Such men are rare and seemingly unapproachable after a certain point. We laugh together quite a bit and our personalities seem to click in a peculiar way but as soon as I feel I am beginning to know him better he's off like a flash and seems nervous and wary.

C has gone out looking for friends to drag back but hasn't returned and I'm glad as I'm still reading the *Confessions*.

Dr George Burroughs,[29] the husband of the only woman tutor, wants to take some photographs of me. He thinks I'm a beatnik but all such terms are ridiculous. They are supposedly naturalists, free-thinkers, living outside social convention but the term is used to describe any person with long hair, rather dirty and in any way individualistic. Type-casting of any sort is ridiculous. I looked rather beautiful tonight. If only my personality were half so attractive I would have so many friends instead of men who whistle and gape and stare.

Some of the students here find our humour peculiar. It entails the blank face, the offended look, the double-take, the rudeness and the irrelevant obscure conversation. C and I are extremely rude to each other. A filthy rag in the gutter and she'll beg me not to leave my coat in the street. Or I'll say, 'It's a pity you've got such appalling acne, it merely

---

[29] Dr George Burroughs, PhD, BSc. Senior Lecturer, 1961: Professor of Education, University of Birmingham, 1965-76. He and his wife, Lucy, who became Head of the University's Art Teachers' Diploma Course, were widely travelled and in the course of his University career, Prof Burroughs worked in a number of countries, including India, Pakistan and Venezuela.

emphasises your overall plainness'. We like the sick jokes coming over from the States:

'Mummy, mummy, I don't like my little sister.'
'Well, just put her to the side of the plate and eat something else.'

There are dozens of these jokes and some are really cruel, the nastier the better. JPD knows all of them. This is an age of tension, of pills and neurosis, of fast living and money has become a god - not mine, personally, but the world in general. Of verbal wars between dangerous men, of vast scientific discovery. It's an era of growing equality but through money, nothing more. It's appalling and fast moving - no wonder our humour is cruel and sick. Men are self-consciously laughing at themselves while they rush around after money and power.
I wish Bernie would come back. He makes me laugh.

Monday 8 January 1961, Varna Road, Birmingham
We went to a party in a rich house, luxuriously furnished and centrally heated and the place and the people dripped of money. We were definitely out of place and it was made obvious and of course we danced like mad things and didn't help matters with our behaviour. Hideous girls in expensive but awful clothes and pompous young men with slick hair and conspicuous suits who just couldn't dance - they have no blood, no rhythm, no humour, only money in their pockets and a limited, narrow experience of life.

We've been asked to leave the flat by the weekend. They don't think we're old enough to live by ourselves! How sweet. It's dark outside and I have no idea of the time; it's a peculiar feeling, like the loss of a sense like sight or hearing.

Perhaps Rousseau is right when he says that women in general are incapable of abstract thought. Women think in progression, by derivation. Are there any brilliant female abstract painters?

Tuesday 9 January 1961, Varna Road, Birmingham
Last night a very good party at the college, jiving all the time, everyone as drunk as kings and in fine humour. Today the Committee was told 'no more parties'. We've sat in the flat most of the evening, miserable and utterly depressed.

Friday 12 January 1961, Varna Road, Birmingham
And so the teaching course goes on with dull education books and far worse, the schools themselves - musty, old, dull and altogether nauseating. Old ladies with beards still teaching, all brogues and dropped busts. Most of them are senile and silly and completely unsuitable as educators. They don't educate, they curb and tentatively push in the wrong places. But this is not a book on education.

Last night a session in one of the student's flats. A really interesting chap, good-looking like a fictional Christ but quite short. He has a beautiful room with an Indian atmosphere [*in his parents' house; they were missionaries*]. We listened to Indian music and Dylan Thomas reading Auden and a record of T S Eliot reading his poems and Monty, the fool, recording idiotic but amusing monologues.

Then a 'beatnik' started reading his crappy poetry under a spot-lamp and we were intensely bored but unable to stop him, even with yawns and rude remarks. He just would *not* stop, the idiot, using every gimmick and nonsense he could.
We have to be out of here by the weekend and have nowhere to go.

Yesterday I left the school in horror and dashed into a pub next door for half a pint and a cigarette and old folk sat with their Guinnesses and prattled on about socialism, betting and other people, speaking angrily and yet pathetically, about rich folk.

I've cleaned out this filthy place again and am sick of doing it. I remember clearing out filth from other flats with as little thanks.

Sunday 14 January 1961, Varna Road, Birmingham

A stolen day and I've worked very hard. Done a great pile of washing - no small task when each kettle of water has to be boiled. I've cooked and cleaned, read an education book and done the shopping. Alone, I'm compelled to work but with someone here I sit and talk and am idle. My skin, other than on my face and neck, was engrimed with dirt. The whole place is dirty.

No poems incubating.

Tuesday 16 January 1961, Varna Road, Birmingham

Six-thirty in the morning. I have to go miles to a bloody school and I'm dreading it. I could easily watch the clock tick on without moving. But I must seek the pompous smells of schools and live through a day of total incongruity.

At least the day can last only so long.

Thursday 18 January 1961, Varna Road, Birmingham

Teaching today in a school for deaf children was an experience worth having. The terribleness, the pathos of the nature of human beings. I feel surrounded by infirmity. It's not *me* that teaches, goes through all the motions. And I'm losing myself; I'm becoming the person I hear speaking with my voice in another language. I don't want to work out a project to educate these unfortunate creatures. I want to sit and mourn their misfortune, wonder at the terribleness of their situation and feel for them. I don't want to record systems and procedures and devise methods. I want to watch and feel and keep silent if I wish.

We have to be out by Sunday. Last night we went from place to place knocking on doors but only Indians answered who didn't know what we wanted.

Bernie is applying for jobs in America.

Monday 22 January 1961, Handsworth, Birmingham

Installed in a room the other side of Birmingham, lodging for a month in the house of the missionary couple whose son looks like Christ and goes to the Art College. They've been so kind to us and the rent is only one guinea a week.

C is already off with the fellow upstairs. There are several students somewhere in the house. I've heard them talking loudly since they found out there were two girls in the house.

I feel tired and ill tonight and glad to be here on my own. I feel I'm going mad, my brain hammers in my head. I'm empty now of poems, of writing, except philosophical essays on education, on which my heart barely rests. My heart, my soul is never touched except when I think of him.
But if I begin to sadden I can divert my thoughts quite easily, like turning over a page, with regret but no nearer to crying tears as I am to being the cause of any. I sometimes wonder if Derek's heart is mending now after this its second break. I hope so.

Wednesday 24 January 1961, Handsworth, Birmingham
It's good, living in this house; beautiful rooms, with a couple of interesting men and fags and books and music.
Will I ever have a room of my own? But I'm not sure I want a resting place. At times the idea is as dreadful as that of not having one.

Tuesday 30 January 1961, Handsworth, Birmingham
In college now and just out of a session of essay reading which I hate. I was told my writing was difficult to follow but when each sentence is read several times it can be rewarding. To me, my written thoughts are condensed and logical and quite within an average intelligence to follow.

Living in this house is wonderful. On Friday night we played records and talked of ghosts until four o'clock.

On Saturday night we saw a Charlie Chaplin film and then decided to gate-crash a University hop. We ran like maniacs through the city and then combed the university building for an opening but the place was barred like a prison and it drove us wild to hear the music inside.
We tried to talk our way in with the stewards but were refused. We tried all the windows. Finally a student opened some windows high above some dustbins. We were through like dogs, covered with dustbin

rubbish and laughing our heads off. As I landed I saw a room full of people; it was the bar and they hissed and cat-called and jeered but we rushed on.

We had to have a conference in the bog because there were still more barriers to get through. We stole pass-out tickets and C got through but we were left. The others scoured the dance floor and eventually dropped tickets down to us, and then we were all in and jived until midnight. We were dirty and those idiots gaped and nudged and were incredulous and we loved it.
We jived until the sweat dripped off us and then Ty and I hitched back.

How can I describe the pleasure of this house with its crowded elegant rooms filled with Indian objects and the smell of them? The bare staircases and the noise of people?
Last evening we sat in darkness by the fire, talking. And then we went for a walk in the howling gale and came back to talk with the young man from upstairs until three this morning. There is such freedom of interest, humour and movement. And so we argue and the house smells of India. All is alive again.
Ty and I talked a lot as we were walking. He's going to the Royal College for an interview today.

Friday 3 February 1961, Handsworth, Birmingham
I set off early this morning for the School for Deaf Children but lost my way, I can't think why. I completely lost my bearings and waited at the wrong bus stop for nearly half an hour. I stood, drenched to the skin, in a doorway of a factory, factories all around and strange buses and dirt and rain and everything was grey and dismal and cold. I felt ill and suddenly saw a car not two feet away and the driver was shaking his fist and yelling. My lungs hurt and I couldn't think clearly.

The whole pattern of the day changed. I walked into the basements of shops and bought beads and two cups and a saucer I can't afford. I wandered about feeling ill for nearly three hours, hardly aware of my surroundings, like a leaf carried along by circumstances, offering no resistence. I am a living leaf, curled up inside itself and at the moment feeling ill, and alone and tormented.

I miss Balsall Heath and the coloured people and the shuffling humanity. All is tightened whiteness here, without colour and no extremes. I would like to move back into a coloured quarter, purely coloured, not bitterly flavoured with whiteness and mixed with vice.

No writing, no poems. I feel so colourless, so supercilious, so surfaced, so empty. I know I'll never write another book, which is probably just as well. So dead, so feeble, so surfaced, so incapable, now, of realising stolen hours.

Saturday 4 February 1961, Handsworth, Birmingham
Last night talking again until one-thirty.
Reading Van Gogh's *Letters.* If only one person would think of me as I have thought on these men that are dead. Just one, for one moment, would suffice this craving for posterity which is in all of us, which is mortal, by which we conceive immortality.

After making a strange and grotesque pot in college I went quietly insane in the basement of a huge store and bought seven cups for sixpence each. I long to buy saucepans and bowls and wooden spoons.

Friday 10 February 1961, Greenfield Crescent, Birmingham
We've managed to secure this grim, damp room for a while. It's filthy and the whole house has a wretched gloom of filth and it stinks. The place is just for women tenants and is run by an old womanish-janitor.
We moved with regret, loathe to leave a place so pleasant, so clean and some interesting people - now this loathesome den.

This endless moving, these bleak lodging rooms, these Balzac lodging houses - the worry over money, the business of keeping clean and getting enough to eat, all this, and the endless search for friends. Yet despite all this frustration, work and worry, a hopeless and sadistic humour. I see nothing in the future.

Rows again about going out. I can't afford to go out. C paces the room as if caged. The outside has for me little attraction lately. It's true I want to go out and jive all night but I hate being asked to dance by spotty young men or fat ones or hideous ones, all this man and woman superficiality, this fluttering of eyelashes, this small conversation, I detest it. I like only to be with people I know for dancing. I have no friends in Birmingham, not real ones. I have a few acquaintances through a certain brand of humour, that's all. The men here hear wedding bells if a girl asks them round for an evening of records and talking. Their minds are about three-quarters of an inch wide. They're like small boys, a trifle lost and muddled, ill at ease and on guard, being away from home and security.

Or is it that I overestimate my desirability? I'm certainly not in great demand. I'm not listed as an eligible young girl and typed as odd. Perhaps I'm still too steeped in adolescence to interpret my actions, my thoughts, my true aspirations. And so the years go by and what am I? I'm nothing.

Sunday 12 February 1961, Greenfield Crescent, Birmingham
This place is very dirty, the filth engrimed in the paintwork and the net curtains were filthy rags breathing dirt. The air is breathless but filth impregnated but now we have our pictures stuck on the walls, our coloured blankets, my clock and cups and we have cleaned the place it isn't so bad. At least it's large, big enough to walk across.

Now we sit, tired, waiting for the shilling's worth of gas to work out with none for the morning and no food. Once I get my books up here I'll feel more settled. At present I'm in pieces.

Thursday 16 February 1961, Greenfield Crescent, Birmingham
I've been working all evening on teaching records which I don't like. Haggerty told me he liked reading my essays and I'm glad because I respect him and suspect he has a good brain.

I stick up pictures, line shelves, as if this filthy flat is mine. C doesn't seem to take much interest. I'm too much of an egocentric to quarrel

with that. My side of the room has nearly the glory of my old room, cut out pictures that mean something to me, colours, shapes, things. Without them I dissolve - they bring me together. I need them, as wheat needs sun yet I have a great wariness and loathing for possessions.
I would like to have nothing, no possessions whatsoever, to stand without them.

This dreadful light makes my eyes run and screw up. I'm beside myself these days - I haven't dug deep into my flesh lately. There's no friction inside me. No excess, there's a level, yet it isn't experienced, it's not positive enough for that. It's just an existent non-recordative state.

Sunday 5 March 1961, Church Road, Moseley, Birmingham
In yet another flat, a very good one, with hideous bourgeois wallpaper, four in all. But it's at the top of a strange 'Jacques Tati' house with a winding fire-escape at the front which all the tenants use to get in and out. The door to each floor leads off this staircase, unpainted and rusty. The doors are always left open and people say that in winter snow blows in but still nobody shuts them. The landings are used as drying yards and the street is a long way down.

The landlord of this house is a true Steinbeck character. His clothes are really old and he never wears a jacket, but a trilby hat always on his head, and he eats all the time, and has a dachshund and never sleeps - he sells coal, milk, spuds, televisions, cars, wirelesses, orange drinks and all this junk is kept in an old garage in which he lives. The yard at the back is filled with junk and infested with rats, scampering in amongst the overflowing dustbins with no lids.

This flat has a televison and a wireless! It's so rude, *obscene*, to have a television. We wanted to live here since we first saw the house from the road in November.

Last week I was teaching full-time. The human being in me kicks. I don't know where or what I am. I'm hiding in a teacher's world. I have nothing to write because although I'm alone I've exhausted my revelations of solitude, so limited have they become.

Monday 13 March 1961, Moseley, Birmingham
I came out of the lecture room to find Roger standing there. He stayed here last night and again the tumult of role reversal when we're together but I can do nothing. He went without saying goodbye.

There was a party on Saturday - it became a mad-house, great swarms of people, all drunken and laughing - not me, for a change. I was with J. He's about six foot three and looks Malayan but is in fact West Indian, very handsome, very quiet, with beautiful hands. There's a strangeness, an excitement about him. At first I thought him beautiful but dull but last night we went to the Tokyo 61 Club with Monty and C and then into the country in pubs and lanes and graveyards and Monty made up crazy verses all the way back.

And in his house last night we talked, we three strangers. As J and I sat in the car talking afterwards, I have never talked with such honesty with any man yet he's a stranger. He's a pure existentialist. He deplores marriage; he has a calm dignity and something that is pure. For him, experiences are only parts to be discontinued. He sees marriage as a vain attempt to prolong a few moments of ecstasy. My own personality is entirely opposed to this yet there was nothing that angered me in his thinking because it was so logical.

Tuesday 22 March 1961, Moseley, Birmingham
On Saturday I bought a Windsor chair for ten shillings.
Yesterday I wrote part of a poem about my father's grave. I teach. I sat talking to J again yesterday. There is a part of me that could love him. It's intangible, but it's there.

Thursday 24 March 1961, Moseley, Birmingham
Last night we vamped our way into a party at Priory Road and we livened it up a bit.

And so it goes on, this life, a constant suppression, adaptation, an everlasting fight for balance, for reason. I finish teaching tomorrow at noon for two weeks. Short release to the rest of me.

Monday 28 March 1961, Moseley, Birmingham
I've been typing out my notes all this week. I love to have something to do, cut and dried and in order. Filed and readable. This book is my exception.

We've been so broke we've gone without food, two days eating potatoes neat, no fags; at the moment I've just poured boiling water over tea leaves used three times already. We've been on raw cabbage and spuds for a week. I'm going home on Saturday, hitching down. Can't afford to march again this year. It's terrible without cigarettes. I've already borrowed £10 from next term's grant [*total grant was £30 a term*].

I've been getting letters from JPD who is earning money. R has a fine flat near the Coleherne [*a well-known gay pub in Earls Court, a few yards from the Troubadour*]. I will join her in May. I don't want to leave the kids in the Deaf School but I've pined for London so long.

Peter Ustinov on television [*talking about the death penalty which was still in existence until 1968*]: 'I don't see how we can presume to destroy what we can't create - we give a man the worst three days possible of being alive - death is incomprehensible - it is life we give him, life of the most terrible calibre. We don't allow him to take his own life, therefore death is not the punishment, but life.' He said it briefly, with brilliance. Another man hanged this morning, another will be next week. It's obscene.

I am in an erratic calm. I don't know where I'm going and I don't really care. I have great faith in my strength because I saw it built, bit by bit.

Friday 3 April 1961, Yeovil
Tonight I watched a programme on the appalling conditions in the Congo. It was terrible. I felt like rushing over to help those fantastic people working there. The beautiful children, so very beautiful. I just happen to write this about a renewed revelation on human beauty and suffering because I had this book and pen near me. A thousand such

turmoils of rage and remorse and fire pass through me in the course of being alive one week.
I miss Birmingham and the flat. I hitched down to Bristol with T [*C's boyfriend*]. We were on the road for six hours and laughed all the time. An old woman on the train from Bristol said I looked too young to be travelling alone!

There's nothing here for me. No room, all that was me obliterated so finally with cream wallpaper, no colour left. I stand in what was my room, my life for so long, and it's impossible that these four desolate walls were once so vivid, containing the essence of a whole existence.

Today 20,000 people gathered in Trafalgar Square to protest against nuclear weapons. I should have been there. Twenty thousand in London, not including thousands in Scotland and Wales, and thousands more in Sweden, Germany, etc. The bloody government can't ignore it any longer but they will try, the blasted fools.

The March started on Good Friday from Aldermaston and ended today at two-thirty in London. Thank God people are thinking, thinking for the idiots who scoff or take no notice and think for Christians who are too busy at Church meetings to think, to wake up, to breathe. Canon Collins, Michael Foot and Frank Cousins were again at the front and Joan Littlewood.

Four Japanese students were forbidden to march which is appalling. It makes me see red when the television shows shots of idiot creatures looking weird. They never photograph the hundreds of housewives and ordinary people. I was going originally before I fell broke.

Saturday 4 April 1961, Yeovil
We went though a sea mist and some wonderful country - Cerne Abbas, a village that fascinates me. Memories of Freddy Friar at the art school, swinging from the girders in his great billowing monk's habit and massive sandalled feet - and Rampisham, such wonderful memories.

A letter from T in Bristol who is also homesick for Birmingham.

Last night Brian came over and tonight I caught a bus to Montacute and we sat in his studio, which is a converted chicken run, and talked about his painting. It is good, broad, free, bold abstractions.
We talked of Derek and his new Pop Art phase. Lawrence Alloway[30], a friend of Laurie's, who lectured us on Monday, is a key exponent. I like Brian, he's free of pretension and less precocious than Derek.

The smell of paint, the talk and the music and the walls lined with photographs and press cuttings, all this, this is my essence, recently suppressed. I will never paint again but this is my world, I can't escape from it. The feeling, the familiarity when I am once more with these painters.
How can I even consider an attraction for someone like J when he has none of this? He's right when he says he has nothing to offer that I want. He knows better what I want than I do myself.

Wednesday 9 April 1961, Moseley, Birmingham
I brought Barbellion up this time. I needed something I was essentially familiar with. I'm getting in a state again, a feeling of great isolation, of feeling, of hatred for everybody. I came back feeling strange, isolated, distraught as though life was re-started into a routine I didn't realise I dislike so much.

Back to that foul college again, like back into a dull, uncomfortable dream. I can't wait to get to London again. I don't feel as if I've ever been in a classroom before. Isolated from everything I've ever done, ever felt, ever been. I am a nonentity, nothing, I have no bearings.

---

[30] Lawrence Alloway [1926-90]:artist, influential critic and commentator. With Robyn Denny, Richard Smith, Sylvia Sleigh (Alloway's wife) and other students at the Royal College of Art in the late Fifties formed the Situation Group, the first to embrace American popular culture and the work of Jackson Pollock and Barnett Newman. Alloway is reputed to have coined the term Pop Art: he emigrated to the USA in 1962 to work as curator at the Guggenheim Museum in New York.

I might write my thesis on phobias and hallucinations. I have enough. I'm so sick of life, the most docile existence wearies me. I've thrown a mood tonight and embarrassed everybody. I had to. I feel so isolated.

Tuesday 10 April, 1961, Moseley, Birmingham
Desperate now because I can't find the first notebook [*in the journal*] anywhere - it's gone. It's the key journal of them all, vital to the whole balance. I couldn't have lost anything more important to me.

I hate this course, all this discussion; the very word 'education' irritates me. I fell asleep in this morning's lecture and now an afternoon of boring lectures with this loss hanging over me.

Back at the flat now and the book is nowhere. I *must* find it. I'm sure I brought it to Birmingham. I feel like tearing the whole city apart until I find it. I feel I've lost a hand, worse, a bit of my mind. It's the essence of my early adolescence and necessary if I am to write any more words. I must find it. I can't concentrate. But I've got a bloody thesis to do for a start.

Saturday 14 April 1961, Moseley, Birmingham
Less disturbed about the book today though the sense of loss is great but I'm really getting my teeth into my thesis, 'Psychology of the Criminal Act'. It's very unbridled at the moment. I have dozens of pages of notes and part of it is yet to be assembled.

What is more, I feel a new energy and even primed a four feet by four board on which I want to paint an important picture. I never thought I would want to paint again. My NDD paintings arrived yesterday. Roger is truly wonderful to me. I only hope I never really take advantage of it.

I've been working solidly for two days writing here in the flat where I have some peace. I am completely engrossed in the subject and it's helping me to come to terms with my own phobias and obsessions. I have a great appetite for learning again, like a re-birth.

It would seem that the loss of the first journal is being compensated with a frantic intake of ideas and facts. There was some important material in that book. I must retrieve it.

Sunday 15 April 1961, Moseley, Birmingham
Two days ago a Russian man [*the astronaut, Yuri Gagarin*] survived a trip around the world in a spacecraft, outside the Earth's orbit.
It's barely conceivable, at least to me. It's tremendous but impossible to imagine his feelings on his return to a crawling, familiar planet.
At last man has conceived and proved how to get off its whole life prison - tremendous things will be discovered and seen.
At last man has seen the earth from the outside - as in my poem, Alien Earth.

But our most progressive discoveries are laden down with political cattiness, jealousy and humiliation.
I saw a direct relay of Gagarin's reception in Red Square, Moscow. It was fabulous. Thousands of Muscovites cheering, old Khrushchev standing staunch and pleased, the loyalty, the pride. It was moving, Gagarin's servility, his courage. He was so proud yet he retained such humility and Khrushchev and the other leaders were kissing him.

Later I listened to Macmillan and he evaded every question with mutters and intonations of voice. He's so solid and irritating; he has no feeling, no drive, he's a placid conductor, no more.
Kennedy has started his prison reform. He's getting rid of Alcatraz for a start.[31]

In reading for my thesis I've discovered I'm subject to narcissism, love of self, an extreme introspection. This is hardly a revelation!

---

[31] Alcatraz: notoriously tough penitentiary for hardened offenders, known as 'The Rock', in San Francisco Bay. It was eventually closed by John F Kennedy on 21 March, 1963.

Monday 16 April 1961, Moseley, Birmingham
A bright morning. Alone and already painting. Watching the rats in the dustbins - a pregnant one dragging itself up the side and scrambling over the top, its belly bulging out on either side. C hates them, is petrified of them but I like to watch them.

I can see the garden of the kids' Home and the Indian boy is walking round and round on his own. He's always alone and makes me feel wretched. I keep meaning to go over and help them.

Half an hour later - I've just been talking to some of the kids over the fence. There are thirteen in the Home. Very difficult to talk to them. How many bees have you caught today? I feel exhilarated! I gave the Indian boy my tobacco tin in which he has captured six bees. He's a prisoner himself and he stamps on them.
We're friends now.

Tuesday 17 April 1961, Moseley, Birmingham
A new book and a vague belief that in fact I took the first notebook home while I was at Greenfield Crescent. My relief if I do find it will be immeasurable.

I went into college today but had to come back to paint while the enthusism lasts. Painting has really absorbed my being again. At last something is coming, some concrete and tangible evidence of certain thought processes.

Sunday 22 April 1961, Moseley, Birmingham
What have I to write? A week's reading and teaching, a week's surface living.
I've applied for more jobs in London and my future remains in a mist. I was alone again all day Friday and most of Saturday. I need time on my own; it's more essential than food and far more desirable. I use every minute and none is wasted.

I seem to have lost touch with Anne. Been writing to Eva who seems happy with a good husband - the one who called me a scrawny bitch -

and an ideal sort of existence in an isolated cottage with animals, no children, and friends and jazz, etc. I'm missing all that.
I see all my former friends finding degrees of happiness yet my path is solitary. Such separation will eventually break me.

Sunday 29 April 1961, Moseley, Birmingham
Back in Birmingham after a long and dreadful train journey with a carriage full of gaping men. Then a row with a foul bus conductor and a long walk with my arms breaking off.

Home for the weekend where I've been typing non-stop. Peter was home and it was good to see him and the relationship between my mother and myself is a little easier. She has lent me the typewriter for a while.

And what a relief to find she hadn't burnt the notebook after all. Arguing with her as usual about Nuclear Disarmament and she is just beginning to see we are right. We also argued about Communism. At least arguing is a development.

Alone here tonight and wondering about my future. I must ignore the temptation to stay in the Deaf School here in Birmingham. I *will* go to London. I must, else I'll vegetate and I refuse to take the easy way out.

Tuesday May 16 1961, Moseley, Birmingham
I haven't written for a long time though I have often felt like it.
The Spring Anthology has come and my poem is weak, as I knew it was.

Last Friday I finished teaching and was quite sad to leave the kids; only I adapt so easily I've almost forgotten them and it's only Tuesday.

I was asked to attend an interview for a job in Abbey Wood but it's twelve miles from Waterloo. I shall live in South Kensington [*rather a sad case of wishful thinking*] so it's out of the question. I'm going for an interview in north London on Friday. Then I shall go back to Somerset to write my thesis. It's impossible to write it here.

The rats breed and thrive. I have a great desire for a mouse and have walked miles in vain looking for a pet shop that will sell me one.

*

LONDON

10 July 1961, Coleherne Road, Earls Court
In London at last. Bernie and I both working hard washing up at the Boltons [*another gay pub in Earls Court, close to the Coleherne*] until three each day and then using the rest of the day watching people who come to the flat to talk.

A letter and the return of my thesis from Professor Morris[32] who seems genuinely interested in my writing and ideas. Also a card from Dr Burroughs. I did quite a lot of modelling for him as he's a keen photographer and I went to their flat several times and he took dozens of photographs, some were nude studies on the lines of Bill Brandt. He likes me and is very complimentary. His wife is a fine woman, energetic, knowledgeable - in fact, they're an extraordinary couple and the most stimulating friends I made in Birmingham although I only knew them well in the last month. A few years back they spent a year travelling in India and their flat has a Westernised Indian flavour which sounds vile but is not.

---

[32] Professor Ben Morris; Professor of Education, University of Bristol 1956-75: Tavistock Institute of Human Relations, 1946-50; Director of the National Foundation for Educational Research, 1950-6; Visiting Professor of Education, Harvard University, 1969-70. Published numerous papers in educational and psychological journals.

Professor Morris talked with me on the last day of term and was most complimentary. I feel at ease and in no way inferior to these people who I know have intellects and experience far superior to mine. I am pleased at their interest and their praise elevates. I had Credits on both Education Theory and Teaching. I knew I'd done well but my written paper was atrocious.

I miss nobody in Birmingham but think with affection of C and T and expect to see them again in London. At the moment I feel confident in my isolation. Bernie and I share a humour which binds and there is a real friendship. We came to London together on the train. A little subdued, three days since the revelation. Behind his personality he has ten years of living with homosexuality - complexities and problems beyond my experience or understanding.
As soon as we were in London he resumed his *real* identity, he was as he is and I suddenly understood. I knew him still but part of him was a stranger.

14 July 1961, Coleherne Road, Earls Court
Late now and Derek has been round. I feel a detachment I never thought possible. There's no bitterness, no compassion even - barely, it seems, a close friendship.

R spends ages getting my hair straight and trying to make me make the best of myself. She always looks fabulous and gets really impatient with me.
JPD entertains everyone for hours on end with his scandalous stories.

Spent some time in Eric's gallery [*the Portal Gallery*] looking at some paintings by Patrick Hughes[33]. He said the last time he was there he'd propped a whole batch in the street outside and someone stole the lot. But he was really calm about it and said he'd just have to paint them all again! One was of a fried egg on a green and blue background.

---

[33] Patrick Hughes: painter. Studied at Royal Academy School. First one-man show at the Portal Gallery, London, 1961. Lived for a period, 1980-3, in The Cheslea Hotel, New York. Author of three books on humour and was married to painter/writer/fashion journalist, Molly Parkin.

2 August 1961, Coleherne Road, Earls Court
Another film of the last war; the absolute madness and horror of war. War games. Clever men who must play at directing thousands of other men to murder en masse.

*

On Sunday last R and I hitched to Somerset and on the way I had the most evil of migraines. I could barely stand. I was sick several times and in such pain throughout the night I couldn't sleep at all. I lay in a painful stupor until one o'clock on Monday [*at R's parents' house*] unable to conceive of a way of getting the thirty miles to Yeovil. R's father gave me a lift to Chard and I shall never forget getting out of the car, almost dead with pain and knowing I had, somehow, to get home. I felt like begging him to let me stay curled up in the back of the car but he was gone. I tried to walk towards Crewekerne. Eventually got a hitch but couldn't speak. He must have thought I was insane or on the run. I hitched another car to Yeovil and then barged into a café and was sick in the bog.

All day Monday and Tuesday the pain didn't cease but today it's eased off. It feels wonderful - no pain, a beautiful sensation. I realise more and more that health is the most important thing in life, for life is suffering enough without the added treachery of pain.

8 August 1961, Coleherne Road, Earls Court
My birthday. Twenty one. I don't care one way or the other. Every night I feel I must get my thoughts in order but each day goes by without leaving the slightest impression, no evidence of living.

Between R and myself there's an antagonism which is basically friendly but we are such differing personalities. We argue about people mostly. I refuse to enthuse over many of her acquaintances. My interest lies with different people and I feel no urgency to gather acquaintances about me. And we are sorely without money and with a huge rent to pay each week [*three guineas a week*]. We have literally no money for food. I don't know if I have the job in the Grisbi [*coffee bar in New Kings Road*].

My one pair of shoes have huge holes in the soles and I'm cutting up Tampax packets to go inside.

Last night a Frenchman came to the flat as he was given the address by a man in Florence so he need not fight for de Gaulle against Algeria. He'll be either imprisoned or sent to a futile war if he sets foot in France. He's relatively safe in England.
Enrico and an Australian architect were also here and they talked politics most of the time. Not half an hour before Enrico arrived the Frenchman asked if we knew a certain director and we said no, indeed not, but after he and Enrico had been talking for a while they realised it was each other they'd hoped to contact in London.
We never seem to know people's surnames.

At least the company was not filled with pseudo-corruption which seems to be the vogue of the blasé. At least there was some interest in the conversation, some reality.
And so I go on, constantly nagged by R to become glamorous and more socially acceptable - whose society? Certainly not mine.

Been arranging my half of the tiny bedroom I share with M [*girlfriend of Shake Keene, jazz musician*] which is like a confined army barracks, blankets included. Two nights ago I woke to find Shake and M in the room and remembered the houseboat in Richmond.
I feel trapped in my own freedom.

I was walking slowly along Earls Court Road to buy cigarettes and I saw J, who looks like Christ, and I remember him from the Troubadour last summer and we sort of ambled along in sections, inspecting each other with an enforced nonchalance, a neglect. We were both disinclined to speak or even animate our faces in recognition. He looked terrible, haggard, wretched and haunted. It was not the occasion to speak. But we know each other all the same.

In Wharfedale Street, opposite the flat, there lives a man who plays the guitar in the Troubadour and he has a brown-haired girl living with him. She sits behind a stall in Portobello Road on Saturdays.

I get sick of people decrying homosexuals. I can't tolerate their general remarks and their despising terms. R nags me to stay away from Bernie until I could scream to be left alone with my own friends, my own judgement. I can't joke about 'queers' anymore.

I hate this hanging around waiting to start work, having no money and feeling nervous and not very happy. R has arranged a party for my twenty-first at JPD's flat but I'm not interested, it's their party, not mine. C sent me ten fags, some yeast tablets and a flannel. She's sweet and I've begun to miss her company.

We have insane rows with the mad couple upstairs. They're hideous and live in a bitter campaign against the world and its other residents beginning with this house. We only have to close a door and they start banging, incessantly. They drive themselves mad with an obsessional self-inflicted rage. They sometimes stand at the top of the stairs and shriek and scream like mad things, going on about the rules of the house and having 'men in all night', etc. Sometimes they just start banging for no reason which is really infuriating. At night it's a bit frightening. I've heard them talking with hatred about 'the blacks' - probably referring to Shake.
They're vile, bitter, revolting creatures, tortured by hatred. I would say he's an ex-army man and she's a half-baked cow. He has just screamed 'Shut up!' down the stairs for no reason and has now started on the furniture.

As I was writing a few minutes ago my mouse darted across the room like a miniature torpedo and I've had to chase him. He refuses to surrender so he will have to go hungry and sleep in the waste-paper basket again. He's too stupid to find his way back to his box where he has crumbs and water and a bed of cottonwool.

R is good to me but I feel we're looking for different things in life - important things. Our French deserter found me wandering in Earls Court Road this afternoon and has arrived with a Swiss man with six shirts to iron.

My mouse has just walked up into my bed and as I grabbed him his face *dropped!* He just couldn't understand how one minute he was free and the next utterly powerless in my hand. Sometimes I feel an overwhelming aloneness.

Sometimes I wish I were about fifty years old with an old husband to sleep with for comfort; to rest, with no mental problems and my life spent and just waiting for death.

All is bombs and more bombs and we nuclear disarmers cry for reason and humanity - and still more talks, more hopes and more despair - we're ruled by blasted bombs. I'll probably die before I've lived, before I'm thirty. And all my friends and contemporaries. I watch this small mouse, instinctive, furry, with whiskers and little feet and no brains and he doesn't know that he will be blasted from this earth soon. He'll go the same as me.

London around here is so quiet, like a stage-set. R on at me to go to the Troubadour but I will not. I spent last summer sitting in that place as this journal will confirm. I sat and was curious and alive to the problems put over by layabouts and geniuses but they're the same as me and their familiarity bores me. It's like living in a mirrored box. I told her I'd rather spend an evening in a snack-bar with a juke-box than in the bloody Troubadour, sitting in the dark, eyeing interesting people who are so earnest and smug and sincere and have as many problems as women on their lists. They play my own game. When I see a young man looking like Christ I feel like screaming because they're my people by choice, by the way we live, but they bore me. When I see girls with long straight hair and lots of eye make-up I feel angry at their familiarity for I know them so well, every one of them, for they are me.

9 August 1961, Coleherne Road, Earls Court
Sitting here in my room, by the window, staring at the convent, a desolate, barren building directly behind the house. We are separated by unused London gardens. The nuns wear grey habits and large, beautiful white cotton head-dresses. They seem to wash, mend and sew all the time. I feel a surge of freedom when one comes near the window. There's something melancholy about nuns - shackled women.

I saw one of them mopping a floor on a landing and another came up the stairs and spoke to her. I wonder what they have to say? Yesterday several of them were sitting in a room farther down the house and they were sitting in a crude circle, sewing.
As I sit by the window I usually put the mouse on the sill and today I was so busy watching the nuns he has disappeared.

I've just seen a nursing nun talking to an old man in a dressing gown, as he stood straight and dying at a window. And then she followed him up the stairs. When one is dying it's a crime to escape from one's death-bed and take a glance at the world outside which is still living. It's wrong to quicken death and they seem to prolong a gentle process of dying, especially in a nursing home where one pays to die to a pattern.
I've seen him painfully ascending those stairs at four o'clock in the morning, like a ghost, a reluctant mortal. He might have crept to the lavatory to die instead of his official cell. Perhaps only the backs of the houses in Coleherne Road know he tried.
Sometimes I'm sure we're all reluctant mortals. I can see the nurse talking to a shape that must be the old man's bed. I feel like screaming.

I just saw a nun move across the garden amongst the trees. How can I be reconciled to life when I use the most sacred, dearest name ever given in the hearts of these nuns as an oath? I use Him and His life as a joke yet to these nuns, these other women not fifty yards away, He *is* their life. What discipleship, what admiration! Has Freud this? Has Jung, has Picasso, has Bertrand Russell? These are revered names to me yet I wouldn't shut myself away from society to acknowledge them. It would seem futile. Each to his own god.

Bertrand Russell was stopped from speaking in Hyde Park last Sunday. Anyone would think he was going to insult the royal family or something.

Another card from Dr Burroughs, a photograph of Giotto's frescos at Assisi. I wish I was there. We can't even afford electricity to run the wireless or even the light. And we have no food left. I've received several revolting birthday cards. What a blasted waste of money. I would much prefer a shilling for the gas. People forget what it's like to be poor. Literally, without *any* money at all.

Reading again Barbellion's *Journal.* I always go back to it and when I'm depressed I devour it. To think that this person, this spirit so like mine, lived in Cromwell Road, not two hundred yards from here. One day I will go and ask at the Natural History Museum whether his wife and child are still living. I'm nearer to him than ever his child could be. I wonder if his wife remembers him with such reverence.

11 August 1961, Coleherne Road, Earls Court
This afternoon I walked to the Natural History Museum to enquire about Barbellion. I signed a book and was handed over to an elderly but tall man who was musty and zoological. His eyes looked at me as though they were more accustomed to peering at insects and yellowed books. I felt somehow too full of blood or something in these reptilian surroundings.

So this was Barbellion, these smells, these sombre officials, this warm, dry, pondering atmosphere. I was followed through the Museum by the spirit of this man.

The elderly man knew the *Journal* well and had come to work there the year after Barbellion left. He said that the last member of the Museum staff to remember him was his great friend, Robinson, referred to as R in the *Journal.* He died only three years ago. I wanted to see the room in which Barbellion had worked but it seemed rather a juvenile request.

I asked if the original manuscripts were in the Museum but he thought Barbellion's wife has them - nothing is known of the daughter.
He showed me some 1912 pamphlets Barbellion had compiled on bedbugs. These musty pamphlets on insects seem incongruous with his nature and mean nothing to me. That isn't what I'm looking for. They bring me no nearer the man. Two musty pamphlets. I felt very reluctant to leave. I felt that I hadn't done enough, that there was more, that with more searching I would find him, still in his room, sadly dissecting mosquitoes. But there was nothing left. New staff, new bones, new acquisitions, new air. I felt his absence so strongly, like a presence.

As I was talking to these officials I saw them as the very men Barbellion saw, looking into the same insect eyes. They had no idea what he was going through, feeling, knowing and mine was just another obscure enquiry. They just knew him as young Cummings, who wrote pamphlets on bedbugs and left because he was ill. Cummings from the Zoology Department.

I sat outside for a while and watched the pigeons, reluctant to leave and hating those birds for their stupid strutting impartiality.

Walking in Kensington today I felt too tall and too long in the face and rather uncomfortable and having lost my search for Barbellion I was walking erratically and inclined to stoop.

Last night I was drinking tea in Bernie's flat and it was raining, simply pouring with rain, falling in great sheets. I love the rain, it elevates me. It was sounding loudly as it rushed down the drains and into the gutters, moving the windows in their frames. We hurried along Earls Court Road under a huge black umbrella, laughing as usual.

As I sit in the flat writing these things it's getting dark and winter is coming. We're very hard-up. R is working in the Coleherne tonight shrieking with the leather boys.

Had a letter from the LCC informing me that my salary will be £708 per annum. I don't care a damn how much it is as long as it's enough to live on. I must get a calendar for I lose count of the days. I don't even know how long I've been in London, and Birmingham seems like another life.

I was trying to explain to R my great fear of open spaces and large objects. I'm overcome with apprehension, for instance, in the Natural History Museum where there are great stuffed mammoths and things. Even that section of tree trunk makes me nervous. I couldn't stand directly in front of it. And that great suspended Blue Whale!
Sometimes I consciously frighten myself by imagining all the great plains and spaces there would be if all the seas dried up. The Grand Canyon would terrify me.
An empty town would frighten me beyond words and any empty room has the same effect.

I stood for more than two hours for those blasted costumes again. [*R was designing costumes for a theatrical company and had roped me in for fittings.*] It seems such a dreadful waste of time but I can hardly refuse. R can't really understand how I can live without sex. It's no trial whatsoever, compared to some.

12 August 1961, Coleherne Road, Earls Court
Working in The Grisbi from ten till six; working hard with no one to relieve me the whole eight hours. Couldn't even sit down. Talking with students and layabouts and fat lecherous Englishmen. It's a dump.

It's late now and M has just phoned to say she's found an American who is in London looking for a guitarist. He's just arrived from Germany where he's on tour. His name's Bobby and he's one of the Inkspots. I've only vaguely heard of them. She and Shake met him in the Downbeat and he's coming over tomorrow to meet me.

14 August 1961, Coleherne Road, Earls Court
He's very sweet, plenty of money and plenty of humour and looking as only a coloured boy can.

15 August 1961, Coleherne Road, Earls Court

He leaves for Germany again tomorrow where he may give up the Inkspots and go back to New York. I'm sad now, feeling a loss, having got used to his humour and his personality. Talking in his southern drawl, just like Broonzy. We talked of the jazzy apartment we would have, with the biggest brass bed in London, if things were different.

20 August 1961, Coleherne Road, Earls Court

A man at the Grisbi seems to have taken me on as his sort of Pygmalion; that I will never be and it's a strange presumption on his part. All these lecherous young and old men. I get so tired of it all.

Derek rang up while I was at work as he's back in England. He said he'd be round very early in the morning before I go to work but I know him so well and can guarantee he'll never wake in time. My heart is wary but retains its detachment - just.

Middle-aged men seem so anxious to hand over half their incomes and provide cottages in Devon or house-boats in Chelsea. I'm bored. I wish I were somewhere else.

R and I went to a boring party given by some boring Australians in Cornwall Gardens. The basement was crowded with more boring Australians and one boring Turkish painter. Earls Court is now a new New South Wales. R and I embarrassed two idiot young men with our crazy twenties jive and then insulted the rest. Hideous young men with fresh faces and fat bums and inane smiles. We laughed at them to their faces and then left, half-cut, doing zany walks along the length of Earls Court Road.

21 August 1961, Coleherne Road, Earls Court

Now that Derek is somehow more accessible I've been reading the section of the *Journal* when it was bad. It's true and sincere but too emotional. I see now just what a state I was in. But I have come to realise that it is still, in fact, him that I'm concerned for, inevitably.

This morning I went into a record shop and spent an hour browsing through the record sleeves, imagining the music, wanting money to buy them. I found one of the early Inkspots records but his picture wasn't on it. I work over the weekend and have Monday, Tuesday and Wednesday free. I hate the communal weekend - one always feels that one should be enjoying oneself.

Much later and a solitary evening reading Plato's *Last Days of Socrates* with renewed relish. Things within it that I've written myself. I wonder if knowledge is, in fact, recollection. It certainly seems so.

22 August 1961, Coleherne Road, Earls Court
I was just sixteen and now I'm twenty-one and it's just the same. We went to a lousy film yesterday evening. He's as uncontactable as ever. I can see a million faults and no new values and I was bored but tonight I feel like walking straight round to West Kensington to see him. I won't, but he's the only man who could make me. There's no way out because when I fell in love five years ago I integrated myself.

25 August 1961, Coleherne Road, Earls Court
Another day slopping around serving coffee and food and trying to read in between these petty services. Dreadful pompous young people with money in their pockets, fresh faces and silly grins. Well fed, well set up for dead living. Always enough, if not more, in their pockets and in their stomachs and not nearly enough in their hearts or in their heads and pure nonsense in their mouths.
I despise them but must serve them food and accept their money gratefully.

Re-reading Plato's *Protagoras and Meno.* I love these writings; what an inadequate phrase - its clarity reminds me of Bertrand Russell, its logic, its humanity.

28 August 1961, Coleherne Road, Earls Court
Last night reading again C W Valentine's *The Normal Child.* Work yesterday was exhausting. I fell down the steps of the Grisbi and cut

my knees and served the customers with deep-red blood running down my shins.

I was walking behind Derek in Old Brompton Road on my way to work this morning.

I watched my mouse for an hour last night; small animals are so unselfconscious and without pretension. Not only are they far simpler than humans they're far sweeter and *much* prettier to look at.

Watching the nuns again with a sense of isolation and a sort of envy.

1 September 1961, Coleherne Road, Earls Court
I could scream every time a customer comes in but only two days to earn some money. Always this endless worry over money. I feel like removing myself for several decades so weary am I of my body and the process of keeping it alive. And yet Josh Kirby was here last night and despite my poor head and stomach we sat indulging in verbal madness for literally hours on end.

London is cooler now and the tension and panic over the Bomb and the Soviet Union is now gripping the majority of the population not just a few.

5 September 1961, Coleherne Road, Earls Court
My thinking has been leading me to a decision that I've been subconsciously postponing. Now my doubts have gone - I'm an atheist. My reason won't allow me to be otherwise. I stand with no other security than myself and other human beings.
The only power is in men. It's taken me a long time to finally rid myself of years of Christian indoctrination. Fear and insecurity breeds gods and religions.
I still believe Christianity evokes goodness in some people but as a religion of supernatural myth I can't condone it. There is goodness and evil and greatness and virtue and beauty but there is no God.

10 September 1961, Coleherne Road, Earls Court
I've just returned from Somerset where I've been typing out this book. I have a great determination to get the journals typed in sequence because as they are, in seven separate, and losable, books of various shapes and sizes, they somehow lack unity and precision. I will feel much more at ease when I have them as a complete unit, a continuous piece of writing.

Talk is of war[34] and tomorrow I hope to be at a mass protest in Parliament Square. Last night I met Bernie and TG coming out of the pub and we went back to the flat and talked about the reality of war. But on the surface we still plan for a future and I long to buy a cheap sweater to teach in and a brighter bulb for this dull room and now it's very late and I've stayed up clearing out drawers and lining them with newspaper and thoroughly sorting myself out.

This afternoon I did the shopping in Portobello Road [*it was already the place for the young and fashionable to be seen on Saturday mornings*] and I still think its excitement as a past-time is over-rated, even for the ambitious.

The war could come tonight. One would think that I'd be sad that no one will read these ramblings. Not at all. I have read Barbellion's ramblings and Delacroix's therefore mine are also read, time over and therefore they cease to matter.

12 September 1961, Coleherne Road, Earls Court
I've been happy today, a rare and marvellous state. I've completely taken stock of my few possessions. I've sorted out every scrap of paper, stacks of newspaper cuttings, pictures and letters. I've thrown a

[34] The Bay of Pigs: there had been an ill-fated invasion of Cuba in April, 1961, by 1,500 CIA-trained anti-Castro expatriates; failure was due in part to J F Kennedy's cancellation of air-strikes, resulting in the death of more than 100 men. Many thought that a full-scale nuclear war between the Soviet Union and USA could erupt at any time. The tension remained and in May, 1962, after the discovery of Soviet-built nuclear missile installations in Cuba, JFK threatened retaliation if USA was attacked.

lot away but a few gems remain. I've re-stuck my wall cuttings and got myself ready to start teaching tomorrow. Human beings need so much space. This room is so small [*my half was about 8ft by 4ft*].
To have a *whole* room - how marvellous!

14 September 1961, Coleherne Road, Earls Court
I've been teaching for two days [*Shelburne Girls Secondary School, Holloway Road*]. The system is chaotic and the school is in three buildings hundreds of yards apart. I have a special class consisting of fourteen Greek girls, four English and two Turkish. Normal classes have forty-six. They're all noisy and precocious but interesting. I felt no nerves at all. I do what I have to do without really thinking about it.

17 September 1961, Coleherne Road, Earls Court
In an hour Trafalgar Square will see its biggest sit-down protest yet. Bertrand Russell has been put in gaol for seven days along with a lot of the Committee of 100. A shadow committee has carried on with the arrangements for today's rally. It's been banned by the Government and there's a fine of £2 for anyone going anywhere near the Square and there's a risk of going to gaol and this could mean losing one's job. Thousands more would protest were it not a crime to speak against insanity in a free country. Suddenly we realise we are not free after all.

The pamphlets being distributed have become quite hysterical since Russell's imprisonment. G is in jail and so is Russell's wife. It's intolerable. I feel so ashamed. I should be there. I feel so frustrated by it all and so helpless.

1 October 1961, Coleherne Road, Earls Court
I got mad at one of the kids today and almost sloshed her but just managed to control it. The stories I hear of the home environment of these girls are amazing and some are very pitiful. Teaching has lost its novelty.

My half of the room has begun to have its own aura and my desire for possessions, precious icons, has returned and I think to hell with the bombs and bloodshed and misery. Any phase in life is a prelude to another, a waiting for something, and living is dying. Reading Freud.

Derek came tonight and I felt dislocated, very detached yet thrown back into a vague remembrance that was disconcerting for a while until I again cut myself off.

5 October 1961, Coleherne Road, Earls Court
To know I could go and buy some food if I'm hungry is a marvellous feeling. To have more than 2/6d [12½p] to spend on necessities is wonderful. At times I've been very poor.
There's a constant antagonism between R and myself but I think it will clear.

9 October 1961, Coleherne Road, Earls Court
On Friday I went with little awareness to a dance at the Royal College and met Taj, a Sudanese third-year graphics student, born in Khartoum, oddly enough [*my father is buried there*]. He made me realise how different people from the East are, despite a Western-style education. He talks of things completely out of my experience and we're so different I have to think before I speak.

I've seen Derek several times lately and he seems unbalanced and unhappy and I pity him.

I've been buying books, books, books, all second-hand - Rumi, Katz, Plato, Koestler. I devour them. Books, music and time, these are my gods. I'm sick of physical things and relationships are getting me down. Too many people; every night out drinking with them; other people disturb me.

School goes on - sharp voices, curt replies and the constant façade of discipline and order to hide chaos and human stupidity and aggression. Can aggression and self-love exist together? I'm not sure.

27 October 1961, Coleherne Road, Earls Court
I've been wanting to write for a long time but the aptitude for writing personal thoughts has slackened almost to the point of non-existence. Perhaps because I'm less unhappy.

But I must record a marvellous three days in Cornwall with Kullmann[35] at the Rose Cottage wedding near Mevagissey. The wedding was a fiasco, with Kullmann cracking eggs all through the service and getting up the vicar's nose. They're all at the RCA and they pay ten shillings [50p] a week rent between the four of them.

We drove down in the back of Kullmann's van, with my mouse in its basket and Dave Hockney[36] very quiet and nice. During the thunderstorm he sat under a huge black umbrella in the middle of a really muddy field and all through the party, while Kullmann and the vicar were shouting at each other, he was trying to dry his socks.

The families down there are ideal; their children are wonderful -adult, hardened, essentially child-like but not childish. Old cottages and dogs and mud and gas-light. I see what I most desire and shall never have.

Kullmann driving everybody mad with his relentless truth expounding. He is the most extraordinary person I've known and knowing him has been an extraordinary experience. He has a brilliant mind and is impossible to defeat in an argument.

---

[35] Michael Kullmann M.A.(Oxon): Philosopher; Tutor: Department of Liberal Studies at the Royal College of Art, 1958-62.

[36] David Hockney: artist. Studied at the Royal College of Art,1959-62. He has enjoyed more international and popular acclaim than any other artist of his generation. After his first visit to New York in 1961, he produced the series of etchings, *The Rake's Progress.* Always diverse and innovative, since 1975 he has designed a number of stage sets for a production of Stravinsky's *The Rake's Progress,* Mozart's *The Magic Flute* at Glynebourne and for three other productions at the New York Metropolitan Opera House. Retrospective Exhibition, Tate Gallery,1988. Exhibition: Flowers, Faces and Spaces: New Paintings: Annely Juda Gallery, 1997.

1 November 1961, Coleherne Road, Earls Court
A sudden change in a pattern and I feel completely disconnected. The crux of the matter is that R has invited a girl to live in my room [*Enid Faers, student in the Fashion School at the Royal College of Art*]. To me this is shattering, a prison sentence. I came back to find my most private place invaded, my books, my photographs exposed. To me this is an unforgivable violation. R knows this; time and time again we've discussed this need for privacy yet she does *this*. It's an appalling situation yet the girl is very nice. She's tiny and glamorous, with huge dark eyes. [*She used to apply two sets of false eyelashes to the top lid and stick on, individually, a single row along the bottom. She also applied tiny black and white target transfers to her finger nails.*]

It would be much fairer for R to have her in *her* room, which is much bigger and she doesn't have this obsessive need for privacy. She has done a cruel thing. She also told me I was unbalanced, in fact, going mad. What an insane thing to tell anyone. It numbed me. She has blatantly shattered my one necessity for balance and I'm bewildered and greatly injured, and I will never forgive her.

8 November 1961, Coleherne Road, Earls Court
It would seem that I have had nothing to write for a week and therefore haven't lived, but my lack of words, on the contrary, indicate that I've lived more intensely, or rather that my time has been more completely used. I haven't lived more intensely, but a milllion slight impressions have bombarded my consciousness. My last piece of writing recorded bitterness at the situation in which I found myself. I've searched for a room and cannot find one and now I'm again temporarily resting within these walls.

In anger, and somewhat desperate for I knew I was to blame for my blatant selfishness, I said I would get out and at once felt a great relief. Not worry or remorse but relief, a new lease of freedom. I wanted to get my belongings out of the house and if need be sleep in the street surrounded by them so great was my urge to rid myself of these people and the horridness of the situation. Verbal violence is so depressing. Knowing I have declared my independence of R has given me a freedom which lightens the worry of finding a room to live in. To find a room is, in fact, almost impossible when I can look only at weekends. Most of them have been taken before the advert goes to press.

Last Saturday I walked the length and breadth of Earls Court, following up addresses on notice boards but each door had a large note pinned to it: SORRY, GONE. I have my books, the most precious of my belongings, piled up on a small chest of drawers and my huge paintings stacked behind my bed.

Once again I feel like a wretched soldier, having only a bed space and an open locker. My suitcase is packed but with the latch left open and my pictures once more stripped from the walls. I am once again starkly faced with the fact of living on my own. It's a state that both exhilarates and frightens me. On the one hand is my fervent need for solitude, without which I cannot live. But on the other hand, my nervousness, the erratic ramblings of my mind and imagination have proved to make living alone at times a torture I cannot bear.

Shortly after the terrible rows with R two weeks ago she told me that I was becoming more and more unbalanced. The sound of that word remains in my ears and I'm very afraid. It was as if, at last, I had driven someone to say it, to confirm my own self-knowledge, to verify the fact. Not in anger, not in spite, but in truth. My show of utter selfishness forced it from her and it has obsessed me ever since. My first desire was to rush round to Lexham Gardens and tell Bernie.

Yet I had begun to feel that I had acquired a new balance, that I had strengthened my grip on reality; for once my time has been completely taken up with work and relationships, not self-analysis. But it would seem I was wrong and I am, in fact, still sliding downwards. My position has been marked at last.

It is true that my relationship with Bernie is unusual - it could hardly be otherwise. And becoming involved with Kullmann has thrown me more deeply into the world of anger and protest and socially abnormal behaviour. But he has only carried me further along the line of social incompatibility. And it's strange but although he's so erratic, neurotic and verbally violent, he relaxes me. I feel no strain in his company yet he has the most strenuous personality it's possible to imagine. His whole life is spent in verbal agitation and argument, his mind is a weapon of discourse and antagonism. He is revered to an extent for the brilliance of his mind and his verbal eloquence but hated for his power over people's personalities and compunction to deflate pomposity. Strangely, he does not dominate my personality, it remains intact because it's subordinate. One only uses one's personality to full strength in the face of one that is weaker. One becomes overbearing in the face of stupidity, complacency and illogical thought and prejudiced actions. Kullmann reacts violently to this and I understand him exactly. He appears to be a man full of hate and antagonism but it's a perverse, inherent love of humanity that ignites his violence. Like him, I curse narrow-mindedness because in bulk it causes hunger and racial prejudice. I, too, despise illogical thought because it allows superstition and creates wars.

For Kullmann to be so positive can only result in trouble. He's so disliked even Hugh Casson [*Prof.Interior Design, RCA*] made some ridiculous accusations against him and there was a hell of a fuss and they nearly threw him out. I waited outside when he was summoned to Casson's office. He, Kullmann, oddly subdued, but it seems to have been resolved. He amplifies trouble until it becomes deafening and lacks any social conservatism, an admirable thing in the abstract, but in reality it creates an almighty mess.

He's a man burning himself out. But I see him in another perspective. On the very rare occasions when he's with people whose brains he can begin to admire, like Samson[37] and Steiner[38], he can withdraw from his endless verbal attack. He can begin to listen and appears as a boy of eighteen. He's like this especially when he's with Samson, who worries

---

[37] Frederic Samson: Philosopher; Tutor, Department of General Studies, RCA, 1961-77.

[38] George Steiner, MA.DPhil. Extraordinary Fellow, Churchill College, Cambridge. Professor of English & Comparative Literature, University of Geneva. Influential writer, philosopher and cultural commentator.

for his safety [*we always expected to hear that he'd been beaten up*] and so obviously respects and loves him as he is because he knows him. When I see this, when I witness the love and respect from men like these, I think that the mass of bums who hate him because he disturbs their complacency can go to hell.

To him the average Royal College of Art student is an imbecile. No wonder his life is a hell of frustration trying to interest them in philosophy. They just don't want to know and resent having to go to his lectures. He knows incredible loneliness. Few people see him relax and stop talking even for a moment.

On Sunday night we went for cider - more arguments with the cider drinkers in Weston's cider house in Harrow Road - it's a wonder he's survived - and then back to Norland Square where we both fell asleep listening to some Beethoven. And when I woke in that weird room the needle was still aimlessly circling the record. I felt beside myself, alien. My soul was removed and I felt timeless, dead. And there was Kullmann, sound asleep, tensely relaxed, the nearest to sleep he can get. A few nights ago he fell asleep in the middle of a sentence and carried on with it as soon as he opened his eyes. His mind never seems to sleep.
On impulse I left and came back to Earls Court by taxi, still on the boundaries of this other world.

A few weeks ago we were in the Queen's Elm [*a favourite haunt of artists and writers in Fulham Road*] and I suddenly saw Dom Moraes, barely able to stand. He looked so shattered, so dead to life that I was afraid and felt deserted. This face that I had been familiar with for so long, the face that meant those poems, suddenly, stark and drunken not two feet away. Seeing his drunken eyes I felt to be in the presence of treason or shame or reality or some death and wondered where his poetry had come from.

One night Kullmann and I found a Greek engineer who had an intense inquiry into life. We took him drinking with us and he seemed relieved and grateful to have at least two friends in the world. The next day he phoned and said he must see us and we met him and talked. Loneliness is when one's actions have no consequence on another person. It's also a lack of self-illumination.

And then there is Taj, the Sudanese. He, myself and Kullmann have a remarkable relationship. He cares for Kullmann and says I relax him a little; likewise Kullmann, who likes Taj, says I am good for him. And then there is Bernie with whom there is no physical contact as such but we have a great mental alliance and shared humour. Each of the four of us is very different but we have a great strength which I can't define.

And now I must write of my meeting with Dr Burroughs. We met in the West End and we had dinner in a posh place with waiters and things. I had to wear my wellies as my only pair of shoes were being mended.. I've always been on the other side before. And he told me that the tutors in Birmingham didn't know what to make of me. Haggerty didn't know if my essays were very good or just plain bad. Then Professor Morris read them and insisted they were above average. In fact, he said I had remarkable ability. Dr Burroughs seconds this but I'm still a mystery to them all. He's always writing urging me to continue to write and paint. But I tire of this personal outpouring. I no longer write poems.

Maybe I'm foolish and over-susceptible to praise and kindly encouragement but write I will. The Professor was taken with my originality - how gratifying to a fanatical individualist drowned by a million doubts! This acceptance of me as a person, and this concern for my writing, is so important. I can only accept their belief for I can see no reason for them to pretend. Dr Burroughs has now been made senior lecturer at the university. I hope Professor Morris contacts me. I need these people, for encouragement and for a new belief in my mental capacity which is, as always, smothered by the frustrations of living.

10 November 1961, Coleherne Road, Earls Court.
I have eased the situation by adapting to it. Tonight I have denied myself the doubtful pleasure of a bar-party at the Royal College merely to attempt to adapt, that is, abandon the idea of finding a room in Earls

Court, quickly and at a low rent. Now I have re-arranged my corner and drawn a chalk line down the middle of the room. I have fixed myself a desk space, about one and half feet square in all, but it's enough. And I have fixed myself a shelf for my beloved books. I couldn't stand to see them piled up like junk.
My enemy is the person who attempts to deprive me of my solitude.

I was to have gone to the College with Taj but by the time he arrived I had already given myself to creating my new surroundings and he was lost in his persuasion before he began. Now he is upset and moody.

Kullmann will be in Oxford now, lousing up someone else's weekend. He's a social barbarian. Again the other day we nearly got thrown out of an Indian restaurant because he was verbally attacking the rest of the customers and talked loudly of the Tories eating Royal shit and people licking bishops' arses, etc. His language is foul but it means nothing to me because I understand the anger. Taj was with us and so was Samson; a wonderful man. People complain and protest, move away or just glare at Kullmann as he rants and raves. He's a bitter man, hating love and yet exalting romantic love above all else. He rants about his wife - he has two small sons - and seems to despise her. Every now and then he screeches up to her house in his battered blue mini van, tells me to wait outside, charges inside and grabs various mats and things and throws them in the back, cursing like mad.

When he admits loneliness, he has a great dread of solitude, I go to his room and we sleep and when we wake we go about our business. Our quietness provides a direct contrast to the fierceness of his public image. He regains a measure of himself and I provide a prop. He makes love to quite a number of women but we rarely do. We just sleep and free each other of solitude, as far as we are able.
As with this morning when he drove me to Holloway I never know whether we will see each other again and I never think to ask. We just leave each other. This is my role. Although I'm emotionally concentrated on this complex relationship I know it is temporary.
Sometimes I have to go to see Bernie in Lexham Gardens where I feel at home.

13 November 1961, Coleherne Road, Earls Court.
I have been looking at my poems again and happy to throw several away. When I get a typewriter I'll send a few copies to Dr Burroughs and Professor Morris. Having no typewriter is a constant frustration. I need one. I have needed one for the last three years. I hope later on to finish typing out my journals.
No person has ever read even a portion of them but I believe them important, at least to me for they are the basis, the vehicle of my development. I long to stop being a person, a teacher, who has an odd obsession with my own written thoughts. But writing them is a necessity. I am a writer. I was always a writer and yet it was smothered and pushed to the background.
Only today I've realised that this, in fact, is my eternal frustration. I was forced by circumstances to become involved with visual art and all my enthusiasm went into the world of paint and pencil and the smell of turps. But all the time I was a writer obliged to attend art college. During the first year I was writing poems every evening. I wrote hundreds but only two remain. Then writing *Anyes* night after night.

And then the children's book. All my creative energy went into this at nights and during the day I was a frustrated person having to work in the wrong medium. I hated the paint, the very texture of it. There were days I could have screamed with irritation and boredom. Most of this frustration comes out in the journal but it wasn't until today that I realised how devastating it was to have to paint when all I wanted was solitude and time to write.

Now I have evolved as a teacher and still haven't the time to write. I teach art but I live books, words, mental formations. I own no art books and have no interest in them. There's an emotional indirectness about visual art.

The reason for those unhappy years cannot be easily given but now I can see that wanting time to write was my main frustration, my love for Derek being the other.

The relationship with Taj has possibilities but somehow my interest isn't there. For a relationship to have substance it needs challenge, indifference, pain. Roger never realised that to love me at all, let alone so obviously, was the worst thing he could have done. I hate people to love me. Perhaps it's the masculine trait in my personality. I have a great capacity to love but I have never come to terms with being loved.

Teaching has become a shifting routine. The girls are quite tough to handle. They swear all the time and fight like cats. Though in theory I can't really object for, once outside the gates, I swear as much and as violently as they do.

13 November 1961, Coleherne Road, Earls Court
Kullmann came tonight unexpectedly. His father died today. I care so much for him.
Tonight the wind is howling, exciting, an exhilarating night. A quick Indian meal with Kullmann and then I ran, ran, ran to Lexham Gardens and Bernie was away and I sat and talked with TG [*his partner*] and then walked quickly against the luscious wind to Nevern Square to see Taj but he was out. I sat on the stairs and wrote him a note, watched by a man in a doorway and the woman who was loathe to let me in. I left undaunted, exhilarated by the luckless visits and this magnificent weather. The sheer grandeur of the wind and rain, the strength behind it. It carries me with it. It possesses me and I cannot be depressed for it ridicules time and disproves the whole of civilisation. We have a unique communion. A howling wind may kill me with authority - it would be an unequalled submission. I have lost my fervent quest for a room with complete solitude. I have found a temporary place in this one - yet I know I must soon move and take the next step.

15 November 1961, Coleherne Road, Earls Court
I began to write last night but I had mislaid my pen and hate writing in biro. Instead I finished reading Zola's, *The Masterpiece*; it was very moving and how well I know Christine's state, but despise her for being in the same state that nearly destroyed me. It's strange but I have so little pity or sympathy for women but wish I had a few more as friends. [*Being so insecure I saw all women as threats*].

I sat fingering some poster paints today belonging to one of the girls and the smell of them brought it all back, the four long years, the smell of paint, airless rooms, easels, the flesh of models, wood smells, turps and oil, laughter. For a moment I remembered it all. And while I was drawing they started making a bigger row than usual and I yelled at them to shut up and I was suddenly again in a life-class cursing some fellow student for disturbing my concentration.

But I was trying to create the self-discipline of an art school with children, which is impossible. Mental processes create their own disciplines. These girls have very surface and weak mental processes therefore they have no powers of concentration nor any all-consuming interest in their work.

For the first time I almost hated them for their insensitivity and stupidity, instead of accepting them as they are, creatures of instinct, without insight and of limited intelligence. I had arranged to take two fourth years to the Victoria and Albert at two-thirty but they didn't turn up. I wasn't the least bit angry and merely caught a bus back and got on with some work.

Taj and I have begun to form a more sympathetic relationship. So much about him is interesting and admirable but I have never experienced before the factor of race being a barrier to understanding. His whole background, his essence, his philosophy is that of an Egyptian and it's so foreign to me. He's a beautiful sienna colour and with all his other qualities he would seem perfect but there's this weakness in communication. The Middle Eastern nature of his behaviour and thought patterns makes me uneasy. It's all a bit traditional and tied down and somehow unprogressive. I like people who are free of the traditions of their race and society. He's very much part of his.
For the first time I have realised that I am essentially Western and my interest in the East is Western.

I seem to have adapted to the teaching world but I doubt I'll stay in it for more than a year. I need enforced study. Reading Kullmann's question paper for his students, I felt envious of their legitimate opportunity for writing their thoughts.

Dr Burroughs's interest has elevated yet confused me and I almost dread my meeting with Professor Morris. I feel their faith in what I do is unfounded, unplaced, that I haven't this exceptional writing facility at all but the whole thing is a delusion, a fraud. Dr B's and Prof. M's knowledge of my written work amounts to my four essays and my thesis. These are not my work. They are intellectual by-products. They know nothing of the existence of these journals or my poems. They don't know me and they don't know my work. I almost fear their knowledge of it for I doubt its real worth.

As soon as I can get copies of my poems I will send them even though I am apprehensive. Not that I fear criticism, I need that. But I fear that the raw me will prove less original, less exceptional than they believe it to be. I fear a loss of esteem for I need their encouragement.

Living conditions are much the same. A friendship forming with Enid but this continual antagonism with R - but I try to remember that she did a lot for me.

Several vile Christmas cards from various school girls - what a loathesome irreligious waste of money. I have urged them to put their money to starving children instead but to criticise all that is held dear by dull minds is to make a lot of enemies. I provoke them into arguing about God and the bomb and the colour-bar in England. Some of them are horrified when they hear me question God or condemn the monarchy and hate me for it; and some of them absolutely despise me when I argue against colour prejudice and tell them I have coloured boyfriends. They look at me with disgust. This isn't easy to take from young schoolgirls and they can be absolute bitches. But to know what I believe and to believe it without compromise and to pronounce these beliefs is the most exhilarating thing.

23 November 1961, Coleherne Road, Earls Court
Another day of endless grind, constant pushing and shouting and reprimanding and all the petty fuss and hard work in schools. Some of the staff have incredibly narrow and amoral minds. Full of the bitterness, intolerance and petty pride in small powers and privileges. The scheming and plotting against colleagues and the blatant arse-licking of ordinary men.
Today, my last three and sixpence on two books, my chief joy in life. One of Kant and one of Ethics.
Reading steadily, money short.

25 November 1961, Coleherne Road, Earls Court
This morning I hurried to South Kensington to meet three girls from the school. We went to the Natural History Museum and then to the Victoria and Albert. I walked around while they clattered about on too high heels and they giggled and idly glanced at beautiful things without caring. And I had to be in the Natural History Museum without mentioning that Barbellion was there or ever existed.

Then, going through the V & A, gazing at those fantastically beautiful ring, pendants, icons and windows - with them laughing and the noise of their silly heels getting louder and more ringing - I felt despair at their indifference and their hopeless ignorance of fine things, and of great beauty. We talked of clothes and boys and pop music, which I like too, being so near them in age, but I realised there's nothing more to them than this. They are kind-hearted but can also be bitches and tough and there's nothing more to them than that.

This evening I've spent in reading Epictetus: *Moral Discourses*. My books are my main anchor on life. Taj rang at ten-thirty wanting me to sleep at his place tonight; he was drunk in the Queen's Elm. I refused to see him as he hadn't bothered to take me there in the first place.
I still haven't seen Kullmann but his existence remains vital.

3 December 1961, Coleherne Road, Earls Court

I haven't written for several days - the last few have been chaotic. This small room, once shrine, has been littered with sleeping and visiting persons - getting ready for the RCA dances or sleeping off the night before. My feelings can be assessed and I have wasted a great deal of time. I went with some bloke to the College dance, all dolled up in a black boa and lace, etc. It was lousy, very crowded and really deafening, even from South Ken station. Everyone was dazed, but not drunk, and bored. Saw a lot of the 'Rose Cottage' people which reminded me of that weekend.

A poignant moment when I heard amongst the uproar loud booing and hissing and there was Kullmann on the stage, drunk and telling jokes. He looked so small, pathetic and bitter and nobody liked him. But his presence was electric to me. I watched him leave the stage and went to find him but he was way out and on another wavelength.

I understand him and feel such compassion for him and felt incredibly sad to see him go. I feel a great alliance with this hated, truthful man, a true revolutionary with tremendous spunk and if he is vile and obscene that is by the way.

4 December 1961, Coleherne Road, Earls Court.

Nothing to write; this tiny room is always full of RCA students, odd beds on the floor, borrowing everybody's clothes, cadging money and fags and people creeping in at odd hours and I have to climb over heaps of bodies in the morning, before it's even light; no time for food and then the hell of the tube.

A letter from Dr Burroughs offering a room, very kind.

7 December 1961, Coleherne Road, Earls Court

A good evening with Prof. Morris. Much later now and I'm full of beer and playing my beloved Elvis records. I realise again that it's only with drink that I obtain a degree of indifference to the problems of being alive. I lose myself so happily. The room is crowded as usual but I am in a timeless reverie. Taj was in the pub and made a silent scene. We talked about education all evening. I talk constantly of Kullmann and feel I must see him before he goes to Switzerland. And so life goes on. We talked of Lawrence Durrell and Dom Moraes.

Everyone's gone off to another party and I am alone now, playing Elvis and Brook Benton records. A marvellous solitary condition. I must get drunk more often.

11 December 1961, Coleherne Road, Earls Court
I find myself caught up in two rather strange relationships with middle-aged men - one with Dr Burroughs and the other with Prof. Morris. The former writes often and has begun to refer to me as his beloved daughter whilst at the same time raving about the qualities of my bosom. I received a letter from the Professor to say he would be in London again and would I meet him. I am going round to see Bernie so I won't be able to see him for long.

12 December 1961, Coleherne Road, Earls Court
Instead of seeing the Professor I went to an awful bore of a drag show in Notting Hill Gate. There were literally eight other people in the audiance. I was the only woman in the place except for the four lesbians on stage. It was quite funny but a bit boring. Should have gone to meet the Professor instead. Bernie is sceptical of both relationships. He says I'm either very naïve, over-estimating my intellect, or under-estimating my sex appeal. But it seems perfectly straightforward to me.

16 December 1961, Coleherne Road, Earls Court
Derek came here this morning and I felt estranged. But it's a forced estrangement, so real I almost fool myself. I sometimes pass him in the street with barely recognition and no afterthought and yet were I to allow myself to think I would know the truth.

A card from Kullmann. I miss the bugger. Feeling very solitary, bored, uneasy and tired of life. There is a great space, a lapse in living and the world seems at a stand still, reflecting myself. I can't write. Small death.

20 December 1961, Coleherne Road, Earls Court
Time to myself at last. Finished school yesterday - God, the noise, the constant voices of over-excited children until my head almost splits. Stolen time now, school forgotten, left behind in north London. I talked with two Indian students deposited on me by Derek, who came and went. I feel excessively detached and self-sufficient. Not looking forward to going home on Friday. I left my two students and hurried to Nothing Hill Gate to meet my brother - went to the pictures and I ate apples and was bored with the film and there was a flatness about everything, no dimension: then we ate egg and chips, played jazz and drank cups of tea.

Late now and again in lovers' company, as always, night after night, no space to myself and unable to get down to my work - no solitude, only this constant communal living which I both hate and need. I'm like a cat who is independent, needs solitude, yet needs companionship too.

23 December 1961, Yeovil, Somerset
I stood in my room in Earls Court, hating to leave. I have visited Anne and Dan and their baby son and feel alien. It's a past world now.
Recently a further encounter with Derek in the flat and we went to G's, an Indian student's place for a meal, and Derek left at seven-thirty and insisted I stayed. G and I talked for several hours about his Indian upbringing and colour prejudice in England. This seems to be my role of late, a listener to Eastern reminiscences.

I was in a bad temper on the way south. I loathe train journeys, particularly in these circumstances and in this hideous season.

Tonight we went to Rampisham as of old but it and we have changed. I no longer envy my married friends and greatly prize my freedom. Perhaps my desire for independence reflects my growing egocentricity.
I feel tired and disconnected down here and no emotion seems to register.

24 December 1961, Yeovil, Somerset
A wasteful day except for a visit to Laurie Fricker in Taunton and long discussions with Anne and Dan about capital punishment, colour prejudice and sex education. I talk so much of Kullmann; he has such an influence on me. I remember him with no regrets only a great compassion, there's no other word for it. I miss London. Here my mind clogs up and my personality is diminished in a vaguely unpleasant familiar past. I am so changed. Independence. Mine exhilarates me! I am re-convinced of my mental stamina and balance.

*

2 January 1962, Coleherne Road, Earls Court
Three days ago I started on the mammoth task of typing out my journal. It's laborious work, not very interesting in places, the hurried scrawl difficult to decipher - sometimes impossible - but I feel it's worth doing. I've been typing almost non-stop, using only two fingers. I've got through only twenty pages of the first notebook and the task of typing seven or eight books will no doubt take me until next year.

The snow is thick. On New Year's Eve I went sliding through Chelsea with Taj and we drank a lot and then walked miles in the cold to a party and it was boring and we got touchy and then almost made love in a white and frozen park. But it was five o'clock in the morning and there were already several odd persons about. God knows how we got back to Nevern Square. I left him in his flat sound asleep and ran along Warwick Road; familiar streets changed white and making me feel very free and somehow excited.

3 January 1962, Coleherne Road, Earls Court
A great day! I have at last got another Barbellion *Journal.* A first edition of the *Journal* and a first edition of *The Last Diary* and a second edition of *Enjoying Life*. What a treasure. I'm so happy. I was rummaging about on some step-ladders in the second-hand book shop near the Boltons [*Earls Court Road*] where I often prowl and get most of my books, and the name BARBELLION was like neon. I got all three books for nineteen shillings and sixpence. So happy at last. Also a

marvellous book on *Opium* by Jean Cocteau, an extraordinary document.
I read *A Last Diary* tonight. I am determined to get Rousseau's *Confessions* tomorrow. I have handled them so often in the shop and wanted them for six months now. The Barbellions are small, dark navy blue books with roughly cut edges and altogether marvellous.

A long walk in the snow through the backstreets of Kensington with Eni looking like a cowboy in my tight jeans and heavy overcoat and rain boots. Freedom to shuffle through dirty loose snow without a pass, or a past even; the air is cold and London is so silent.

5 January 1962, Coleherne Road, Earls Court
A chance to write and a change from typing. The journal makes slow progress. I only managed four pages today and even less the day before. Today on my shelf I have two more books I doubted I would ever see there - the two volumes of Rousseau's *Confessions.* So now I have Rousseau and Barbellion, two kingdoms side by side. Books are my life, little else.

At the moment I'm disorientated, no incentive, no solitude. No emotional crisis. No pain. I feel cramped and unable to expand. I'm physically girdled to three feet square of space into which I have crammed my soul. And so cups of tea and cigarettes and snatched seconds of solitude but by the time I am accustomed and begin work they are ended.

Reading again Barbellion's *Journal* I found this fantastic reference to 'swallowing landscapes and swilling down sunsets'. And then I read his essay on 'Journal Writers'. There are so many diarists I must read, especially Marie Bashkirtseff.

Typing through the journal it's interesting to see the course my personality has taken since I realised the solitary nature of all existence. I'm a character now with ideas of iron strength - and in the last few days I have seen them evolve from unreasonable, wild, instinctive outbursts of feeling, written without understanding, some ridiculous and some I would find intolerable now but they remain as relics of a stranger's past. But I'm surprised and pleased to find my views on royalty, capital punishment and colour prejudice so vehemently expressed so early in the first notebook.

The thought of solitude tantalises me. My soul needs space to wander in, not jammed in a corner with other people forever in my eyes, my ears, my head, my very being, until I begin to doubt the very existence of my soul. Once I spoke to myself, constantly, and a soul answered.

Tonight, in the pictures with Eni and Tom[39] I was anxious about the journals and obsessed with the idea of obtaining a fire-proof box in which to keep them.

Reading Barbellion's article, 'Journal Writers', I can verify that we write journals under unsympathetic conditions. It's a great incentive. Today, again, it all came over me and I fell into a cast iron depression and any attempt to push me out of it were useless. This oppressive urge for solitude at times becomes intolerable. I'm oppressed by the constant presence of other people. I'm mentally and bodily in a cage. I would write more and more if I were on my own. I would allow my mind to wander much further and if it wailed no one would hear. And my soul, I would find it again, renew an acquaintance I can't help remembering.

16 January 1962, Coleherne Road, Earls Court
Another day's teaching, managing twisted temperaments, bolstering up confidences, stripping excess confidence. Moulding, checking, controlling. These few weeks are an eternal wait for the other room to myself when R has gone [*the larger of the two rooms, overlooking the street*]. A lot has passed. I have a list of friends to ring but don't care to. Reading Simone de Beauvoir's *The Second Sex*, interesting. I am

---

[39]Tom Watt: furniture designer, lecturer. Studied at Royal College of Art, 1959-62. Contemporary of David Hockney, Derek Boshier, Peter Phillips, Peter Crutch, etc. With Terence Conran's team under Rodney Fitch, 1969-73. Lived in the Coleherne Road flat for a year and married Eni. In 1968, after a bad motorcycle accident, in which his face was re-arranged to resemble Elvis, he lived with the author and her daughter in Notting Hill.

essentially female but I wonder if I am resigned to it. My self-sufficiency and love of solitude is almost masculine.

I've been reading *The Journal of Eugénie de Guerin*. In general I dislike women painters, poets and writers, especially women journal writers. There's much in Eugénie's journal I find interesting but her religious mania leaves me cold.

Kullmann will be back in London as the Royal College starts again today. I have dismissed Taj. Derek is the one man in my life but the knowledge no longer dominates me.

Eni is out tonight and I have become accustomed to her company and feel strange. R is away on her honeymoon and the place is much easier to live in. To live with such antagonism and mistrust is impossible.
Something will prevent me from the paradise of my room. I have waited three years, lived with this desire, all the time jammed in a corner with one foot in another bed. Next door is empty now, except for her things. I can't believe it will ever be mine.

A meeting with the Professor arranged for the 23rd. I haven't written to Dr Burroughs for so long. C phoned from Birmingham on Sunday. I look back on that year with great nostalgia. I must contact Bernie. I live in a world of journals and the revelations of others and my own self is blurred. I must accept these invitations and get out and make love and get drunk and remember I am human. I shall become alive again and life will have two surfaces.

21 January 1962, Coleherne Road, Earls Court
Back again after a whole night of parties, one after another, four in all. We travelled across London and out to Wimbledon and gained nothing. But earlier, Kullmann and I went to the wrestling at Shepherd's Bush, marvellous. I thought I would hate it but I didn't. It was sheer burlesque, so staged and obvious, the coupling of an effeminate blond-haired white with a tall, aloof, all powerful-black called *Black Butcher* Johnson, who moved in a beautiful way and his body was burnt sienna and very exciting. And also *Dr.Death* - the audience hated him most -

in a bout with *Prince Swahili* - it was real theatre, and they have a drink in the pub afterwards. The crowd was yelling out crude wisecracks and witty remarks throughout. I loved it. One coloured woman in the crowd was almost hysterical and young boys were having a great time crawling along the spaces between the seats.
I am without money again: three pounds to last eleven days and that's not counting the rent. I get so depressed with it all and Kullmann is up to his neck in debt as well.

Another violent row with R before I went out this evening - she can't stand Kullmann. Again the accusations; I'm deranged, neurotic, unbalanced, a liar, to be pitied, prone to persecution complexes and a thief. It's now a battle as to who gets the flat outright.

For the first time, at one of the parties, I was jealous of Kullmann's pursuit of an arty pug-faced girl with a pronounced pout who spoke in the most inane way, posing with her head thrown back as she talked. I almost smashed her face in. It's not so much jealousy, he's always charging after women he fancies, as much as an absolute contempt for that sort of girl. I feel an affinity with Kullmann that is not possessive. It's only sexual magnetism that creates possessiveness - there's far less mental jealousy, though it does exist. This is how all relationships should be. No marriage. Marriage is a relationship aborted.
Kullmann is minding his two children today. Sometimes he dreams in Russian. How strange.

26 January 1962, Coleherne Road, Earls Court
Oh, the troubles, the rows, the screamings, deceits and hatred that have swept this house. The landlord refused my application for tenancy by phone and it took three hours of precipitous talking to get him to change his mind. R must be out by 1st February. Until I see them go and that room absolutely bare I daren't even comtemplate my solitude. Fate seems anxious to deprive me of it. Just another tenant to him but *life* itself to me.

18 February 1962, Coleherne Road, Earls Court
Now I'm in my fought for space in this world, this island between four walls.

19 February 1962, Coleherne Road, Earls Court
I've lived to the enth degree. Kullmann took me to meet RW [*another painter at the RCA*]. A night of snarling and rebellious talk in a backroom in Notting Hill Gate, overpowering in its over-crowdedness. RW came here. Fantastic human being. Life on the edge. Intensity too high. Two days of great living, vital communication, the vitality of conviction - the urgent undertone of rebellion - lives mixed up in the bitterness of civil wars.
The routine of school was almost unbearable today and I have no interest in the kids whatsoever.

21 February 1962, Coleherne Road, Earls Court
I think perhaps the longest week I have known. I don't know where RW is, if he's still in England or whether he will come this weekend as he intended. Time is immense. It's like a damned machine that needs oil. So much for these obsessions of mine, they disrupt my whole being and irrationally disturb.

23 February 1962, Coleherne Road, Earls Court
I left the school today with something like affection for those vicious young bitches, with all their violence and rudeness, all their lies and thieving and deceit. There's a certain exhilaration in dealing with a bad class, giving as good as them, mastering them. But at times this week it's been an eternity so that I could have shot the lot of them or simply let them tear me to pieces. They sap my personality, they rip shreds off it, pick it over, inspect it, and criticise in the most honest manner.

26 February 1962, Coleherne Road, Earls Court
On Saturday night I sat for several hours waiting for him to come and it was agonising. Then I met him in the street and we went to a party and then he came here. He's ultra-sensitive, but there's an elusiveness about him and I can only suffer from it.

I only write these days when I am frustrated, either mentally or physically. These pages have become a substitute for either violent curses or love. Sick, half-finished sentences. Each as useless as the next.
I was at the kitchen window watching the snow and the strangeness of the street; the sound, the drawing up of strangers' cars, greeting voices and doors slamming; I drew his name in the condesnation with my finger and drew a heart around it. Fool. I am desperate to see RW and feel a strong desire to run to Bernie with my problems - we're such friends.

28 February 1962, Coleherne Road, Earls Court
I spent three hours typing through my first journal which I always call the Book. It's very boring in parts but illuminating in others. Naturally, I am asking myself why I am making this exact copy of it. Why? I'm not sure but it creates a task, it provides a chance for reverie, nostalgia. It occupies me. It uses time that would otherwise be equally wasted on some other futile preoccupation.
Many men and women are snakes hidden in all manner of grass. Is life merely a long and drawn-out discovery of a fiasco?

2 March 1962, Coleherne Road, Earls Court.
Typing pages and pages of notebook Six, the Birmingham one. Eni is out. Brian came and almost drew me out of it but I felt devoid of life, feeling, past, knowledge, everything. Last weekend I was living for tomorrow, now I don't care. I realise I have lost.
A depressing brief epilogue with Kullmann last evening. The depths.

4 March 1962, Coleherne Road, Earls Court
As I predicted, a rather miserable weekend of suspended expectancy. He didn't come. He phoned tonight instead.

5 March 1962, Coleherne Road, Earls Court
Living in an illusionary state reminiscent of the one, summer 1960, again the numbing disappointment I know will come. Working on the journals tonight. Felt a sort of panic before I sorted them into some order. I've deciphered and typed notebook Seven and am now, after a

mammoth night's work, half-way through book Six. Book One is about one fifth-typed. I have a year's work on this. Relief.

10 March 1962, Coleherne Road, Earls Court
It revolts me, angers me, bewilders me that people enjoy life! For life grinds, spits, hits below the belt without stopping.
I sat and read some existentialist prose last night and hated being a bloody woman: women are not philosophers, they bring in issues that are irrelevant. I am just a woman and even as a woman I fail.

Shit. My typewriter has broken and I've just come in from a wander around South Kensington, feeling bad. I honestly don't know what to do with myself or my life. But my mental aspirations are limitless. Childbirth is the main female experience therefore I must experience it. I can't side-step, ignore or avoid it. Eni said last night that I was a defeatist with men. True, I sat with my feet on the mantelpiece reading philosophy instead of digging through the pubs until I found him. I don't see the point of this for either he wants me or he doesn't. I was so absolutely defeated with Derek I have no fight left.
I will attend Kullmann's lecture on Wednesday.

Early evening now and I am drinking steadily, alone in the flat and smoking myself sick. I have cried. Have just been out to buy a bottle of gin and I've rung Bernie and he won't drink with me. I have rung Laurie seven times and now I am drunk. Well, well, well...
I am drunk and in despair. I am considering going to the Queen's Elm. I am drunk. I am going mad.

11 March 1962, Coleherne Road, Earls Court
Last night was a moral decline. Eventually Bernie took over and we went to the Queen's Elm and talked about homosexuality. I was very drunk. I am now drinking the dregs of my bottle of gin. It's been tempting me all day. Bernie was marvellous. I dread work tomorrow. No hangover, just numbness. God, I'm sick of life, so bloody sick of it, why write, why love, why live, why, for Christ's sake *why?*

12 March 1962, Coleherne Road, Earls Court
In desperation I've written to Kullmann, the crucified. In a very depressed state. Hardly the energy to write. Suicidal.

17 March 1962, Coleherne Road, Earls Court
I intended to buy and drink my gin this evening - it's ten now and I've only just started it. People come and deprive me of hours in which to lose myself. I am less miserable this weekend but still despair.
Meeting with the Prof. on Wednesday - long discussions.

18 March 1962, Coleherne Road, Earls Court
I don't know whether I'm going to go on living. I write this in all seriousness and without melodrama. It's not entirely this passion for RW - it just triggered off a whole well of hate, love, despair, defeat, everything. I can't afford to smoke and drink as I have been doing. I owe rent. I hate myself. I'm like a person who is so deranged that they believe in the existence of someone who is dead. This blind hope baffles and horrifies me. I go on when I can't even grasp the fundamentals of the situation.

Now it's creeping towards Monday and with it comes a dreadful hopelessness. Will nothing ever shatter this disbelief? I believe if he rushed round here now and shot me in the stomach I would believe he did it because he loved me. Last night I sat and contemplated my wrists and was exhilarated at the knowledge of my blood going through and the realisation that I have the power to sever the arteries and then know unconsciousness.

Three fifteen pm. A morning and afternoon of intense consciousness and less despair. I've been reading without stopping, the newspapers mainly. Again a welling up of excitement over literary things, compassion for Algeria, etc. I don't read, I eat facts and they are consumed by me and consume me in turn.

I was going to visit Brian but feel disinclined to leave my room so industrious have I become. To go outside might break this hopeful spell - I, who have enough to eat, a room - compared to the fear and misery some people live through. I merely have an erratic hopeless passion for a person I hardly know.

21 March 1962, Coleherne Road, Earls Court

Once again, a man who is completely self-sufficient, ambitious, egocentric. The same, just a different name. Again to hear every hope shattered as they talk - always this frank statement of facts which I demand and yet die each time it's delivered with such terrible coldness.
I didn't go to work again this morning. I feel stripped. Damn everything. Damn the whole fucking world.

22 March 1962, Coleherne Road, Earls Court

A new defiance. I went and found Taj at the Royal College and we drank in The Queen's Elm and met JPD and we snarled and hated and triumphed over life, over love. We laughed at our suffering and had the seering strength of bitterness. Taj is impossible to be with for long but I find him terribly attractive and he has a marvellous flat so I will go there, dowse myself with Sortilège and triumph and forget and obliterate the memory of truth or love.

26 March 1962, Coleherne Road, Earls Court

This morning I opened my eyes and cried.
Derek was on the televison in a Ken Russell film.[40] I watched and it meant nothing yet he was once my life, Christ knows.

27 March 1962, Coleherne Road, Earls Court

A night drinking in the bar at the Royal College, hardly hearing the talk of students. But late tonight an angry defence of Kullmann. I rage at unfair criticism of him but it's a singular and thankless loyalty for he wouldn't walk a flight of stairs to see me.

Again this morning I woke and cried and then went to work.

---

[40] Ken Russell's documentary film *Pop Goes The Easel* featuring Derek Boshier, Peter Blake, Pauline Boty and Peter Phillips.

2 April 1962, Coleherne Road, Earls Court
Strangely exhilarated - it's the weather, this howling weird wind, there is madness, aggression, the wind rushing about making people seem superfluous, cars reduced to toys. Rain.

6 April 1962, Coleherne Road, Earls Court
On Wednesday night I went to Kullmann's play [*he was directing Goethe's, The Visit, at the RCA. Tom Watt and Nick Jensen were playing eunuchs, an inappropriate piece of miscasting, though Tom's guitar playing was authentic*]. We met again with a distance between us that each seemed unwilling to breach. He's so changed, quiet, morose, no shouting, no speeches, just a sadness or is it resignation? Next to Derek he has had the greatest influence on me and we have an affinity which cannot be broken.

Eleven o'clock and bloody depressed; no money at all, hungry, cold, miserable, still sick, no money for gas or for the bus-fare to South Ken for the Dance at the RCA; no money to get in, and all because I bought that fucking wireless that doesn't work.

15 April 1962, Coleherne Road, Earls Court
Once more spending a lot of time with Bernie. Endless talk and lots of laughing.
A weekend of typing, working solidly on deciphering the journals.
Once more I am consumed by this room, again in love with my shrine. Surely this is the resting place I have pined for over three journals? Now I am here, I have a room, I have my belongings, I have a job, I have friends. I am not happy. But again I live for these four walls and hurry back each day to the solitude of my temple.

18 April 1962, Coleherne Road, Earls Court
End of the Spring Term. Tired.
Earlier JPD and I played like puppies doing judo throws. Earlier still and a visit from Derek who remains distant but inexpressibly familiar. His presence is a reminiscence and I could not now conjure up the anguish even if I wished it.

On Monday Dr Burroughs and his wife took me out to dinner. I still see no real justification for their interest but they are very sweet.

19 April 1962, Coleherne Road, Earls Court
After seventeen hours of sorting out and typing I have, at last, completed typing out notebook Five. I felt like screaming with irritation at times, sick of my own self-absorption but I am stubborn - I set out to type this damn journal and I'll do it.

29 April 1962, Coleherne Road, Earls Court
Since my return to London [*after two days in Somerset*] I no longer have any enthusiasm for my journals and my half-finished task. I have again the feeling they're worthless and my time is being wasted, that I'm merely a disillusioned introvert.

My last two days have been filled by an intensive delving into some murder cases of the last century. I have read the cases of some fifteen psychopaths. I find them so interesting - I feel for criminals, especially murderers. I walked late one night to see 13a Finsborough Road [*not far from Coleherne Road]* and peered down into the basement where Ronald True murdered Olive Young. I've always had an interest in the mentality of murderers - my thesis was on the criminal potential in all of us. I feel it in myself.

Alongside this recent preoccupation with murder and law, a renewed interest in Stanley Spencer. His journal is shortly to be published. The place at Cookham was one of the first places Derek took me, the paintings were magnificent: the chapel was locked and we had to find the old man with the key. From what I can gather he, Spencer, was rather like Kullmann in some respects.

7 May 1962, Coleherne Road, Earls Court
Back at school and depressed. This existence [*being a teacher*] rubs out my own, eliminates it. Life becomes dreary and without any horizon. Were I rich I would first purchase *time*, great quantities of it in which to read, to write, to exist without ties, without routine, without other people. One is not allowed to be solitary. The kids appeared as

they are today, nothing, weighing me down. I hated them today and will hate them even more tomorrow.

11 May 1962, Coleherne Road, Earls Court
Heard a fourteen-year-old at school mutter to no one in particular: 'Can't wait to get in me grave an' 'ave a bleedin' rest.'

My life is very solitary of late, which I like. I see no one from the time I leave the school until the morning. Preoccupied with dying my hair. I feel no need for any other person or persons. I occupy myself and am totally self-sufficient. One only feels lonely when one feels one has something to contribute to the enjoyment of other people.

17 May 1962, Coleherne Road, Earls Court
Conditions at school are chronic. A chaotic day trying to fit forty-six huge quarrelling, giggling adolescent girls into a minute art room. No new paint whatsoever for the last twelve weeks - painting on newspaper with lemon-yellow powder paint - endless daffodils - what else, for God's sake? The LCC should be shot.
Every evening I am exhausted, too tired to read, write or think.

I have some beautiful branches in a pot on the floor with silver green leaves just spreading. I have almost blonde hair at last. I am now more complete than I have ever been. People clutter me up, I have no need of them, their company is neither here nor there with me. I have no fear of death or life. I have no longer enough love of humanity to fear a mass death by bombs or radiation. I have ceased to interest myself as I once did. I love no other person. I have no balance to restore. Loving nobody, I am not miserable. Just disembodied.

Yet when I am with people, drinking, I talk fast and laugh and seem human but I am not with them, they are familiar stones, littered about, that I occasionally knock against and the jolt sets me talking.

18 May 1962, Coleherne Road, Earls Court
The silver leaf branches. All that beauty for 1/8d. An evening drinking beer with Bernie. Thank God it's Friday.

19 May 1962, Coleherne Road, Earls Court
The silver leaf branches, more beautiful even. Again the depressive Saturday night feeling - the sounds of people in crowds, in twos, not in isolation, the parties that appear fun but are pathetically drear.

Out again tomorrow with Nick Jensen[41], another Royal College student. I have been out too much lately and have lost myself. I have diffused pointlessly. No typing recently and I long to get my fingers on the machine again but the human in me finds me out in pubs.

Kullmann was further up Portobello Road with his wife and kids - I felt trapped, anxious not to see him but curious. We missed each other. He's capable of making a street, a city, electric. He's a great man, an all-consuming spirit. But I would not move two yards to put myself in his path. He is someone else's present now, perhaps his wife's.

21 May 1962, Coleherne Road, Earls Court
Life screams. Drinking again. Life epitomised in the curve of an eyelid. Jesus Christ, life ruptures me. Beer, cigarettes and the dull monotony of myself.
The very fact that I want to piss exhilarates me. Understand. Comprehend, for Christ's sake, comprehend.

*

21 June 1962, Coleherne Road, Earls Court
There seems no necessity to write when one is in some degree living. The knowledge, the awareness, the essence of my relationship with Nick looms large on my conscious. I cannot put it aside; it's become

---

[41] Nick Jensen: designer. Studied Industrial Design at the Royal College of Art, 1959-62. Has combined a career in industry and teaching. Lecturer in Design; Alfred University, New York State, 1969-70. Lecturer, University of South Bank, London, 1970-95.

integral but without a hurting presence. It has a sensuality that lacks sophistication. We spend fifteen hours in bed and can't help smiling.

Back now from a delightful evening with Laurie and happy about his new job as a lecturer at Edinburgh University. I have such regard and affection for him he is one of the people I want to be happy though we are far removed in many ways. Whenever I am with him, which is infrequently for no real reason, merely the circumstances of life, I wonder why I don't fall in love with him; he has looks and great charm - I know of no more charming character - vivacious and interesting.

We met Shake [*jazz musician*] in a pub in Notting Hill Gate. I was so glad to see him again but always feel too feminine and superfluous in his company, he is so wise and huge and black and benign.

*

The week in Hay [*Anne's husband, Dan, was the dentist there*] was marvellous - Bernie came too. Have acquired some more cheap, greatly desired books in a really good second-hand shop there[42] and put back the entire André Gide *Journal* for two guineas. Very excited about this but no money to send for them as yet. Greatly in debt and frankly uneasy.

14 July 1962, Coleherne Road, Earls Court

A chance to think now that Nick is away, yet still there is little reason to write for I have become a placid creature, no passion left only intense finite feeling. No great love now for humanity, no yearning for mind, no pity even. I am now a human being like a completed article and very dull. Is early development the only violent, passionate, beautiful stage? To get excited about God, life, love, politics again would exhilarate me. I live now merely to be fit to work in order to eat and work some more. Life is a soggy pit which we tread like mules.

---

[42] Richard Booth's first second-hand shop in Hay in the Old Fire Station. The Welsh border town is now one of the largest centres for second-hand books in the world and hosts an annual Festival of Literature which attracts many successful authors from all over the world.

Now I've tasted an integrated state it doesn't really appeal to me. One becomes annihilated, amalgamated into another person, no matter how strong the individuals. Above all the loss of solitude antagonises me and I could not live without it. In great debt now.

We go to Naples on 6 August. Derek leaves for India, Laurie leaves for Edinburgh, Roger soon to leave Oxford, Taj goes back to Egypt and so on. People diverge and sometimes it seems drastic, these life separations, making cohesion between souls so temporary, so futile.
Jesus, I've gone to seed mentally since the journals. I am unaware. My criticism is habitual, my perception routine, no new force enters my system. I have half the intensity of three years ago and I despise myself for the dullard I have become.

29 Sunday July 1962, Coleherne Road, Earls Court
Back to a solitary orderly life. Eni has gone to Stafford to design shoes and I'm alone in the flat, very contented during the day but, I must admit, apprehensive as soon as it's dark outside and people have stopped walking in the streets. My room is back to its quiet austerity, everything in place and in order. But as a person - am I ordered? Solitary once more, but temporarily, and possibly on the verge of making a decision to integrate myself. This is the existence that is more essential to me. I need time to myself, hours and hours of it. I'm essentially a solitary person. Individuality, I know it, I'm at ease with it, as a study it never dulls. Its facets for ever turn and show themselves multiplied.

I have made no effort to contact anyone tonight yet would welcome an intrusion by a friend.
As for Nick, I miss him and look forward to his coming back on Friday. I'm at ease with him. He's strong-willed and very constant in his ideals which I admire. He has a totally technical mind yet despite this and the battle of wills in many things, we adhere to each other in an extraordinary way.
We stuck a pin in the atlas so it's Naples Monday week [*by train on a students' ticket through Holland, Germany and Austria for £9. Hitch-hiked back through Switzerland and France*].

30 Monday July 1962, Coleherne Road, Earls Court
The joy of waking up alone!
A silent flat, empty and TIME, time, weighted like gold, a hundred times more desirable. I will go out and do some shopping and then come back to this heavenly solitude and savour my isolation and try to finish deciphering notebook Three, the second longest of them all.

1 August 1962, Coleherne Road, Earls Court
Like hell I will. I've been working for hours on the bloody journals until I'm bored to tears and thoroughly sick of them. What drivel most of it is. And here I am writing more of it to bore me another time perhaps! I can't settle to anything until I can put the bloody typewriter away and package the journals and forget them.

Looking forward to Nick's return. I've never had an affair so ordered, so un-urgent, the most mature of them all, yet the least demanding, none of the sweat and tears, the scenes and the heartbreaking jealousies. Some breakages but not despair.

With this calmer, near happiness state goes my blonde hair. I still have a dark personality but my hair is now blonde - many shades of blonde, unfortunately. I don't really know what made me do it. I started bleaching it the first day I went out with Nick. This new lightness epitomises our affair, not by any means lightly taken but for me a new sphere without that dreadful, stifling jealousy. He is the one man I would trust with my life. He has a steadfastness, a man's quality.

2 August 1962, Coleherne Road, Earls Court
At three-thirty this afternoon I finished typing notebook Three, a momentous task. I had to force myself to finish it. I was much more alive then - and feel a little ashamed of the comparatively superficial person I am now. Complacent, lacking in fire. In the company of this girl of seventeen I am dead. I seemed to have been always miserable. I'm rarely miserable now and my mind is less elastic, not as all-embracing as it was then.

Am I ever fired by anything now? I am as acutely critical, but perhaps more tolerant - or is tolerance an excuse for complacency? I still question most things but experience rarely takes me by surprise. I am less naïve, more confident but less exuberant - is it only the naïve who are really alive?

Italy on Monday. No chance to write. I will fear for my journals, my mind, when I am away.

*

1 September 1962, Coleherne Road, Earls Court
We returned to England last Sunday, almost a week ago - reason, no money. I almost wish I had kept a journal of some kind but impressionistic writing is often superfluous and boring. I have all the details in my memory but have little desire to write about them. The feelings, the thoughts which were fired by all the things I saw, all that happened, they pile up like silt in my mind and will all come out eventually.
The bond I feel for Nick increases. Now he is away I feel a little lost. We play like children, we quarrel, we rub against each other as individuals, we adhere to each other as lovers. In some ways he is stronger than I - he has more will and more drive. After crossing to The Hague we had three days of rattling along in crowded trains on slatted seats - through Germany, Munich, where a couple gave us a bed, a massive feather one badly sunk in the middle - Austria, unreal it was so beautiful, Switzerland - southern Italy, bloody fantastic. Drank lots of wine. Nick's revolting little tent which he made himself - very embarrassing alongside the swish German ones - some great lifts and now I am brown and my hair is almost white from the sun.

2 September 1962, Coleherne Road, Earls Court
I miss Nick tonight. I've done nothing today. My precious time, my beloved solitude has no appeal: instead it weighs and moans and is becoming unbearable. Occasional reading and long-drawn-out-mouse-watching. I rely on this little creature for small distractions.

Poor Nick, I put him in some frustrating situations: he, on the ascent of his aspirations, I, on my decline. I dread starting work again. It promises nothing but dreary hard work, boredom and desperation.

6 Sept*ember 1962, Coleherne Road, Earls Court*

Back within these familar walls. Reading all evening: *The Life of Oscar Wilde.* I could fill this book at one sitting with thoughts, ideas, but having the words of Oscar Wilde still on my eyes I cannot. Perhaps I'm a reader not a writer, after all.

Late now, a cold blustering night, very dark. My room once again excites me and my solitude once more offers a sweetness of familiarity and that same anticipation. This is a meeting sometimes longed for which never fails to be rewarding and I never leave myself without a little gain, more self-knowledge and added strength. And yet if Nick came at this late hour, in the middle of this meeting, I would leave myself without a second thought and be glad of the intrusion and revert to an effervescent animal union as easily as waking.

9 September 1962, Coleherne Road, Earls Court

Really miss him tonight. Reading again throughout the day.
Over the last few months having to reconcile myself to the knowledge that I am nothing, merely a human being, no more. I read and am excited by what I read but never write. I could have written every sentence I read, every idea, every thought, every conclusion is my own, innately, but I never write. Just when I begin to regain a little of myself I am thrust back into the nerve-wracking business of teaching. Tomorrow, Jesus, nobody can know how I dread waking up to the reality of it. After Naples, Sorento, Germany, the freedom, to that! Teaching has killed me in more ways than one.

11 September 1962, Coleherne Road, Earls Court

Not a day passes without an odd, disassociated moment when I miss Kullmann. I feel a great hole in my existence. I am aware of his absence. The others knew him, about him but not the person, the crucified live-wire that he is. I can't believe that others still partake of him, participate in him, digest his ideas, gnaw at his personality, chew his substance, devour his essence, if, that is, they realise him at all. If not, they see only a small, eccentric, vitally obtrusive individual without any conventional grace or charm. Kullmann, the great antagonist, the agitator, the man living perpetually at boiling point. To the lazy he's unbearable, to stagnant minds an intolerable fanatic. The machinery of his mind never failed him. I have yet to meet his equal. I have met more obviously humane thinkers, minds as logical but no one with such an electric dimension. Perhaps he will burn himself out.

That place will be a shell without him [*he was sacked from the RCA*]. A pioneer indeed to demand from an *art student* to comment on the *Existence of God* or to enquire as to where they might find the past. I think Derek and Hockney like his lectures but most of the students are outraged that he expected them to *think*! What, they have said to me, has philosophy to do with art?!
His sacking was outrageous but nothing will silence him - I doubt that death will. He would antagonise the angels and question God as to his own existence. Some things are so large people can't see them, so used are they to assessing small quantities in human beings - normal vision isn't sufficient to focus on such an individual.
I have no contact with him now but my assessment of him has never fluctuated nor has the estrangement of circumstances decreased his value. I miss him.

13 September 1962, Coleherne Road, Earls Court
Tonight it's cold and dark and very clear. Memories of last winter creep back. And Kullmann, again his memory is so vivid I wonder if something has happened to him.
This existence of incongenial arduous work and long solitary evenings, one after the other, with no alternative - I long to go out and drink again.
Bernie will not be back in London yet and I've lost touch with Brian and Laurie. How few friends I have. I feel caged and irritable, alone but not lonely.

26 December 1962, Coleherne Road, Earls Court
I feel the need to write for I am once more isolated. For some months life was much happier - I saw emotional security and it was marvellous. Now that has ended. Reading through the previous pages I was once more dragged through, impersonally, not feeling it, the violent, desperate days of Kullmann and RW and eased into the affair with Nick. How dull and easy the latter appears - not so - it is, or was, a relationship that had its share of despair and jealousy: the scenes, the tears, yet also a lot of happiness.

When Nick left I began to gather possessions again, the days of austere bleak surroundings are gone. I have resorted to objects to mark my insecurity. I need them to clarify myself. If this affair ended now it would not be the most drastic one but certainly the most endearing and the one I would miss the most.

New Year's Eve 1962, Coleherne Road, Earls Court
After such a combined existence for nearly a year I find myself once again making that solitary and painful walk to the pub to buy myself two quart bottles of beer and twenty fags which I can ill afford, bring them back here and spend the night alone.

I am sick of tears and heartache. At times like this I hate him. I hate his thirst for supercilious company, for gay times that are a total waste. I refused to spend New Year's Eve in the splitting company of strangers, the endless chat and giggle. Now I must pay for my wilfulness with a really wretched night watching the clock, trying not to care, not to feel the dreadful loneliness creeping back. I hate him for being as strong and wilful in his endless quest for social prowess - so typical RCA.

Everyone is with people they love. He's at a party and I am heroically wretched on my own. The one night when he could have foregone a party - there are enough to choose from and he only came back to London on Saturday.

Ten o'clock and listening to Luxemburg; it makes it worse hearing this twist music, knowing that he's twisting and doing what he loves doing,

oblivious of my loneliness. I love twisting too but I hate strange dances where I know no one - crowds frighten me. I'm afraid I'll be bored, afraid of so many things, afraid of my seering jealousy, afraid of depressive moods.
Thinking back I've loved several men and though I find it hard to believe, I suppose I will again. I am not as naïve this time. I'll never be free of them. I will love other men, once I am free of this one.

*

1 January 1963, Coleherne Road, Earls Court
The heartache when he leaves. Men don't feel even short separations half as much as women. He's gone back to his room to work now and I'm just wishing the time away until I see him tomorrow. I feel dead without him. Men don't really suffer this. I can't wait for the time when he's no longer a student, the time when we can live together again, but no, it's an illusion. I will always wish my life away, always wishing for a future that will be happier.

I sat in last night and then Bernie came round and we had a marvellous time at a camp party; then I rushed back at midnight and Nick arrived at one minute past twelve. Better we had never lived together, but it was wonderful.

3 January 1963, Coleherne Road, Earls Court
We meet in the morning like any lovers, not the lovers we were. But then a wonderful afternoon as it used to be. Men, they love in spasms, never constantly. To them love is a fever that takes hold occasionally, they know nothing of love as a continual, overriding presence. In the past I would have thought this affair almost perfect - he is faithful, he is kind most of the time, he loves me as much as he could love anyone but, for me, the desire to possess is overruling. I have no patience, always this all-consuming urgency. I only hope that when it does end, probably because of my impatience, it won't make me any more bitter than I was before I met him.

I have never learned the art of emotional chess. I have no subtlety when I'm in love. I shout it. I am overruled by it. I need to live with him as we were. This intermittent happiness gnaws at me and I know I shall send this affair crashing by my impossible demands on a nature that is set, and rightly so, not to answer them blindly.

4 January 1963, Coleherne Road, Earls Court
I hate to return to an empty room. I need him. He says he's working. I dread the rare nights we don't see each other. My instinct urges me to run along Old Brompton Road to South Kensington [*he was living in a room at the RCA Common Rooms, next door to Charlie Watts's girlfriend, Shirley, later his wife, one of the many beautiful young girls I was so jealous of at the time*] and bang on his door until he opens it.

17 January 1963, Coleherne Road, Earls Court
A period of adaptation, painful at times, sad all the time and bringing a new sense of isolation. I'm having trouble in getting a release from the school and prospects are clouded with insecurity. I must get out! I must do something to demonstrate the change in myself. The novelty of love, of loving someone and of being nearly worshipped has worn off for him. He has changed and has ruthlessly cut me off; he has found that he can do without me, that he has no need of anything beyond social aquaintances. He fights attachment heartlessly. He cannot forgive me for initiating him into a full relationship. He isn't ready for it and is rebellious and fighting back with cruel indifference. Like the other RCA students he lives on ambition.

This treacherous weather is terrible, no water at all, bitterly cold and the snow in the streets is solid, packed and very hard and dirty, with rubbish gathering in the gutters. There's no warmth anywhere, only coldness. The tubes are always late and it's chaos. It must thaw soon.
It's lucky I can live without another affair for I feel no enthusiasm other than for two friends - I need not fight for their affection, neither is it decreased by time nor suffers any disturbing variations.

31 January 1963, Coleherne Road, Earls Court
I can't explain what happened, only that I live for and through the person I love, he doesn't. A week's separation to him is nothing. I cannot adapt and therefore we decided to leave each other completely. How can a man be moved to tears and then spend days away without a thought? Are men so alien to women?

He came back after a while which makes it worse but in a way more bearable. He is a drug I must have in order to live. If I only knew there was an end to it all, some end, whether bitter or good, at least an end. Each time these terrible things happen I feel my sanity ebbing away. I didn't go into school but I must work to live. I can't just lie down and cover my head until it's all over. Death is the only way out. It wouldn't hurt him for long and he'd get his precious freedom.

The terms of a man's love are so limited, so pallid in comparison to a woman's. Did I sense all this from the beginning of my consciousness - this underlying sadness?

1 February 1963, Coleherne Road, Earls Court
Knowing he's with other women is unbearable. Pride prevents me from catching a 30 bus and joining them. That place, RCA, has been a constant source of pain. One of those beautiful sensual women will always win in the end, against the odds of love and intimacy, against real feeling. They grasp and take all of my life, these anonymous, dolled-up women. No wonder I hate the place.

2 February 1963, Coleherne Road, Earls Court
A much calmer and more reasonable outlook. We were happy this weekend and he said again that he did want to marry me one day. He has actually condescended to see me mid-week for an hour or two which is something, I suppose.
I find little peace in him now, little security but I am bound to him by an indefinable feeling of love.

3 February 1963, Coleherne Road, Earls Court
I woke on Saturday to find a note which I knew would be there saying that the break was necessary. I am numbed and hardened but very unhappy. Drink and two friends are my only consolation.
Tonight I left them and went from pub to pub and drank calmly. It's unbelievable after so much intimacy. Two people could not have been more intimate nor more loving. I will go back to the pub now and rest in semi-oblivion until ten-thirty. I dread that he will come and this nightmare will continue.

11 February 1963, Coleherne Road, Earls Court
The last month or two has been a nightmare. The whole affair has been a deep and spreading disease. Intimacy and dependence grew like a cancerous growth embedding within it my whole emotional balance. He had become my life and separation seems to resemble death, even now. But death must be a void not a positive hurt.

I can't sleep or eat, nor assemble myself to perform the most perfunctory actions. Sometimes, loving him as I do, I cry out like an animal unable to believe such unhappiness. He will be sad too.

Late last night Eni brought up a hasty and desperate note from him. I must be strong and regain my independence, my dependence on my own thoughts.

13 February 1963, Coleherne Road, Earls Court
We met in the street and have no defences.

15 February 1963, Coleherne Road, Earls Court
Last night, happiness that I have no means of expressing. The last week has been a most important one for me. I have seen my own, not his, need to grow up. I have at times utterly hated myself for hurting him as much as he has, and will again, hurt me. He is a true lover for he loves without the desire to possess.

How will this affair finally resolve itself? I always see the end as though unhappiness is inevitable. He's climbing Snowdon this weekend.

16 February 1963, Coleherne Road, Earls Court
Tonight I am content. I must learn to love my freedom again. Have I learned patience? I must be an impossible lover for such a rational, far-seeing person like him. How stifling a love such as mine must be. He's tried to escape but found himself unable. *He* should be pitied, not me, for he's in the grip of an upheaval he is as yet unequipped to cope with though his heart forces him to further it.

18 February 1963, Coleherne Road, Earls Court
A glorious day of freedom. I've religiously washed and ironed my few worn clothes and lovingly mended them - they hang, heavenly rags, in a dirty cupboard space with the paraffin.

My bed is surrounded by photographs of beautiful men and pink roses. Nick climbed up the drainpipe and came through the window at three in the morning. We were happy this weekend. Sunday was like heaven must be - in a dark, lazy room, sculptured, with my work around me and he, fast asleep in bed. I sat in the chair and drank tea and watched him. It was all the more beautiful for being sudden, temporary, a prelude, perhaps, to less happy moments.
We slept all day and for the first time he was peaceful and not fighting for complete freedom. He seems to have found it.
Does happiness always have an unreal quality?
Living has become lighter and I wonder for how long.

*

Long before my flesh has gone
I shall have flown from here
Effortlessly spanning immeasurable spaces
Eternity, the down thrust of a wing

The journal ends on 18 February 1963 but the following three entries were scrawled on a blank sheet of paper.

Friday 22 November 1963, Coleherne Road, Earls Court
President Kennedy was shot dead today. This has shocked the world and literally moved thousands to open tears.

Saturday 23 November 1963, Coleherne Road, Earls Court
Kennedy's assassin shot dead while handcuffed.

Sunday 24 November 1963, Coleherne Road, Earls Court
The world is in mourning for Kennedy - all the newspapers are full of it and likewise TV and radio. Everyone shocked and shopgirls in a dither, unable to give correct change; small groups in the street discussing the tragedy as though their own brother had been murdered.

*

In addition to the assassination of J F Kennedy in Dallas, Texas, 1963 was also the year in which Nelson Mandela was sent for trial; Dr Martin Luther King led the Civil Rights march on Washington DC; Alcatraz was finally closed; Sylvia Plath died; the Beatles hit the charts; the scandal broke over the Profumo Affair and The Nuclear Test Ban Treaty between USA, UK and USSR was signed.

INDEX

*